On the Threshold of Eurasia

ON THE THRESHOLD OF EURASIA

Revolutionary Poetics in the Caucasus

LEAH FELDMAN

CORNELL UNIVERSITY PRESS
ITHACA AND LONDON

First published 2018 by Cornell University Press

Printed in the United States of America

Library of Congress Cataloging-in-Publication Data
Names: Feldman, Leah, author.
Title: On the threshold of Eurasia : revolutionary poetics in the
    Caucasus / Leah Feldman.
Description: Ithaca : Cornell University Press, 2018. | Includes
    bibliographical references and index.
Identifiers: LCCN 2018002248 (print) | LCCN 2018005984 (ebook) |
    ISBN 9781501726514 (pdf) | ISBN 9781501726521 (epub/mobi) |
    ISBN 9781501726507 (cloth : alk. paper)
Subjects: LCSH: Caucasian literature—20th century—History and
    criticism. | Azerbaijani literature—20th century—History and
    criticism. | Russian literature—20th century—History and criticism. |
    Poetics—History—20th century. | Insurgency in literature. |
    Azerbaijan—Intellectual life—20th century. | Caucasus—Relations—
    Russia. | Russia—Relations—Caucasus. | Caucasus—Relations—
    Soviet Union. | Soviet Union—Relations—Caucasus.
Classification: LCC PK9030 (ebook) | LCC PK9030 .F45 2018 (print) |
    DDC 899/.96—dc23
LC record available at https://lccn.loc.gov/2018002248

For my family,
who taught me the meaning of hospitality

CONTENTS

Acknowledgments

Describing the world of Fyodor Dostoevsky's poetics, the theorist Mikhail Bakhtin wrote, "There is almost no word without an intense sideward glance at someone else's word" (1997–2012, 6:227). This vision of authorship as both an intertextual and intersubjective phenomenon not only inspired the writing of this book but structured the process of its composition. To say that I am indebted to the many great mentors, colleagues, family, and friends who have shared their minds with me over the course of writing this book would perhaps not capture the animating force their words played in igniting and guiding my own. In many ways, this book is a set of sideward glances at other people's words, written and spoken, a collection of moments in which the self fragments into that brilliant multiplicity of scattered thoughts that find their way into a fluid dialogue.

This book would not have been possible without the contributions of several individuals and institutions. The language training, research, and writing of this project were funded by generous contributions from the

American Council of Learned Societies (ACLS), the Princeton Institute for International and Regional Studies (PIIRS), and the Institute for Advanced Study (IAS) at the Central European University. I thank the fellows at PIIRS and the IAS for many lively discussions, which have shaped this manuscript.

I hold a deep gratitude for my mentors and colleagues in the field who have provided support and inspiration since graduate school. I thank my mentor and friend Aamir Mufti, who has taught me to approach the discipline with a humanist and yet tirelessly critical and worldly mind; Paul Bové and the *Boundary 2* collective who continue to shape my understanding of critique; Anindita Banerjee, who has guided me as a junior scholar, balancing the worlds of Slavic and comparative literature with such generous intellect and professionalism; Bruce Grant, whose mentorship in the field and deeply humble, genuine and brilliant scholarship on the Caucasus and former Soviet Union continue to inspire me to become a better scholar; Azade-Ayse Rorlich, who first introduced me to Azeri literature and instilled in me the rigors of a historical approach; Dragan Kujundžić, whose mentorship has sparked a sense of play in my approach to theory; Altay Göyüşov, who continues to teach me about the nuances of Azeri language and history; Omnia El Shakry, whose brilliant mind, deep humility, and genuine curiosity has long set an example to which I aspire, and Elizabeth Richmond-Garza and Tom Garza, for first exposing me to the words of Bakhtin and the practice of academic mentorship. I thank many other great interlocutors whose work continues to push me to think and who have offered insight and support as this manuscript took shape: Ali Behdad, Nergis Ertürk, Rebecca Gould, Stathis Gourgouris, Sam Hirsch, Nilüfer Hatemi, Katya Hokanson, Güliz Kuruoglu, Harsha Ram, Michael Reynolds, and Nariman Skakov.

I thank my colleagues in the Department of Comparative Literature at the University of Chicago for their mentorship and support. I am especially grateful for my comrades in Chicago who have made the city and the university feel like a home for the past three years, sharing thought, practice, and dreams of communal dwelling: Adrienne Brown, Peter Coveillo, Patrick Crowley, Harris Feinsod, Andrew Ferguson, Adom Getachew, Ghenwa Hayek, Faith Hillis, Rami Jabakhanji, Patrick Jagoda, Anna Kornbluh, Emily Licht, Liz McCabe, Nasser Mufti, Kim O'Neil, Julie Orlemanski, Na'ama Rokem, Zach Samalin, Christopher Taylor, Sarah Pierce-Taylor, and Sonali Thakkar.

Last but certainly not least, I thank my family by blood and love for their ever-abounding patience, care, and sense of humor. To my crew from Cali to NYC and Budapest to Baku for listening to me rant about revolution for many years and for making life fun, interesting, and beautiful: Sara Brinegar, Amy Brouillette, Nassie Elzoghby, Leila El Shakry, Dani Fazekas, Elizabeth Gelber, Krista Goff, Kate Hamby-Goodson, Natalia Janossy, Vladimir Kropatchev, Cetta Mainwaring, Marcy McCullaugh, Marites Naca, Tom Popper, David Ridout, Nina Silove, David Simpson, Dan Stern, Stephen Sykes, Kyle Wanberg, and Sandee Willis. I am also so grateful for my dialogic buddy Hoda El Shakry, who has patiently read so many versions of this manuscript, who shared my early fascination with Bakhtin, and who I feel so lucky to have the chance to continue to think, laugh, and cry alongside. To my grandparents, Evelyn, Ned, and Harold, who encouraged my early curiosity in the world; my cousins, Brittany, Brooke, Erik, Erin, Lily, Melissa, and Robin, and my uncles and aunts, Britt, Barbara, Carol, Doug, Hetta, Jon, Lili, Maurice, and Nedelyn, who have brought much love and laughter to my life. Finally, with all my love to my parents, Henry and Betty, for their unending support, my brother-in-law, Rusty, for teaching me about drill bits, and my sister, Jessica, who inspires me every day.

Note on Transliteration

Russian transliterations are based on the Library of Congress system, with exceptions made for established English-language spellings, such as Dostoevsky rather than Dostoevskii. Azeri transliteration follows the Latin alphabet adopted by the Republic of Azerbaijan in 1991.

ON THE THRESHOLD OF EURASIA

INTRODUCTION

Heterodoxy and Heterology on the Threshold of Eurasia

You're Komsomol, I'm "nonaligned"
But my heart is yours
Inseparable from your light.
Though I'm an idler of the revolution
My road is the wide one that you traveled
And our word is "ready!"

Sən komsomol, mən—"bitərəf" . . .
Fəqət mənim qəlbim sənin
Nur çəşməndən ayrılamaz,
Mən inqilab tufeylisi olsam belə bir az
Yenə yolum sən getdiğim geniş yol
"Hazır ol!" bizim parol . . .
(Refili 1929, 45)

In the poem dedicated to the death of Lenin, the poet and translator
Mikayıl Refili outlined the position of Azerbaijan in the tumultuous period

of the Bolshevik revolution and the consolidation of the Soviet multinational empire. Refili defines himself in relation to the state bureaucracy as "nonaligned," drawing on the hybrid Persian-Arabic loan word "biteref," literally without sides. Pledging his heart to Lenin and the Soviet cause, Refili's verse marks the inseparability between early Soviet politics and romantic poetics. The imagery of the heart, spiritual light (*nur*), and the open road, tropes of classical Arabo-Persian poetry, contrast Refili's use of the Latin script and free verse. For Refili, the *parol*, password or promise, weaves his lyric subject and Lenin into an intimate dialogue across political and cultural lines through the Soviet Komsomol, the Franco-Russian *parol* (word), and its Turkic rhymed command *hazır ol* (be ready).[1] In so doing, Refili locates political awareness not in party membership but in a space of romantic love, *without* or *between* (*biteref*), and in the process of an aesthetic, semantic, and political negotiation across the Russian, Persian, and Turkic cultural divides that surround the Caucasus. Refili's poem from his 1929 collection *The Window* (*Pencere*) offers an alternative view of the Bolshevik revolution and consolidation of the Soviet empire in the south Caucasus.

The Bolshevik revolution of 1917 remains a mythic turning point marking the moment when St. Petersburg—which Peter the Great declared the center of imperial Russia's modernization and westernization, its "window onto the West"—was swept away by the formation of a new empire centered in communist Leningrad. The legacy of these twin empires as a *translatio imperii,* or imperial succession, still looms in the shadow of the Cold War and Putin's 2014 interventions in Ukraine. However, the imperial imagination always seems to return to the topos of Eurasia.

Following Emily Apter's invocation of translation zones as both the process of imperial transition, *translatio imperii*, and translation studies, this book unfolds a series of Russian and Turkic intertextual encounters, which expose the construction of literary modernism as central to Soviet empire building, through the transnational circulation of texts and ideas between Russia and the Caucasus.[2] Rather than replicating the orientalist imaginary of Eurasia, as Russia's infamous Janus-faced vision of an empire trapped between the geopolitical and ideological constructs of Europe and Asia, I offer an analysis of understudied Turkic archives, placing them into dialogue with the Russian works that were monumentalized into a Soviet world literature and cultural canon.[3] While structural differences underlie comparisons of the state formations of imperial Russia and the Soviet multinational empire, the formation of political subjectivity in Turkic Muslim literature produced during the revolutionary transition offers insight into discursive continuities in the *translatio imperii*, as well as the role of literature more broadly in the creation of alternative forms of political subjectivity on the imperial periphery. I argue that the topos of Eurasia exposes nodes of intersection between discourses of Soviet national identity and Russian and Soviet orientalism, as well as the interlinked imperial disciplines of structuralist linguistics and anthropology, which sustained the privileged position of literature in their formation.

The urgency of an exploration of the discourse of Eurasianism is motivated by the terrifying revival of neo-Eurasianist geopolitics spurred by the work of Alexander Dugin. Once a fringe political theorist, Dugin has not only gained Putin's ear but over the last five years has expanded his influence across global New Right movements, including the US Traditional Workers Party and the French GRECE. As Dugin frames in a recent interview, "Eurasianism is the creation of an alternative to liberalism," in which liberalism embodies the persistent force of the West, whose "dictatorship" can be fought against only by reclaiming the geopolitics of Eurasianism.[4] More than a political theory, Eurasianism for Dugin traces a historical continuity to the tradition of Russian and Soviet scholarship in linguistics, ethnography, and geography and its influence on the development of structuralism and anthropology.[5] As an orientalist enterprise driven by a vision of the sociopolitical value of language and literature, for Dugin (2010) Eurasianism formulates an existential understanding of a people, a history of being (*Seynsgeschichte*) based on a geopolitical model of the coordinated efforts of traditional religious societies to build a new world order within the contiguous landmass of Eurasia. Drawing on the work of the twentieth-century Eurasianists and nineteenth-century Slavophiles, Dugin (2012, 2014) argues that the historical evolution of a Eurasian people is inseparable from the space of the Eurasian landmass.[6] The application of geopolitics to discourses of (post-)Soviet victimhood more broadly has nurtured the emergence of nationalist discourses in the post-Soviet space, which armed with postcolonial post-Soviet scholarship, has championed a vision of return to an authentic national culture.[7]

As I elaborate below, the term "Eurasia" not only describes a geographical region situated between the European and Asian continents but also opens up an entire system of economic and political relations across the former Russian, Ottoman, and Persian empires, centered along the Caucasus Mountains at its southeastern border. The orientalist vision of Eurasia—born in the work of Russian poets, politicians, geographers, and linguists—promoted Russia's liminal position between the ideological poles of a rational and modern "Europe" and a spiritual and revolutionary "Asia." Framing the revolution and its aftermath as a dialogue between the constructions of Russia and Europe from the vantage point of the Caucasus accounts for the ideological formation of Eurasia and its impact on these historical, cultural, economic, and political differences on twentieth-century literature and aesthetics.

During the revolutionary years from 1905 through 1929, from the first labor mobilizations through the end of the New Economic Policy, an alternative literary aesthetics emerged in the Turkic Muslim South Caucasus. The influence of romantic poetics as the basis of this new avant-garde, in turn, informed pan-Turkic, pan-Islamic, and later Soviet Eurasianist imaginaries. Viewed from a historical perspective, this romantic poetics, while defined by romantic genre conventions, was also motivated by a concern for the affective power of poetry to influence politics. One of the foundational figures of historical poetics, Alexander Veselovsky describes the affective dimension of sentimental poetry: that is, the ways in which literary texts give form to emotional experience, highlighting the simultaneous historical persistence (*perezhivanie*) of poetic form and personal experience ([1904] 2016, 255–73). Moving away from the imperial locus of this vision of affective poetics, writers in the Caucasus drew on the experience of cultural, linguistic, confessional, and political heterodoxy. In this way, the literature of the revolutionary period in the Caucasus poses a crucial paradox between the convergence of a deterministic discourse of imperial identity and the flourishing of variation and hybridity in forms of heterology and heterodoxy. These two terms describe the formation of literary modernity, as at once an *archive* of texts characterized by its linguistic and religious multiplicity, and as a *praxis* that challenges a monolingual, monologic canon, reliant on a static vision of European modernity and its attendant universalizing doxa. Cognizant of a diverse multilingual and heterogeneous archive of Russian orientalist scholarship, romantic and avant-garde aesthetics, Arabo-Persian-Turkic poetic conventions, and Muslim modernist cultural reform movements, Muslim writers and thinkers thus positioned the Caucasus on the threshold of dominant political structures and poetic forms.[8] The decentralized locus of these literary aesthetics on the Soviet periphery and the formation of what Refili described, anticipating the postcolonial movement of the 1950s, as a "nonaligned" vision of Soviet literary modernity, in turn, exposes the geopolitics of uneven development in the context of Soviet modernization during the cementing of its empire.[9]

Explorations of Marxist aesthetics from the vantage point of the (post) colony are hardly new. However, postcolonial theory as distinguished from anticolonial writings, as Dipesh Chakrabarty observed, was born in the West (2010, 45–68). The epistemological distinction between the historical Marxist-Leninism of the Soviet empire and the Western Marxism of postcolonial theory hinges on a fundamental disjuncture between theory and praxis in Anglo-American academia.[10] Indeed, this disjuncture has resulted in a contentious relationship between postcolonial theory and Slavic studies, which is only recently being remedied.[11] Marxist aesthetics imagined through postcolonial theory produced in Euro-American academia was shaped by Sartrean existentialism and Althusserian structuralism. In this way, postcolonial theory framed anti-imperial discourses through a post-Marxist inquiry into Anglo-French orientalism, postmodernity, biopolitics, and feminism as debates that arose within the geopolitical landscape of the hegemonic forces of Euro-American capitalism.

As Timothy Mitchell (2000) contends, the conditions of modernity on the colonial periphery are the consequence of a response, or *structural adjustment,* to colonial subjugation. Mitchell's argument leads to aesthetic claims, namely that "the colonial-modern involves creating an effect we recognize as reality, by organizing the world endlessly to represent it."[12] I argue that historical poetics, formalism, and semiotics present literature as central to representing an alternative vision of colonial modernity. From an intellectual history standpoint, this connection is articulated through the reliance of semiotics on the Marxist-Leninist speech acts of Soviet linguistics and, more broadly, historical poetics's concern for the imbrication of literature with sociopolitical life.[13] In either model, a decentering of capitalist modernity is not achieved in a colonial mimesis of a phantom West, but rather in the act or event of speaking back, in enunciating and engaging in a dialogue with the West as a space of representation. This shift in focus on the perception of peripheral modernities does not aim to validate the hegemony of a Eurocentric aesthetics but rather to ask what other types of aesthetic forms such encounters create.[14] In turn, this book addresses forms of heterology and heterodox praxis that emerge through intertextual dialogues in the "peripheral modernities" produced during the revolutionary period in the Caucasus.

Taking up this challenge, the disciplinary aims of such a comparative praxis reconciles the intellectual history of Eurasianist discourses of empire with Marxist-Leninist aesthetics and poetics across the divide between Slavic and Turkic area studies and postcolonial theory. In so doing, I trace the history and literature of discourses of anti-imperialism in the former Soviet Union to resonant if often dissonant echoes in postcolonial studies, exposing correspondences between avant-garde literary modernity and (post-)Marxist aesthetic theory. This alternative reading of postcoloniality is centered on a variant of Marxist-Leninist aesthetic and political thought that developed in the former Russian empire in an archive of romantic and modernist political and poetic texts penned by Russian and Turkic Muslim writers during the *longue durée* of the revolutionary period from 1905 to 1929.

Linking the Russian/Soviet avant-garde to contemporary postcolonial theory exposes a curious intellectual genealogy that has been obscured by the underrepresentation of work on Central Asia and the Caucasus in the literary field. These realities are fraught by lack of access to language training and archival sources, as well as the marginalization of cultural studies of the region from the disciplines of both Slavic and Middle Eastern studies.[15] Connecting these fields exposes the emergence of Soviet literary modernity at the nexus of the formation of new forms of political and cultural life in the multinational empire, as well as inviting a disciplinary critique of both postcolonial and Slavic studies.

The two topics central to discussions of Russian/Soviet (post)coloniality that frame this book are the geopolitics of *Eurasia* and Mikhail Bakhtin's theory of hybrid literary modernity developed in the concept of the *threshold*. The threshold, as I discuss at length below, at once outlines a literary topos and relational ontology, exposing the interplay between a text and its social worlds by exhuming the historical traces of diverse registers of speech and their cultural content. This framework highlights the imbricated intellectual histories of structuralist linguistics and the Eurasianist movement, which both emerged among Russian intellectual émigré communities in Prague and Paris in the 1920s and 1930s and are echoed in Dugin's neo-Eurasianist designs.[16] Furthermore, the extension of the Russian imaginary of a hybrid Eurasian empire into the realm of cultural identity interpolated the Russian intelligentsia's critique of empire in the nineteenth century onto the notion of a multilingual, multiethnic Soviet federation in the twentieth.[17] The paradoxical coexistence of anti-imperial critique and colonization, I contend, was central to the revolutionary political as well as poetic exchanges between Russians and Turkic Muslims.

The geopolitical and linguistic formulation of Eurasia, in turn, influenced the theoretization of empire in Euro-American academia.[18] This liminal Eurasian geopolitics and linguistic and cultural hybridity has, in particular, endured in post-Soviet academic scholarship on Russian orientalism, as the central ideological framework through which the diversity of the Soviet archive is articulated. In this way, the growth of Slavic studies amid Cold War cultural armament was beholden to forms of liberal multiculturalism that not only grew out of American neoliberalism but were indebted to discourses of Russian/Soviet imperial modernity.[19] In reference to this point, in *Death of a Discipline,* Gayatri Spivak (2003) raises "planetary" forms of critical practice as a necessary corrective to the institutional shift brought on by the defunding of area studies in the wake of the Cold War and the formulation of discourses of multiculturalism as a belated form of postcoloniality in the age of globalization. Aamir Mufti similarly argues that the orientalist project lies at the foundations of the making of world literature. He urges, "what would be needed is a concept of world literature (and practices of teaching it) that works to reveal the ways in which 'diversity' itself—national, religious, civilizational, continental—is a colonial and orientalist problematic, though one that emerges precisely on the plane of equivalence that is literature" (2010, 493). Reading a Soviet-world literary framework similarly requires a critical approach to the role of Russian and Soviet orientalism in the foundations of the geopolitical discourse of Eurasianism and its production of forms of diversity. Attentive to the geopolitics of the Eurasian imaginary, I render visible the imbrication of Soviet imperialism, linguistics, and modernist aesthetic theory. Following Edward Said's critique of Orientalism, as well as Spivak's, Mufti's, and others' interventions, this book contests a vision of Eurasia that functioned not only as an orientalist imaginary but also as an institutionalized canon constituted through the growth of Slavic studies in American academia. Emerging out of Eurasianist discourses, formalist and structuralist linguistics were thus predicated on a binary worldview of Russia and the West.

For Iurii Lotman and Boris Uspenskii, the centrality of binaries to Russian culture lies in the duality of the Russian medieval system. They argue that in contrast to the medieval West, in which "a wide area of neutral behavior" neither "unconditionally sinful" nor "unconditionally holy" was possible, the Russian medieval system was rather based on an accentuated duality of the sinful and holy (1985, 32). While their model relies on a reading of what they call "non-hereditary memory"—that is, cultural constructs that are discursively perpetuated—the claim does not account for any historical cultural accounts that were not included in nineteenth-century political and literary writing devoted to discourses of Russian national identity. To challenge this binary, I engage with discussions of literary modernity and (post)colonial subjectivity from the vantage point of the writings of the Turkic Muslims of the Russian empire.

The theoretical formation of this paradoxical discourse of imperial totality predicated on difference and hybridity can be clarified by turning to the work of the literary theorist Mikhail Bakhtin. While Bakhtin's work belatedly received wide reception in the 1980s, apace with the growing popularity of postcolonial theory, his early writings were penned in the 1920s during the revolutionary period of cultural production on the imperial periphery.[20] While Bakhtin's work considers a range of subjects outside the Soviet sphere, from Rabelais to Dostoevsky, one of the fundamental animating concerns in his work is the construction of literary modernity in relation to discourses of imperial identity. These discourses include Russian Orthodox mysticism as a revolutionary topos, the romantic anticapitalism of the avant-garde, and the centralized control of the arts under Stalinism. Bakhtin's elusive flirtations with Marxist aesthetics, demonstrated in his publications, whose authorship was contested and attributed to his contemporary Valentin Voloshinov, were indeed hotly debated in the 1990s in North American academic circles. Putting aside his personal politics, Bakhtin's inflection of Marxist-Leninist aesthetics perhaps more crucially situates his work within a historical context in which, as Stephen Kotkin (1995) has argued, intellectuals regardless of real political commitment were required to "speak Bolshevik."[21] In this

way, his work envisions a Soviet literary modernity through its interpolation of romantic anticapitalism into a vision of *novelistic discourse*
(Bakhtin 1997–2012, 3:9–179).

The concept of the *threshold* in Bakhtin's work envisions an avant-
garde or modernist position, one that critically reflects on art's relationship to society. In dialogue with Jürgen Habermas's aesthetic formation,
avant-garde poetics generates a form of literary modernity premised on a
post-Enlightenment struggle with the schism among religion, science, and
art (3:19–22).[22] This disjuncture between autonomous art and life, as well
as the sublation of art in the praxis of life, articulates its transformation
on the Soviet periphery through the recovery of a hermeneutics of the dialogic form.[23] The Russian and Soviet periphery, I argue, functioned as an
experimental space for this transformation of life. Drawing on the work
of Bakhtin, I situate this exploration of literary modernity on the discursive *threshold*, which envisions literary or novelistic discourse through a
series of intersubjective encounters between speaking consciousnesses and
their underlying epistemological and historical formations. In so doing,
I expose the ways in which literary modernity in the Russian and Soviet
East during the revolutionary transition and *translatio imperii* was imagined through a series of intertextual encounters between Azeri and Russian poetics. This intertextual dialogue, in turn, drew on resonances from
diverse doxa, including metaphysical and religious concepts in Islamic,
Orthodox, and Enlightenment thought, evolutionary biology, German
romanticism, and Marxist-Leninist materialist theories of language.

Russia's military intervention in Ukraine in 2014 spurred a series of
quasi-historical comparisons to both Russian and Soviet imperial expansion. But, the question remains, what kind of empire was Russia? The
nineteenth-century Russian historian Vasily Kliuchevsky infamously
declared, "In Russia the center is at the periphery."[24] Much of the scholarship on the history of the Russian empire and the formation of the
Soviet Union indeed continues to echo his words.[25] The fall of the Soviet
Union witnessed a burgeoning body of scholarship on the topic of Russia's empire across the disciplines of literature, history, and anthropology.
The case of Russian orientalism, for example, presents a unique challenge
to historians, anthropologists, and literary scholars. How can a notion of
empire, which has largely been theorized through the hegemony of the
first-world Anglo-French empires be reconciled with the Marxist-Leninist

second world sprawling across the continuous landmass of Eurasia? Two major differences emerge in cross-imperial comparisons: the ideological centrality of the West European Enlightenment to constructions of imperial modernity and the geography of the overseas empire.[26] This book positions the long revolutionary period of transition from the Russian empire to the consolidation of Stalin's power (1905–1929) at the heart of Russia's expansion of its Eurasian land empire in the Caucasus. The focal points of this vision of Russian and Soviet imperialism hinge on representations of revolution and the Caucasus as a geopolitical and ideological border or threshold space that was central to imperial ideology, thereby securing the transition from the Russian to the Soviet empires.

This book focuses on a series of literary encounters in poetry, prose, and political essays written by Russian and Turkic Muslim writers, which contributed to the formation of discourses of literary modernity in the transitional revolutionary period. The key concept of the threshold informs the geopolitical setting of my study and sustains the critical framework of this book. The threshold not only describes the imperial periphery and—to paraphrase Kliuchevsky, its central role in the formation of the Soviet Union—but it also identifies the ideology of Eurasian hybridity and liminality, which emerged in textual archives produced by both Russian and Turkic Muslim writers in the Caucasus. The threshold, as a Bakhtinian concept, situates my reading of texts between the constellations of power that underlie orientalist, imperialist, and anti-imperialist discourses.[27] Intervening in historical and aesthetic discussions about Russian national identity to illustrate its relationship to imperial expansion and orientalist production makes it possible to account for the contributions of Turkic Muslims of the Caucasus to imperial and revolutionary politics, identifying critical yet lesser-known discourses of Turkic and Muslim cultural and civic identities—that is, forms of self-ascribed confessional and ethno-linguistic identity that transcended national borders.

The terms "Russian" and "Muslim" signify ethno-religious markers of identity, as Islam and Orthodox Christianity played a major role in defining cultural, ethnic, and civic identity through the early twentieth century.[28] Russian orientalists referred to Muslims of the Caucasus as Caucasian (*kavkazets*) or mountaineers (*gortsy*) to emphasize a connection between the physical topography of the Caucasus and the character of its people. However, most often the terms "Tatar" or "Azerbaijani Tatar" were used erroneously to refer to all Muslims across the empire, not only those Tatar-speaking Muslims of the Volga-Ural and Crimean regions.[29] The term "Muslim" was also employed by Russians to distinguish religious otherness and by the people of the Caucasus as a means of self-identification.[30] Within the Caucasus, Azeri speakers were called "Türk" by Armenians, "Tatrebi" or "Tatars" by Georgians, and "Mughals" or "Mongols" by other minorities.[31] Like the supranational signifier *Türk*, Azeri also drew on wider cultural ties across the former Persian empire, referring more broadly to the Turkic-speaking people, a majority of whom are Shi'i, who inhabit the territory between modern-day Iran and Daghestan, flanked by the Caspian Sea.[32] My use of the term "Azeri" thus emphasizes the porous national boundaries between various cultural identities in the region, the cultural centers of Tbilisi and Baku (the capitals of contemporary Georgia and Azerbaijan), as well as the shared cultural heritage with the Persian, Russian, and Ottoman empires.[33]

These intersecting cultural identity discourses challenge a singular narrative of an Orthodox Russophone imperial space. While confessional and linguistic difference remains one of the observed markers of the Russian empire's distinction vis-à-vis a vision of secular Anglo-French imperial modernity, these forms of imperial hegemony obscure the multilingual and multiethnic constitution of the empire. Religion— Orthodoxy, in particular—played a major role in defining imperial ideology. For instance, in the 1830s Sergei Uvarov—education minister and adviser to Tsar Nicholas I—coined the state slogan "Orthodoxy, Autocracy, Nationality [*Narodnost'*]" to describe the tsar's embodiment of the Russian people or *narod*.[34] However, across the empire religion functioned as a heterodox field marked by intriguing correspondences between various discourses of collective action and unity, such as the Orthodox notion of *sobornost'*, the Islamic conception of *tawḥīd*, and the Marxist international union of the working classes, which I discuss in subsequent chapters.[35] Taking up these intersectional doxa through their poetic manifestations, this book contests national boundaries, and by extension, the idea of national literatures. By rejecting the singular model of national literature, I trace the formation of what I call *supranational* literary traditions that invoked pan-Slavic, pan-Turkic, pan-Islamic, and Marxist-Leninist ideologies, engaging writers and thinkers across the Persian, Ottoman, and Russian empires.[36]

The Eurasian Empire

"The transition from Europe to Asia is more perceptible with every hour," wrote Alexander Pushkin as he recorded his passage through the Caucasus in his travelogue, *Journey to Arzrum* (1974, 17). The story of the Russian and Soviet colonization of the Caucasus and local resistance to it took the form of a dialogue, albeit often one-sided, about the imagined geography of a Eurasian land empire as it was projected across the sublime slopes of the Caucasus. Drawing on accounts dating back to ancient Greece, nineteenth-century Russian orientalist ethnographic, linguistic, and literary representations identified the Caucasus as a threshold space caught between Europe and Asia.[37] Marked by the expansion of Russia's massive land empire and its related distinction as a destination for political exiles, the Caucasus emerged in accounts such as Pushkin's marked by its liminal geography and cultural hybridity.

My use of the term "Eurasia," however, draws on the aforementioned historical movement popularized in intellectual circles between the 1920s and 1930s, which sought to found a new social and cultural form in the arts and sciences, linking biology, history, geography, and linguistics. By building on studies of Eurasianism that trace its intellectual antecedents to nineteenth-century Slavophile nationalist ideology and Russian orientalist scholarship, with its connections to the formation of early twentieth-century linguistics, we can explore Eurasia as a discursive threshold space through which a vision of literary modernity and revolutionary transformation was interpolated in the works of Russian writers and thinkers and their Muslim Turkic counterparts in the South Caucasus.

As Russian writers and thinkers imagined Eurasia, they mapped geopolitical, scientific, and theological epistemologies onto literary representations of Russia's southern colonies, particularly the Caucasus. In so doing, they defined the cultural and economic importance of the territories as central to a modern revolutionary ideology. These revolutionary-romantic discourses generated a crucial historiographic and theoretical foundation that linked anti-imperial revolutionary poetics with the process of colonization, all the while operating through intertwining discourses of geographical liminality and cultural hybridity. Orientalists of the Caucasus, like the historian and Turkologist Vasily Bartold and the linguist and geographer Nikolai Marr, were informed by the notion of a heterogeneous

Eurasian identity that was not united by race but rather by a common historical fate and culture.[38] In this way, revolutionary poetics, more broadly encompassing the Russian and Turkic avant-gardes, served a central role in the transition from the fall of the Russian empire through the consolidation of the Soviet multinational empire from 1905 to 1929. Highlighting these avant-garde poetics thus exposes intersections between revolutionary ideologies that were striated by the geopolitics of the Eurasian land empire.

The topos of the imaginary Caucasus as a projected fantasy of Russia's revolutionary Eurasian identity constituted forms of literary modernity based on a differential ontology. This discourse of modernity was premised on the centrality of difference to forms of being, which were articulated through a romantic vision of totality. This conception of totality through heterogeneity and difference was indebted to Russian responses to Darwinian evolutionism, in which a theory of evolution based on coincidence was replaced with an overarching vision of structural laws premised on wholeness.[39] On the one hand, this model of the evolution and diversity of imperial culture, contributed to the structure of the multinational Soviet empire, while on the other, it relied on an orientalist vision of Eurasian totality. This totality was inscribed in the imagination of a place that was neither Europe nor Asia but greater than their sum. Despite divergent politics, the shared conception of an evolutionist scientific discourse in linguistics and literature also accounts for the aesthetic resonances between Marxist-Leninist and Eurasianist modernity discourses.[40]

In Patrick Sériot's *Structure and the Whole*, he exposes the explicit connections between non-Darwinian evolution and Russian linguistics, tracing the latter to nineteenth-century biological and cultural theories, as well as Slavophile and Eurasianist politics (2014, 24–60). The Slavophile philosopher Nikolai Danilevsky's famous treatise *Russia and Europe* (*Rossiia i Evropa* [1869]) designed a theory of nations that combined religion and the natural sciences into a natural theology based on German romantic connections to homology and responses to Darwinian evolution.[41] Danilevsky's natural theology developed a concept of pan-Slavic unity and superiority through the cross-fertilization of nations and cultural traditions. He compared Slavic nations to the confluence of streams of world history running through Egypt, Palestine, and Byzantium, merging with ancient Greece and the Roman empire (Danilevsky, as described in MacMaster 1954, 154–61). Danilevsky's vision of cultural hybridity was based on Goethe's poetics and Karl Ernst von Baer's biological theories of homology. Indeed, as the Tashkent-based French ethnographer Joseph Castagné argued in 1923, German romantic orientalist ethnography had a major impact on the formation of Bolshevik Muslim politics.[42] The biological model compared organisms with the same type of structure and in so doing constructed an ideal that was particularized according to individual organisms but remained unified under the conceptual structure (MacMaster 1954, 154–61). In this way, Danilevsky projected the future of a pan-Slavic empire through its heterogeneous yet structurally coherent composition. For thinkers such as Danilevsky, Darwin's theory constituted a form of Western materialism that must be rejected for an alternative form of Slavic modernity.

Eurasianist linguistics extended this geopolitical model into the twentieth century, drawing on the disciplines of geography, biology, economics, and a political-military idiom. Following the work of the Russian biologists and geographers Lev Berg and Igor Savitsky, Roman Jakobson argues in "Toward a Characterization of the Eurasian Language Affiliation" (K kharakteristike evraziiskogo iazykovogo soiuza [1931]) that languages are not only bound by shared families, inherited vocabularies, grammars, and phonetic traits but also language affiliation (*iazykovyi soiuz*), a term he appropriates from Nikolai Trubetskoy (Jakobson 1962, 144–201).[43] Language affiliation describes structural similarities that do not stem from shared inherited traits but rather from a continuous geography, as well as a shared culture and history. In this way, it is a comparative linguistic theory grounded in a notion of the linguistic and cultural affiliation of neighboring territories. Jakobson understands Eurasia through its territorial continuity and linguistic structure (defined by a shared consonant palatalization and the absence of polytony).[44]

While such a model promises the lateral affiliation of neighboring languages and cultures not linked by a single nation-state, the very notion of affiliation for Jakobson is tied to political and military organization. For example, Jakobson introduces language affiliation through the analogue of a government's military, political, and economic alliances. Like political and military alliances, for Jakobson language is correlated through several systems (morphological, syntactical, phraseological), and in this way, he concludes, "language is a system of systems" (1962, 145). Crucially, the linguistic structure for Jakobson and the other Eurasianists, unlike the Saussurean model of arbitrary signification, is governed by a romantic conception of wholeness derived from specifically non-Darwianian evolutionary biological models. For example, Jakobson draws on the biologist Lev Berg to support his formulation of the Eurasian linguistic union as a model reliant not on coincidence but rather on convergence to internal laws, and in which hereditary variations are limited by their determined direction. Following German romantic thinkers like von Humboldt, phonological affinities mirror the ecological affinities of plants. In this way, convergence, as a non-Darwinian evolutionary principle, is the central mode of comparison.[45]

Similarly, the work of Nikolai Marr substituted natural selection for a principle of total contamination yielding to cross-breeding forms of language for culture building.[46] Marr's work highlights an intellectual lineage linking Russian orientalist accounts of the Caucasus in linguistics to historical poetics. In both the cases of non-Darwinian nomogenesis and Marrean cross-contamination, the idea of a cultural, geographic, scientific, and economic totality was based on the principle of the heterogeneous character of the Eurasian space and its attendant revolutionary time. These evolutionary biological theories, in turn, informed the conception of linguistic structure. As Sériot argues, Berg's nomogenesis illustrated how internal and external determinism, driven by mimesis or environmental/geographic factors, functioned as structural laws that generated a modern functional system of genetically varied organisms. As structural principles applied to linguistics, mimetic and geographic evolutionary determinism thus became central tropes in Russian orientalist literature. The scientific principles of mimesis, cross-contamination, and geographic determinism furthermore informed the literary imaginary of the Soviet frontier.

At the end of the nineteenth century, Russia's Eurasian geopolitics became central to calls for imperial messianism. Perhaps the most famous iteration of this Eurasian messianism is Fyodor Dostoevsky's description of the Russian conquest of Central Asia. In 1881 he wrote, "In Europe we were hangers-on, but to Asia we will go as masters. In Europe we were Tatars, but in Asia we too are Europeans" (1972–1992, 27:36–37).[47] Penned at an analogous historical moment during the Bolsheviks' southern expansion into the Caucasus in 1918, Alexander Blok's poem "The Scythians" (Skify) imagines Eurasia through the myth of the Third Rome:

that is, Russia's messianic succession to Byzantine power. Responding to the popular French orientalist depiction of the Slavic peoples as Tatars, Blok identifies the Russian empire instead as a band of Scythian warriors. His vision of the Iranian Scythian, in turn, draws on the race theory of the nineteenth-century orientalist Alexei Khomiakov. As an alternative to Ernest Renan's influential ethno-linguistic theory of Aryan and Semitic peoples, Khomiakov instead insisted on the terms Aryan and Kushite, which classified peoples according to monotheistic and polytheistic confessions. Thus Khomiakov identified Eurasia as Aryan, dominated by Islamic and Orthodox cultures, while both China and Germany instead encompassed forms of polytheistic Kushite civilizations.[48]

In Blok's poem, Russia stands as a sphinx gazing with love and hatred between two enemy cultures, Tatars and Europeans. Associating the figure of the Tatar with the Kushite, and the Scythian with the Iranian Aryan, the Scythian warrior represents both Russia's opposition to the forces of westernization and dominance over Asia through the unity of its monotheistic religions—Islam and Orthodoxy. Blok also urges that Russia should be inspired by the spirit of the ancient nomadic Scythians to expand its empire. "Across the wide thickets and forests / In front of pretty Europe / We will spread out! We will turn to you / with our Asiatic mugs" (Мы широко по дебрям и лесам / Перед Европою пригожей / расступимся! Мы обернемся к вам / своею азиатской рожей) (1997, 5:77). Blok appeals to Russia with a self-orientalizing gesture, calling on the Asian-Russian empire to rise up against *pretty Europe*. While emphasizing Russia's hybrid Eurasian character, he nonetheless issues a triumphal, militarized call for expansion to fulfill a Eurasian imperial telos. The doubled signifier of the Scythian warrior announces the Eurasian imperial crusade as an alternative to the cultural and political hegemony of Greco-European civilization. In this way, the Eurasian ideology relied on both the contingency of simultaneously being and nonbeing—that is, both and neither Asian nor European—and a commitment to an ethno-linguistic identity determined by Islamic and Orthodox culture.

The Eurasian ideology was not only one of the driving forces of Russia's cultural imperialism, but it also paradoxically informed the construction of pan-Turkic and pan-Islamic supranational identity discourses. One of the founding figures of Russian pan-Turkism, the Crimean Tatar writer and thinker Ismail Gasprinsky (Gasprali) invoked the idea of Eurasia in his vision of a Muslim utopia—albeit one set on a different mountain range—in southern Spain.[49] In his fictional account of an advanced civilization secluded in the Andalusian mountains, Gasprinksy described his vision of a Muslim Eurasian utopian civilization in his influential dual-language Russian and Crimean Tatar journal *The Interpreter* (*Terjuman*). He writes, "This city reminded me of neither Europe, nor Asia. There, one did not see the huge, compact, mountain-like tall houses of Europe and nothing resembled either the decaying shacks of our Asia, or its filth. Everything was original, beautiful, excellent, clean and [the result of] voluntary [participation]" (Gasprali 2008, 120). Rejecting the singularity of the geopolitical categories of Europe and Asia, Gasprinsky defends the possibility of a hospitable cultural union in the Russian imperial space through the formation of a nonplace, "neither Europe, nor Asia."[50] His utopian imaginary—both a good place and nonplace, or *eu-topos* and *ou-topos* according to the Greek etymology—offers an intervention into Eurasianist civilizing discourse, unified by a supranational vision of Turkic Muslim modernity.

While it is noteworthy that Gasprinsky had often been an apologist for empire, he here complicates the discursive terrain of Eurasianism by envisioning a sort of Eu(r)-Asian topos that replaces Pushkin's geographic, Dostoevsky's political, and Blok's cultural hybridity with an emptying of space and time.[51] For Gasprinsky, the determinism of the Eurasian telos is troubled by the nomadic topology and mythic futurity of his Andalusian society. Eurasianism and its evolutionist biological underpinnings thus not only authorized Russia's imperial hegemony but, more important, informed a differential ontology central to the experience of being in the Russian empire, and through which both Russian orientalists and Turkic Muslim intellectuals mediated literary modernity during the revolutionary period.

Revolution in the Caucasus

The most proximate and enduring imaginary Eurasian topos was projected onto the Caucasus. Indeed, the Caucasus served as a crucial ideological, geopolitical, and economic site in the Russian empire and during the formation of the Soviet Union. After the signing of the Treaty of

Turkmenchay in 1828, which ended the Russo-Persian wars (1804–1828), the Russian empire annexed the Caucasus territories north of the Araz (Araxes) River.[52] Russians traveled to the Caucasus as political exiles, imperial bureaucrats, researchers, soldiers, and adventure seekers. The region most memorably entered the Russian imagination through the poetry and prose of Alexander Pushkin, Mikhail Lermontov, Alexander Bestuzhev-Marlinsky, and Lev Tolstoy, as well as the photography and film of Sergei Prokudin-Gorsky and Alexander Mishon. Short stories and verse—as well as ethnography, geography and linguistics—exalted a romantic vision of the wild and sublime terrain on this border between Asia and Europe and its "brave" but "savage" and "primal" inhabitants.[53] Representations of the Caucasus emphasized the position of Russia on the border of Europe and Asia, a protectorate of European modernity and the heir to Asian "bravery" and "might," as well as a location for political exile and revolutionary dissent.

Pushkin, Bestuzhev-Marlinsky, and Lermontov's writings, which largely described the North Caucasus or Georgia, became the foundation of a general Caucasus imaginary. Both Pushkin and Lermontov were exiled to the Caucasus, in part, for their respective poems "Liberty" (Vol'nost' [1820]), which rallied the people against the tsarist autocracy, and "The Death of the Poet" (Smert' poeta [1837]), which condemned the ruling elite for Pushkin's death. In particular, Tsar Nicholas I feared the poets' sympathy for the revolutionary Decembrists—a group of writers and thinkers who organized an uprising in December 1825 to overthrow the tsar and establish a constitutional monarchy.[54] The most famous examples of what would become the Russian orientalist canon include Pushkin's "Prisoner of the Caucasus" (Kavkazskii plennik) and Lermontov's "Demon" (1829–1839), which recount failed quests for freedom and love set in the Caucasus. Through their descriptions of the landscapes and peoples of the Caucasus, the works emphasize the ideals of *freedom* (*vol'nost'*, *svoboda*), faith, bravery, and a close connection to nature.[55] *Svoboda* evokes freedom from restrictions, while *vol'nost'*, or liberty, refers to political will and a sense of the openness of space. Deriving from *volia*, a form of the Latinate *voluntas*, it emphasizes the role of human cognition in its determination. The poetic imagination of the Caucasus emphasized the role of literature in designing the conceptual topography of an early revolutionary discourse rooted in both a spatial and a political vision of freedom. Indeed, this poetic trend was sustained by state ethnographic campaigns, which defined the peoples of the Caucasus through their natural surroundings, envisioning both the diversity and unity of the Russian empire through the biological determinism of its landscape.[56]

The influence of the Russian imperial imagination generated by Russian émigrés, exiles, and orientalists left a mark on the local Muslim elite communities of the South Caucasus. The 1905 revolution and the consolidation of Stalin's power in the 1930s frame a period during which artistic and political experiments shaped the terrain of identity. The 1905 revolution resulted in Tsar Nicholas II's declaration of new civic laws, including the freedoms of speech, assembly, and conscience. These laws lifted the ban on the Muslim press and liberalized the status of non-Orthodox religious practices, including conversion and the proliferation of new religious sects.[57] The city of Tiflis (Tbilisi), the capital of Georgia, served as the administrative center of the Russian Caucasus and became a cultural center for literary salons and publications, as well as artistic, musical, and theatrical productions.[58]

The oil boom at the beginning of the twentieth century also channeled resources to Baku, making it the second largest producer of crude oil in the world and an important site during the revolutionary transition. From 1905 to 1929, Baku experienced a series of political upheavals, including the fall of the Russian empire, a brief period of noncentralized leadership under the Baku Commune and the Azerbaijan Democratic Republic, and finally the Soviet reconquest of the Caucasus and institutionalization of the Azerbaijan Soviet Socialist Republic in 1920. The economic development of Baku in turn led to the emergence of a Muslim entrepreneurial class that lent its support to a movement of Muslim cultural reform.[59] Focused on education and critical thinking, the movement campaigned for school reforms, launched an international Turkic language press, as well as an internationally touring theater company—named after its benefactor, the entrepreneur and intellectual Zeynalabdin Tağıyev.[60]

The rise of the Muslim merchant class contributed to the cultivation of discourses of civic and cultural identity. After the October revolution in 1917, Azerbaijan experienced only a brief period of independence under the Azerbaijan Democratic Republic from 1918 until the Bolsheviks invaded in 1920. Prior to the revolution, Azeri writers and thinkers associated an imperial civic identity with the event of Russian colonization in the mid-nineteenth century. Russian linguistic and civic identity, in predictable colonial fashion, represented the gateway to westernization and often modernization. However, an Azeri ethno-linguistic identity was also defined through Turkic and Persian cultural spheres of influence, which acquired political valences as they entered public fora, particularly in the local press and theater. Although identity in the Caucasus remained highly regionalized among the working class and peasant populations, at the turn of the century the emerging class of Russian- and French-educated writers and thinkers, in addition to the existing group of Persianate and Ottoman literati, began to promote discourses of identity that transcended Russian, Persian, and Ottoman national identity. Persian cultural influences on Azeri identity, which in the twentieth century were often connected to a critique of Islamic clericism, extended back to the foundational role of sixteenth-century Persian poetry and the Shi'i tradition of the passion plays or *ta'ziyeh* ritual performances on local literature and theater under the Safavids.[61] Despite a great diversity of forms of Islam practiced in the Caucasus, a supranational notion of pan-Islamic Muslim cultural identity was defined through a common association with the *umma*, or the international community of Islamic believers. Similarly, a supranational pan-Turkic identity was fostered through the rise of print culture. These Muslim, Turkic (and Persianate) identity discourses functioned as cultural signifiers that were interpolated in civic contexts through reformist campaigns in popular literary and cultural journals.

While the idea of the cultural fusion of Europe and Asia was promoted both in the writings of Turkic Muslims and Russian orientalists, these Eurasias were used to justify different forms of political and cultural sovereignty. For example, forms of pan-Turkism were tied to both national and orientalist narratives. On the one hand, European orientalists—including the Hungarian Arminius Vambery and the Frenchman Léon Cahun—developed a political ideology of world domination under the rubric of pan-Turkism in order to justify the imperial expansion of the Russian and British empires in Central Asia (Altstadt 1986, 280). On the other hand, Turkic writers and thinkers in the Russian empire generated pan-Turkic ethno-linguistic forms of self-identification as part of local reform campaigns (Altstadt 1986, 280). That is, while Vambery theorized the creation of a pan-Turkic state from the Adriatic to China, Azeri authors instead emphasized the creation of an imagined community of readers through a body of literary, philosophical, and political works, spread by the print boom at the turn of the century.

To this end, the Azeri writer and thinker Ali bey Hüseynzade describes the objectives of his literary journal *Enlightenment* (*Füyuzat*), published between 1906 and 1907, as a project aimed at a progressive cultural unification according to the slogan: "Turkify, Islamicize, Europeanize."[62] Hüseynzade envisions the union of language and religion through a combined reform effort including an "Islamic renaissance" (*islam intibahı*), the creation of "national self awareness" (*milliözünü derk*), and "Europeanization as a synthesis of Eastern and Western culture" (*avropalaşmaq— Qerb ve Şerq medniyyetlerinin sintezi*) ([1906–1907] 2007, xxiv). While Hüseynzade's journal represented a particularly Turkophilic identity, the tripartite structure of his model for "national freedom" (*milli azadlıq*) is informed by a common interest shared by Azeri writers and thinkers of the time in fusing European and Islamic thought to modernize language education and religious institutions. These pan-Turkic and pan-Islamic signifiers participated in the creation of a literary corpus that generated its own history of impact and influence within and beyond the borders of the former imperial territories. The intersection of these forms of hybrid Eurasian identity—whether used in imagining pan-Slavic, pan-Turkic, or pan-Islamic cultural communities—generated a medium for public discourse, albeit one that often operated through interlingual and intertextual dialogues.[63] An examination of the interference between these competing visions of Eurasia highlights a dissonance between orientalist visions of world domination and alternative supranational counternarratives that interpolated the Turkic and Persianate Muslim world. In this way, these intersecting narratives of religious and linguistic identity shaped the revolutionary space and influenced the creation of a modern subjectivity through the circulation of a crucial body of texts that animated discourses of both imperial and anti-imperial identity.

Examining the development of an ideology, or system of ideas, about Eurasia as a dynamic intertextual modality renders legible its role in framing the important cultural function of religious ritual and language politics in the political and cultural life of the empire. In particular, Islam—the largest confessional minority in the former imperial and Soviet space— and Azeri Turkic—which held the strongest transnational ties to the Persian and Ottoman empires in the Caucasus—played a significant role in shaping imperial geopolitics during the revolutionary transition. Placing these two, often-conflicting, Eurasias into dialogue, I outline a critical threshold space-time that reveals both the construction of imperial narratives and the role of heteroglossic and heterodoxic Russian and Turkic responses in shaping and contesting these dominant discourses. The threshold demarcates the geopolitical border space of Eurasia, the temporal shift from the fall of the Russian empire through the formation of the Soviet Union, and intertextual and discursive exchanges between these competing visions of identity. In this way, the threshold not only outlines the Eurasian geopolitical border zone and the *translatio imperii* from the Russian to the Soviet empires but marks the creation of a diverse intertextual topography in which these cultural exchanges shaped the political and historical transformations of the early twentieth century.

While it is tempting to read the revolution in the Caucasus as a political shift from a colony to anti-imperial republic, these heterodoxic and heterologic intertextual encounters between metropolitan Russia and the Caucasus's colonial outposts (*okraina*) of Tbilisi and Baku reveal a different story. The reciprocal, though unequal, cultural exchanges that took shape in poetry, periodicals, theater, and political essays contributed to the construction of an enduring discourse of an orientalist Eurasian imaginary, which even today remains central to Russian calls for imperial expansion. In this way, my portrait of the Caucasus differs from Steven Lee's vision of the Soviet international avant-garde in his *Ethnic Avant-Garde: Minority Cultures and World Revolution* as "inclusive and decolonizing" (2015, 4). I argue instead that the multinationalism of the avant-garde was central to the regulation by Soviet imperial control, from Stalin's purges in the 1930s to continued provocations of interethnic violence in the republics through the fall of the Soviet Union. These Eurasias not only appear in the cultural archives of the nineteenth and twentieth centuries but reemerge in the institutional fora of academic exchange, shaping Soviet and post-Soviet critical approaches to reading the literature of the Russian and Soviet empires. Indeed, the afterlife of Eurasia remains well chronicled in the Russian literary canon, including the many famous accounts of Tolstoy, Pushkin, and Lermontov in the Caucasus, which remain central to North American Slavic department curricula.[64] This canon is also readily deployed in public media, such as in the example of the flood of articles and references to Tolstoy's *Hadji Murat* following the identification of the Tsarnaev brothers as the Boston Marathon bombers. The figure of the threshold, in turn, formulates a reading practice for disentangling the relations of power that underlie these intertextual encounters and their historicization in Soviet and contemporary scholarship.

My literary selection includes works written by members of the Russian intelligentsia who traveled to the Caucasus either as political exiles or in the service of the imperial administration or to participate in revolutionary politics and intellectual exchange. In this way, the book explores the writers who have since become integral to the Russian romantic, realist, and modernist literary canons, and whose works shaped the Russian orientalist imagination. These include Alexander Pushkin (Aleksandr Sergeevich Pushkin), Mikhail Lermontov (Mikhail Iur'evich Lermontov), Nikolai Gogol (Nikolai Vasil'evich Gogol'), Viacheslav Ivanov (Viacheslav Ivanovich Ivanov), Vladimir Mayakovsky (Vladimir Vladimirovich Maiakovskii), Sergei Gorodetsky (Sergei Mitrofanovich Gorodetskii), Alexei Kruchenykh (Aleksei Eliseevich Kruchenykh), Velimir Khlebnikov, and Tatiana Vechorka (Tat'iana Vechërka).[65] I examine the ways in which their Muslim interlocutors referenced, parodied, translated, and transformed their work and in so doing generated a vision of literary modernity in dialogue with Russian orientalism. To this end I discuss the work of Mirze Feteli Axundov, Abbas Sehhet, Mehemmed Hadi, Celil Memmedquluzade, Üzeyir Hacıbeyov, Hüseyn Cavid, Süleyman Rüstem, Mikayıl Refili, and the Turkish poet Nazim Hikmet, with the overall effect of displacing Russian imperial authority. These authors, like their Russian interlocutors, engaged with a broad range of styles from classical Arabo-Persian-Ottoman poetic forms and tropes to a free verse style. Writers such as Memmedquluzade also drew on a satirical tradition of Turkic folktales. In post-Soviet Azerbaijani literature textbooks these writers are often defined by two camps, highlighting their participation either in the popular working-class Turkic and Persian-oriented satirical journal *Molla Nesreddin* edited by Memmedquluzade or the more bourgeois European and Ottoman-oriented journal *Enlightenment* edited by Hüseynzade. Indeed, while the journals themselves played up this rivalry, such a binary vision of Azeri literary production does not account for the many authors who published in both journals, as well as the various intersections and collaborations among these visions of Azeri Turkic, Persian, Ottoman, European, and Russian imperial identity, which circulated during the transitional revolutionary period. These intertextual encounters not only reveal the manner in which the Russian orientalist literary canon was read by Muslim writers and thinkers from the Caucasus, but it further exposes how their engagement with the Russian literary imaginary shaped their own discussions of the relationship among reform, modern forms of governance, and Islam.

Figures such as Refili, Rüstem, Cavid, Memmedquluzade, and Nariman Narimanov participated in the formation of the Soviet world literature project, many of them willingly serving in or collaborating with Soviet institutions and contributing to Latinization and Russian translation efforts. However, there is a risk in romanticizing their role, since they were on the winning side of history. There is another story that can be traced in the tracks of those who challenged the system and were forced to immigrate to Warsaw, Paris, Istanbul, and Berlin after the October revolution. These included the members of the anti-Soviet Prometheus movement that was founded between 1923 and 1926 in Istanbul. Azeri intellectuals involved in the movement included the writers and statesmen Memmed Amin Rasulzade, Akhmed Aghaoglu, Ali bey Hüseynzade, Mirza Bala Mehmetzade, and Hilal Münchi.[66] They also launched a literary journal of the same name, *Promethée*, published in French and funded by a Polish and French anti-Bolshevik resistance with the main aims of combating Soviet-Russian imperialism.[67] The stories of other writers and thinkers who fled to Istanbul, Tebriz, Tehran, and beyond still remains to be written.

More broadly, while the narrative of Russian writers in the Caucasus has become well known, literary works by Muslim writers and thinkers remain underrepresented in contemporary Anglophone scholarship.[68] This is not only because these works were written in Persian and Turkic languages through the mid-twentieth century, but because they appealed to an interest in supranational intellectual traditions across the Persian, Ottoman, and Russian empires, as well as Europe and the greater Islamic world. Indeed, these philosophic, literary, and political works influenced Muslim intellectuals in Turkey, Central Asia, Iran, Egypt, and Algeria. Beyond exceptional cases, meetings between Russians and Muslims in the Caucasus have been more difficult to trace. Mayakovsky, Khlebnikov, and Ivanov gave lectures in Baku in the 1920s, yet their names remain largely absent from the Turkic press. Similarly, they do not discuss the work of their Azeri contemporaries Memmedquluzade, Sehhet, and Refili. The Soviet conquest of the Caucasus generated a series of institutional collaborative productions in the domains of theater, propaganda posters, and film. Archival records of these collaborative projects have largely been displaced, lost, or remain classified. This book thus recounts the story of Russian and Muslim cultural interactions between these institutional and intertextual encounters, as well as rendering connections visible from within the aesthetic tissue of the works themselves. An examination of the cultural topography of the Caucasus in this way offers the opportunity to challenge the orientalist discourse of Eurasian hybridity, not only by rendering legible forms of difference, but by presenting contesting and intertwining ideologies of empire from both positions of cultural and political hegemony as well as marginality.

Orientalism on the Threshold: In Bakhtin's Margins

Since the collapse of the Soviet Union, Slavic and Eurasian studies have introduced the literature of the former Soviet Union into world literature debates—specifically in the field of postcolonial studies. Scholars in the United States have begun to think about the application of Edward Said's *Orientalism* (1978) to the former Soviet and Russian imperial space only since the collapse of the Soviet Union (Alexander Etkind, Monika Greenleaf, Katya Hokanson, Adeeb Khalid, Nathaniel Knight, Susan Layton, Harsha Ram, Maria Todorova, and Vera Tolz).[69] Furthermore, as Afrid Bustanov argues the absence of scholarship penned in the former Soviet Union that links orientalist scholarship to state politics is exemplified by the belated Russian translation and publication of Edward Said's *Orientalism* only in 2006 (2015, xii). Ronald Suny and Alexander Etkind trace the ways in which the fashioning of Russian national identity was imbricated in the economic and political processes of imperial expansion.[70] Francine Hirsch's (2005) history of the national question highlights the role of the institution of orientalist ethnography in the formation of the political geography of the Soviet Union.[71] As demonstrated in the work of Hirsch, Terry Martin, and Yuri Slezkine, scholarship on nationalities policies has provided insight into the character of the Soviet empire.

Nationalities policies were a Bolshevik anti-imperialist ideology that fostered national consciousness as a step in the historical evolution of class consciousness, as well as to combat an emerging Great Russian chauvinism. The policies that emerged from these debates included the creation of organizations such as the People's Commissariat of Nationalities (Narkomnats), which worked to install local pro-Bolshevik leaders and create alliances with national self-determination movements. Martin's vision of an "affirmative action empire" highlights the central state's promotion of nationalities as a challenge to Russian chauvinism (2001, 1–9). Slezkine (1994) instead emphasizes the formation of a philosophical nationalism, through the praxis of translation, which emulated the structure of the communal apartment.[72] Hirsch's work, perhaps most compellingly, positions nationalities policies as a form of state-sponsored evolutionism, a policy of double assimilation whereby subjects' association with the newly created nations formulated their civic engagement with the Soviet state (2005, 63–97). As this scholarship illustrates, the shift in the discourse of imperialism to one of anti-imperialist evolutionism was thus central to political and social transformations from the fall of the Russian empire through the formation of the Soviet Union.

Although many of the critiques of the application of Orientalism to the Eurasian context have been levied against the Eurocentrism of Said's project, few alternative models have taken precedence.[73] However, it is precisely cases such as those of the Russian empire and Soviet Union that offer an opportunity to critically assess and develop postcolonial theory to accommodate a world literary scope. Indeed, this task requires decentering the Anglophone and European canon of world literature, as well as the genre of the novel.[74] The objective of this book is thus not the application of Orientalism to the Eurasian context but rather the task of exposing the imbrications of imperial and anti-imperial discourses that animate literary representations across the empire and their role in the formation of Russian and Soviet literary modernity. Drawing on Said's definition of Orientalism as a corporate institution, my portrait of Eurasian literary modernity also attends to the role of Eurasianism in shaping North American Slavic studies, through the influential role played by émigré intellectuals. In so doing, I highlight the formation and maintenance of a Russian canon predicated on a Eurasianist totality, which emerged in the Russian orientalist archive.[75] By rejecting the singular model of national literature, my discussion follows the formation of imperial and supra-national identity in works produced by writers and thinkers across the Persian, Ottoman, and Russian empires, as well as in Europe. Placing these texts into dialogue, however, requires an attention to the shifting value of linguistic and religious discourses within the transitional political and social space of the revolutionary period in the Caucasus. In this way, the epistemological shifts in the domains of religious and secular politics, language, and speech illuminate the political and social transformations of the early twentieth century.

Mindful of the Eurocentrism of his own project, Said developed an analysis of *contrapuntal* reading and *secular criticism*. He presents con-trapuntal reading in *Culture and Imperialism* (1994) as a method for exposing an entire network of interactions that transcend the dominant narratives of metropolitan history. Said writes, "As we look back at the cultural archive, we begin to reread it not univocally but *contrapuntally*, with a simultaneous awareness both of the metropolitan history that is narrated and of those other histories against which (and together with which) the dominating discourse acts" (1994, 51).[76] The practice of con-trapuntal reading offers an important corrective to the binary constitution of a colonial "periphery" through metropolitan scholarship. Further-more, as critical engagements with Said's oeuvre highlight, his model of secular criticism offers a space for contesting another series of boundaries among imperial, national, linguistic, ethnic, and religious discourses of identity (1978, 2–3).[77] Secular criticism transcends the binary relation-ship between the secular and religious, presenting a heterodox praxis of reading across the boundaries of empire, nation, religion, and language. Framing Said's work as a heterodox praxis also offers a mode for think-ing critically about the role of academic institutions in constructing and maintaining ontological and epistemological distinctions between the Ori-ent and the Occident, or in the case of the Russian and Soviet empires, in constructing an idea of Eurasia.[78] One of the most important elements in this process is a critical approach to canons and the idea of canonicity, whether literary or disciplinary.

As a critical practice for reading literature across cultural discourses, as well as institutional affiliations, Said's secular criticism finds an analogue in Bakhtin's work on the novel, which for Bakhtin is the genre that most embodies his vision of literary modernity. Whereas an engagement with

Said offers the opportunity to intervene in the Eurocentric focus of studies of empire through heterodox praxis, a discussion of Bakhtin's work similarly invites a critical assessment of appropriations of his understanding of heterology in the (post)colonial context. The intersection and complication of these discourses of imperial hegemony and anti-imperial heterodoxy, in the context of the fall of the Russian empire and formation of a Soviet literary modernity, present a compelling context for revising these theoretical frameworks.

Bakhtin's discussion of novelistic discourse outlines the ways in which heterogeneous linguistic histories or heteroglossia (*raznoiazychnost'*) inscribe diverse registers of speech or heterology (*raznorechivost'*) in literary discourse. Often conflated in English translation, these two terms clarify the relationship between intersecting linguistic histories and their animation in speech acts. For Bakhtin, literary or novelistic discourse is constituted through heterology—that is, *in* and *through* the diverse dialogic interactions among literary, cultural, and historical discourses, in which discourse (*slovo*), signifies not only a word but its authoritative function in language (1997–2012, 3:9–179).[79] Bakhtin's writings on novelistic discourse, influenced by his interest in Hegelian dialectics, crucially foreground a model of literary modernity predicated on intersubjective and heterogeneous speech acts. While novelistic discourse emerges from a textual world, at its foundations it envisions interactions between individual utterances and literary forms, as well as the space, time, and sociolinguistic codes that animate them.

While the relationship between the world and the text in Bakhtin's work, as well as Said's, is marked by the shift in the value of language as a primary category for determining knowledge, the relationship between language and meaning in Bakhtin's work is not entirely symbolic.[80] For Said, the text remains founded in the historical moments in which literature is produced and read.[81] For Bakhtin, literature generates exchanges between the speech acts of historically and materially constituted conscious subjects. In *Problems in Dostoevsky's Poetics* he writes that the idea is not fixed as an "individual psychological formation" but rather "the idea is inter-individual and inter-subjective—the realm of its existence [*bytie*] is not individual consciousness but dialogic communion [*obshchenie*] *between* consciousnesses" (1984, 88; 1997–2012, 6:99). In this sense, Bakhtin argues for a sociological rather than a psychological theory of consciousness. The idea is a *live event*, played out at the point of dialogic meeting between two or several consciousnesses . . . Like the word, the idea wants to be heard, understood, and 'answered' by other voices from other positions." For Bakhtin the idea formulates the space-time of an interchange or encounter (*obshchenie*) between individual, conscious subjects. While Said highlights the "worldly" ideological function of literary discourse, Bakhtin develops its ontological dimension through the intersubjective event of being in language.

The parallel between Said and Bakhtin's work also renders legible the endemic relationship between semiotics and anthropology, the notion that cultural models can be understood *as if* they were forms of communication. Literature in this sense is a mode of authoring that organizes experience—that is, makes it intelligible. The Kantian symbolic relationship between the linguistic model and its production of meaning about culture retains a necessary critical distance from the empirical world while asserting its claims to practicality. However, in the context of a discussion of the real violence of the colonial encounter, this disengagement from the political world is rarely possible and presents a problematic ethical relationship between the critic and the literary object. This is perhaps why Said emphasizes his methodological ties both to a Foucauldian model of discourse that exposes relations of power embedded in forms of knowledge about the Orient and an intertextual system of writers and works that generate a collective representation of the orient. The tension between Foucauldian discourse and intertextuality accounts for Said's description of the Orient as both a real and imagined place. Bakhtin's dialogism instead describes these relations of power, not only as institutions that produce knowledge or a set of texts that generate a collective consciousness through repetition but through the sociopolitical function of language. Foucault's conception of discourse relies on a critical approach to the epistemological foundations of the culture, whereas Bakhtin understands discourse through the social life and creative power of the word. Indeed, this very notion of creativity is in part indebted to a line of German romantic thought, as well as the aforementioned German and Russian engagements with evolutionary biology.

The creative vitality of discourse in Bakhtin's work is rooted in many sources including his interest in Russian Orthodoxy, German romanticism, and the avant-garde art of his day.[82] In turn, the aesthetics of the avant-garde, which Bakhtin would have encountered during his youth spent in Petrograd and Vitebsk between 1917 and 1923, also left a mark on his theories of the literary language.[83] These influences surface in Bakhtin's references to popular avant-garde topoi such as the unstable play among the positions of the author, character, and reader that characterize the carnival environment. While Bakhtin discusses these concepts in the context of a historical study of Rabelais, his theory of the *carnivalesque* can be read as a critique of the verticality of Soviet power under Stalinism through its allusions to the Commedia dell'arte, a popular theme within the avant-garde (1997–2012, 4:11–506).[84] Bakhtin's appreciation of the vitality of the word thus hinges on his location within the intellectual history of the early twentieth-century Russian empire as it marks his belated interests in the avant-garde.

Bakhtin's interpreters in Euro-American academia have often read him as a semiotician *avant la lettre*, emphasizing the centrality of intertextuality, as both a collection of texts and their attendant linguistic systems, to his model of novelistic discourse.[85] However, for Bakhtin the text does not represent but *is* an intersubjective event implicitly connected to the truth value of speaking consciousnesses.[86] In this way, his work shares close ties with historical poetics and in particular the work of Alexander Veselovsky. One of the central concepts in Veselovsky's work is *perezhivanie*, which as Boris Maslov describes, carries both the ethnographic sense of survival and the more common connotation of experience: that is, it describes a historically rooted experience that recycles or perpetuates cultural forms (2016, 63).

As a counterpoint to the Eurocentrism of this historical approach to poetics, the Azeri poet Abbas Sehhet introduces his vision of poetic empathy, which I discuss in detail in chapter 2. For Sehhet, the author must submit to his or her feelings in order "to make the word touch the heart of the reader and awaken feeling in another's heart" (2005, 243–45). In this sense, the affective power of literature is shared between author and reader through the historical experiences embedded in the text. For Sehhet, like Bakhtin and Veselovsky, sentiment invigorates the immediacy of the past in the present act of reading. However, for Sehhet this process is connected to the goal of generating a new poetic tradition through, in part, the translation and transformation of a Russian romantic imaginary of the Caucasus according to an aesthetics of empathy. One of the images central to Sehhet's reading is his analogy between writing and a sunset. For Sehhet crucially the moment of creativity in the poetic word is not only inspired by nature but "reveals itself in every particle." He continues describing the passage from day to night: "We (the author) elaborate on our feelings and our dream-thoughts while watching this scene" in order to "awaken another's heart-feeling." Indeed, experience is importantly exemplified for Sehhet in the romantic transient effects of nature: steam rising, sunset, moonrise, and dusk. The natural environment, poised on the threshold of transition, animates the process of empathy and exchange among author, reader, and text.

Bakhtin also identifies the social or active quality of language in the spatial figure of the threshold. The concept of the threshold, although located in the marginalia of *Problems of Dostoevsky's Poetics*, provides a useful model for understanding his dynamic framing of a relational ontology between the individual and the social. In this way, it can be applied to interactions between literary discourse and the social world, as well as between the literary text and the world of the critic. Bakhtin situates a crisis in consciousness in Dostoevsky's work along the discursive fault line of the threshold. The threshold is a *chronotope*, or as Bakhtin notes, the "image [*obraz*] of man in literature" (1981, 84–85; 1997–2012, 3:342). As a defining feature of genre, the chronotope is an important figure for Bakhtin because it brings the historical world, individual consciousness, and the master codes embedded in language into contact. It is the site where the historical traces of multiple languages (heteroglossia) and diverse registers of speech (heterology) are revealed. Bakhtin describes the threshold chronotope in particular as an intersubjective space of dialogization, "the *boundary* [*granitsa*] between one's own and someone else's consciousness, on the *threshold* [*porog*]" where "everything internal gravitates not toward itself but is turned to the outside and dialogized, every internal experience ends up on the boundary, encounters another, and in this tension-filled encounter lies its entire essence" (1984, 287; 1997–2012, 5:345).[87] The threshold chronotope thus describes the points of contact between individual and social codes in language, which are rendered more visible by the ruptures in consciousness exposed in the intercultural colonial encounter.[88]

One of the inaugural applications of Bakhtin's work to postcolonial theory is Homi Bhabha's discussion of intersubjectivity in *The Location of Culture* (1994). Engaging with elements from Bakhtin's work collected in *Speech Genres & Other Late Essays* (1986), he frames nations and cultures as narrative constructions, which emerge from hybrid national and cultural constituencies. In so doing, Bhabha inverts Bakhtin's model, applying an analysis of narrative to culture, rather than applying cultural interactions to the literary text. His specific engagement with Bakhtin focuses on the latter's "attempt to individuate social agency as the after-effect of the intersubjective" (1994, 269). However, Bhabha's location of agency in the after-effect of the intersubjective is premised on his contention that the site of enunciation and enunciative modality are displaced from the intersubjective encounter and thus are unable to individuate and localize the utterance (1994, 270). Notably Bhabha reads Bakhtin's discussion of the chain of communication as a metaphor. In this way, his reading renders Bakhtinian intersubjectivity as a symbolic dialogism that locates culture beyond the text. Contemporaneity, however, is crucial for Bakhtin (as for Sehhet), and I instead insist that the model of the threshold provides both a site and modality for the enunciation of the subject. Bakhtin exposes the synchronized diachrony of the event by drawing on a verbal play between the word for "event" (*sobytie*), and its root meaning "co-being" (*so-byt'e*). The concept of authorship is central to Bakhtin's phenomenology of aesthetic experience, in which the independent position of the author as both conditional to but also outside of the character's consciousness constitutes the sense of verisimilitude in the novel. Dostoevsky's characters, Bakhtin writes are "*free* people, capable of standing *alongside* their creator, capable of not agreeing with him and even of rebelling against him" and "combine but are not merged with the unity of the event [*sobytie*]" because they are "*not only objects of authorial discourse but also subjects of their own directly signifying discourse*" (1984, 6–7; 1997–2012, 6:10). For Bakhtin these cultural exchanges are not transcribed as a narrative but acquire a livelihood and agency within the narrative. They are capable of rebelling against their author and of becoming the signifying subjects of their own discourse. In this way, their agency is constituted *in* and *through* the threshold time-space of the textual event.

One modality through which this vision of the literary event manifests is in the act of translation. In an analysis of translation in colonial Egypt, *Disarming Words: Empire and the Seductions of Translation in Egypt*, Shaden Tageldin adopts the model of what she terms "translational seduction" as "a semiotic and intersubjective strategy of displacement, a mastery of diverted (thus diverting) appearances" (2011, 11). Tageldin outlines three forms of translation as interlingual, intercultural—or the "transaction of epistemic 'equivalence' in economies of cultural exchange"—and intersubjective—or "the translation of one's self to resemble an Other's" (2011, 13). The model of translation, Tageldin argues, fills the lacuna left by Said's incomplete model of contrapuntal reading by describing how subjects negotiate the terms of their transformation. In this way, Tageldin, who also engages directly with Bakhtin's theory of novelistic discourse, compellingly renders the subject's agency to negotiate its own terms.

Like Tageldin's translational seduction, reading on the threshold renders legible the freedom of the literary subject to develop its own signifying discourse. In this way, the threshold is not a hybrid space, if as Bhabha posits, hybridity is understood in opposition to Western history's claims to the "holism of culture and community" (1994, 142). Rather, the threshold is a site in which the subject engages in the dynamic event of dialogue by placing into question the orientalist fantasy of Eurasian cultural unity. The threshold thus not only reveals the ways in which Bakhtin's novelistic discourse is tied to the intellectual history of structuralist linguistics, but also how these intersecting Eurasian imaginaries can render legible forms of literary modernity as central to both imperial and anti-imperial politics across the Russian and Turkic Muslim linguistic and cultural divide. The emergence of porous boundaries among political, linguistic, and cultural epistemologies activates the modalities of intercultural exchange at the heart of translation theory. However, while translations compose a significant portion of the corpus of texts produced in the Caucasus and account for their multilinguality, the heterodox praxis of reading on the threshold describes an intersubjective event. In so doing, it challenges political, linguistic, cultural, and disciplinary borders to expose the representation of a modernist Eurasian imaginary.

While this book opens with a discussion of the diversity of languages, speech, and doxa—that is, the heterodoxy and heterology of the cultural space of the South Caucasus—it concludes with a vision of the foreclosure of these potentialities through the crystallization of Soviet colonial power during the mid-1920s. The first section contests the doxa that cemented a singular idea of the Caucasus and its attendant Eurasian imperial politics. The second section, in turn, chronicles the gradual disappearance

of heterological networks that connected the Russian, Persian, and Ottoman empires with the creation of new forms of Bolshevik national consciousness. However, a linear historical narrative of the transformation
of a culturally heterogeneous Russian empire into a monolithic Soviet
empire would be a considerable oversimplification of the revolutionary
transition. Indeed, during the 1930s, forms of performance such as the
theater and the ballad tradition of *mugham*—or sung dialogues on various
themes—blended Azeri, Russian, and a new Bolshevik jargon, generating
networks of intertwining meanings and diverse registers of speech while
challenging doxic conventions in both musical and poetic genres.

The chronological organization of this book instead presents the development of an orientalist vision of a revolutionary Caucasus from 1905
through 1929 as both a Eurasian imaginary and a real public space that
shaped the aesthetics and politics of literary production in the Azerbaijani
Soviet republic and in the Soviet Union more broadly. It also exposes the
imperial politics and forms of anticolonial subjectivity that generated the
poetics of the Eurasian threshold. The shifting conception of a Muslim
Turkic identity during the revolutionary period, in turn, illustrates the
role of materialist aesthetics and Marxist-Leninist anti-imperialism in the
formation of a supranational Turkic Muslim identity, albeit one quickly
succeeded by Azerbaijani Soviet nationalism.

The contemporary political resonances of these orientalist discourses
and the forms of anti-imperial resistance that developed alongside them
shed light on the nationalist reactions of Putin's new Russia and his so-
called neoimperial expansion. While scholars such as Marlène Laruelle
have traced the resurgence of the intellectual currents of Eurasianism in
the 1990s post-Soviet moment from Alexander Dugin's neonationalist
Eurasianism in Russia to pan-Turkic Eurasianist movements in Tatarstan
and Kazakhstan, this book argues that the intertextual encounters
between Turkic Muslim and Russian writers during the revolutionary
transition a century earlier shaped the resurgent forms of national identity
that have since developed during the post-Soviet period (Laruelle 2012,
145–88). This is not to say, however, that Putin's campaigns replicated
either a neotsarist or Soviet multinational state, but rather that they can
be more critically envisioned as a response to the Eurasian imaginary as a
cultural evolutionist project that took shape on the imperial-revolutionary
threshold. At once a study in poetics and geopolitics, *On the Threshold*

of Eurasia seeks to destabilize a singular vision of Russia's empire as the product of an anxiety about European modernity. It instead examines the interactions between the work of Russians and Turkic Muslim writers as they envisioned the Eurasian imaginary on the imperial periphery and its stakes in the formation of new cultural, artistic, and political forms of life.

Although this book is centered on the particular history of the development of an aesthetic and political project in the Caucasus during the revolutionary period, its implications on the relationship between (post) coloniality and the construction of forms of literary modernity beyond the secular, capitalist West find resonances in work on global modernisms. Additionally, it offers a corrective to the reductive center-periphery binary by thinking through the ways in which Eurasia not only served as Europe's Other, but was reimagined through writings across radically disparate linguistic, cultural, and disciplinary conventions. In so doing, this book offers an alternative reading of literary modernity, which did not mimic the aesthetics of the German/Russian avant-garde or Anglo-French orientalism but in engaging in dialogue with a supranational vision of Persian-Ottoman poetics, Islamic thought, and an internationalist Marxist-Leninist aesthetics generated a new language and shape for poetry. While at once radically local, this story also offers a theoretical model for thinking through a new type of comparative historical poetics, which critically engages with the orientalist vision of Eurasian totality by opening up a hidden archive of intertextual encounters on the threshold of the Eurasian empire.

Part I

Heterodoxy and Imperial Returns

1

Parodic and Messianic Genealogies

Reading Gogol in Azeri in the Late Imperial Caucasus

It is perhaps strange that a book about the evolution of poetics would begin with a chapter on prose. However, for the theorists who hailed Gogol's prose in the twentieth century as an exemplary feature of the world literature canon, it was precisely this critical work of reading *strangely*, of exposing the poetics within prose, which generated the political value of the literary text. One of the best-remembered descriptions of Gogol's prose was Fyodor Dostoevsky's apocryphal claim that all of Russian literature came out of Gogol's *Overcoat*. Indeed, the Russian formalists and semioticians secured Gogol's place as the founder of a revolutionary parodic tradition precisely by foregrounding the materiality of the Gogolian text as the key to his foundational role in shaping Russian culture and the Eurasianist imaginary.[1] Gogol's inclusion in a classic Russian literary canon in US Slavic departments also made him an important source of knowledge about Soviet life during the Cold War.[2] It is thus perhaps appropriately paradoxical that Gogol's work, a veritable *passe-partout*, has over the course of the twentieth century embodied both a materialist critique of capital and a liberal critique of bureaucracy.

Gogol's centrality to the Russian literary canon both domestically and abroad can be attributed to the interpolation of his imagined imperial poetics in a series of revolutions, ranging from the formation of the Soviet Union in the beginning of the twentieth century to its dissolution at the century's end. Indeed, Gogol's words have served a spectrum of political ends at the hands of his critics, from defining the cultural space of the Russian empire in relation to Ukraine in the nineteenth century to championing the revolutionary ideology of the Bolshevik party in the twentieth century. Once an integral part of the Soviet literary canon, Gogol's famous parodic style still remains an important factor in defining the reading practices of post-Soviet scholarship. Gogol's literary canonization in Russian culture, however, assigns a deceptive transparency to the opaque and unequal processes through which his work was appropriated on the peripheries of the Russian empire. How then can Gogol provide a window onto the geopolitical and cultural shifts that marked the transition from the Russian to the Soviet empire and the formation of Eurasianist discourses?

In 1909 Celil Memmedquluzade—the Azeri writer, critic, dramatist, and editor of the renowned satirical journal *Molla Nesreddin*—announced the arrival of a strange word in his journal—a "Qoqol."[3] Hidden beneath the old-script Azeri transliteration was none other than the writer of the famed *Overcoat*. Memmedquluzade's writings inspired by "Qoqol" provide a unique vantage point from which to understand Gogol's representations of the imperial periphery beyond the Slavic canon.[4] Examining the ways in which Gogol's representations of time and space influenced literary production across the former empire reveals a complex network of geopoetic landscapes. Gogol's geopoetics provide the template for Memmedquluzade's architecture of a revolutionary identity, in which representations of the "periphery" acquire a central position. Geopoetics, which describes the intersection between memory and geography, suggests an inherently comparative methodology, which Edward Said memorably described as "the study of human space" (2002, 241). W. J. T. Mitchell (2000) aligns geopoetics with a dialectical triad—space, place, and landscape—drawing on the work of the Marxist geographer David Harvey. Indeed, Mitchell's and Harvey's efforts to synthesize the phenomenological and experiential traditions with French Marxism expose the geopolitical, cognitive and affective dimensions of geopoetics.[5] A critical geopoetics also attends to the ways in which poetic geographies were tied to the institutional structures that authorized them and the social imaginaries that produced them. Such a reading of Gogol and Memmedquluzade opens up a previously unexamined transnational and interdisciplinary dimension of the literature of the Russian empire.[6] The geopoetics of Ukraine as Russia's proximate periphery, which Gogol's work generated, enabled the formal device of parody in his work to be read as the very mechanism for explaining the evolution of Russian political and literary history.[7] Displacing his parodic genealogy to the South Caucasus, however, reveals the emergence of a different geopoetical intervention marked by a more profound experience of colonial alienation.

Memmedquluzade's reception and translations of Gogol illustrate the role of Russian imperial literature more broadly in forging cultural connections and anticipating ruptures between the Muslim South Caucasus, the Russian imperial metropole, and the transnational Turkic Muslim world. The discourse of Russia's simultaneous attraction and alienation from Europe, a window through which the colonial encounter was imagined by exiled Russian poets, can be more dynamically addressed from the experience of the Muslim subjects "writing back" to the empire. Gogol's parody presents a formal model for thinking through the geopoetics of Eurasia through the processes of literary imitation and translation. Furthermore, Gogol's popularity in the Caucasus speaks to the importance of approaching his work not only from the perspective of intra-Slavic relations but through the more radical Other of the Muslim Turk writing from the margins of the privileged positions of Slavic linguistic and Christian cultural hegemony. Such a reading also contributes to a growing scholarship on Turkic-Russian encounters within and beyond the Russian empire.[8]

Gogol's Ukrainian birth and Russophone legacy complicate his place in the Russian canon alongside Pushkin, Tolstoy, and Dostoevsky. Gogol, who indeed instrumentalized his Ukrainian identity for his own literary success, thus presents a somewhat perplexing foundational example for the postcolonial turn in Slavic studies.[9] While such crucial interventions in the authoritative vision of Russian literature emphasize the central role of the Ukrainian periphery on Russian imperial history, this chapter instead focuses on the nuances of the colonial encounter from both within and outside a national Russian linguistic and literary tradition. Memmedquluzade's parodic reception of Gogol's identity (both personally and lyrically) invites a genealogical inquiry into the forms of power that link the Russian literary canon to discourses of Russian/Soviet imperialism and orientalism. In this way, the transnational geopoetics of Gogol's work reveals the ways in which the discourse of Gogolian hybridity, arguably part of a larger discourse of Eurasian hybridity, itself served as a colonial ideology.[10] Comparing Gogol's own ambivalent relationship to the imperial metropole with his work's legacy in the Caucasus reveals how his writings not only produced knowledge about the empire but more crucially shaped the formation of local anti-imperial discourses on the periphery.

Gogol's parodic prose, not surprisingly, features prominently in recent engagements between Slavic studies and postcolonial theory. Dragan Kujundžić accounts for this doubled vision of Gogol in his discussion of parody. Tracing Yuri Tynyanov's and Bakhtin's writings to Nietzsche, he argues that parody functioned as a force for renewing genre, "a mechanism of literary and historical change, as well as a discursive performance by which we measure the cyclical passage of time" (1997, 40–41).[11] Parody here functions as the marker of epistemological shifts in Russian literary history. Building on Homi Bhabha's "ambivalent temporalities of the nation-space," Kujundžić argues that "Parody is the effect of 'translation' from one literary system to another; it preserves the memory of the old system while actualizing the potential of the new" (1997, 39). This capacity of parody to maintain a vestige of the old while generating the new renders it a historical practice; in this sense, it serves as an extension of the reading practice of historical poetics discussed in the introduction. Alexander Etkind (2011) offers a similar vision of Russian history, also reading Gogol through Bhabha to describe Russia's internal colonization as a process whereby post-Enlightenment man is tethered to a colonized double, generated through the experience of loss and division characteristic of the colonial encounter.[12] While both models of self-reflexive or internal colonization expose the poetics of colonial alienation embedded within the Russian national canon, Etkind's project to psychoanalyze Russian history arguably replicates the very Eurasianist orientalist model at the center of its gaze.

Russia's expansion south into the Muslim Caucasus informed the creation of another sequence of revolutionary ideas that challenge the dominant Slavic position from which figures such as Etkind approach the Russian colonial encounter.[13] Internal colonization envisions the colonial encounter from both the intra-Slavic and the imperial perspectives, in which the Other is projected as an extension of the self, as part of the internal body of the Russian empire. The location of the Caucasus and Central Asia as part of Russia's contiguous expansion made these spaces crucial to defining the limits of the "Oriental half" of the Russian empire. However, crucially the Muslim Turk was a more radical outsider to the process of intra-Slavic self-colonization. Parody thus emphasizes the distance between the Russophone and Turkic traditions in which Gogol and Memmedquluzade participated, as well as the possibility of their mutual translation, in part owing to the epistemological currency of the parodic form within both Russian and Turkic literatures. Memmedquluzade's reading of Gogol's work not only dramatizes the relationship between forms of romantic imperial and national identity but also radicalizes an internal alterity within its formal tissue. When Memmedquluzade *translates* Gogol, he does not reproduce the text or even the plot of Gogol's story but transcribes the rhetorical-political violence that animates his work. The reception of Gogolian parody in the Caucasus represents an important epistemic shift or translation of a Russian identity through its historical encounter with an emerging discourse of Muslim Turkic identity.

The year 1905 marked a pivotal moment in the Russian imperial metropole as well as on the periphery. More broadly across the empire in Finland, Poland, Ukraine, and the South Caucasus, national minorities began to react against assimilation policies and discrimination. The South Caucasus was enveloped in violence and unrest after a series of constitutional revolutions that erupted in the Russian empire in 1905, Persia in 1906, and Turkey in 1908.[14] The Armenian-Azeri conflict in the South Caucasus coincided with Bloody Sunday in St. Petersburg, causing Nicholas II to reinstate the viceroyalty (abolished in 1882). Rioting, interethnic violence, and protest fomented in Baku as well as in the countryside. Peasants demanded the redistribution of lands, workers wanted better conditions, and violence was stoked by the emergence of increasingly polarized Armenian and Azeri identity discourses.[15]

The 1905 revolution also brought liberal censorship policies, which generated a boom in local print culture across the Caucasus and Central Asia. The two leading Azeri literary journals of the time, *Enlightenment* (1906–1907) and *Molla Nesreddin* (1906–1931), introduced their readers to Russian and European works of literature and philosophy, printing translations and articles on writers and thinkers including Goethe, Schiller, Shakespeare, Tolstoy, Pushkin, and Gogol. The expansion of the Azeri press, which made literary works available to a broader public, was accompanied by an interest in both class and language politics in the Caucasus.

The Muslim Social Democratic Party (Hümmet) was founded in 1904, and a Conference for Muslim Teachers was held in Baku in 1906.[16] The creation of the Muslim Social Democratic Party secured a bond between the worker's cause and a supranational Muslim culture linked to the international community of Islamic believers. The Conference for Muslim Teachers instead addressed national causes, including the issue of Russification and the promotion of Azeri-language instruction and textbooks. However, the preferred term for the languages of the empire used at the conference was "Muslim language," bridging these two cultural and political discourses. This interest in the cause of "Muslim language reform," which lay at the heart of the objectives of the new journals, signaled that identity was necessarily inscribed within the domain of a supranational Muslim culture, although one articulated in the particular geopolitical space of the Russian empire and more specifically the South Caucasus (Alstadt 1983, 199–209). This print boom in the South Caucasus generated a corpus of texts shaped by the language of the colonial space, which provided a unique vision of subjecthood shaped by the revolutionary transformation of the periphery.

It was in this context that Memmedquluzade introduced Gogol to his local readers. Gogol's journey to the Caucasus during the first two decades of the twentieth century took two forms. His prose was evoked in the pages of *Molla Nesreddin*, and his play *The Government Inspector* became one of the most popular shows on the local revolutionary stage.[17] Memmedquluzade's interest in Gogol's prose centers around three major themes: the relationship between the imperial metropole and the provincial periphery, discourses of modernity concerning Russia's westernization, and the trope of mistaken identity as a model for reading history.

Drawing on satire and parody as political and structural literary forms, Memmedquluzade reframed Gogol's critique of the tsarist bureaucracy through the colonial context and reinvisioned the imperial canon through this Turkic translation of Russian prose. His reception of Gogol's works refracts Gogol's geopoetics through the prism of an Azeri Muslim colonial ethno-linguistic identity. Drawing on Gogol's work, he implicitly situates Azeri literature in a Russian imperial past, exposing the force of the colonial encounter through the materiality of his prose. In so doing, however, he also anticipates a revolutionary break, sketching the shape of an anti-imperial future.

Speaking in Tongues: Ukrainian and Turkic Literary Others

Launching its first issue in 1906, Memmedquluzade introduced *Molla Nesreddin* not only as one of the first Azeri literary journals in the Caucasus but as one with a particular aesthetic and political interest in developing Turkic and Muslim culture. While Memmedquluzade and his work with the journal have been framed in contemporary scholarship through the journal's institutional ties to the Soviet government in the 1930s and an overstatement of the journal's early political and cultural opposition to the pan-Turkism of *Enlightenment,* such a cohesive presentation of the journal's politics is more convenient than historically accurate. *Molla Nesreddin*'s title announced that its founder saw its projected readership as an international community of Muslims familiar with the popular folk character Molla or Hoca Nesreddin (Molla by his Persian appellation and Hoca by the Turkic). Through this appeal to a broad Muslim cultural community, Memmedquluzade indicated that his aims for the journal did not center on a particular ideological narrative (such as those of the jadids) so much as an interest in encouraging social change more broadly.[18] The location and dislocation of modernity between Russia (as Europe) and the Islamic world reframed the journal's claims to generate a modern Azeri literature as a supranational project, concerned with diversity and contingency over national purity. Noting a break from the aesthetic and linguistic forms of the classical traditions of both Ottoman and Persian poetry, Memmedquluzade's prose and the style of the journal's contents more broadly reflected an interest in the variegated terrain of the genre of the folktale and the syntax of spoken Azeri. The first issue introduces the title character and offers a short address to the readers, as well as a description of the broad objectives of the journal. Memmedqulu-zade writes:

> Hey, I came to talk about you, my Muslim brothers. I'm talking about the people who don't like my discourse and make excuses to run from me, such as going to have their horoscopes read, [watching] a dog fight, listening to the tales of dervishes, sleeping in the bathhouse, and other such important desires. But the powers have ordered: say these words to those people who don't lend an ear. Hey, my Muslim brothers! There were times when you heard some of my humorous words, opened your mouths to the sky, closed your eyes as the "ha-ha!" of laughter almost tore your intestines, wiped your faces and eyes with the hems [of your caftans], and said "curse Satan!" Don't assume that you are laughing at Molla Nesreddin. Hey my Muslim brothers! If you want to know at whom you laugh, then put a mirror in front of yourselves and take a careful look at your own faces.

> Sizi deyib gəlmişəm, ey mənim müsəlman qardaşlarım! O kəsləri deyib gəlmişəm ki, mənim söhbətimi xoşlamayıb, bəzi bəhanələrlə məndən qaçıb gedirlər, məsələn, fala baxdırmağa, it boğuşdurmağa, dərviş nağılına qulaq asmağa, hamamda yatmağa və qeyri bu növ vacib əməllərə. Çünki hükəmakar buyurublar: "Sözünü o kəslərə de ki, sənə qulaq vermirlər." Ey mənim müsəlman qardaşlarım! Zəmani ki, məndən bir gülməli söz eşidib, ağzınızı göyə açıb və gözlərinizi yumub, o qədər "xa-xa! . . ." ətəklərinizlə üz-gözünüzü silib, "lənət şeytana"! dediniz o vaxt elə güman etməyin ki, Molla Nəsrəddinə gülürsünüz. Ey mənim müsəlman qardaşlarım! Əgər bilmək istəsəniz ki, kimin üstünə gülürsünüz, o vaxt qoyunuz qabağınıza aynanı və diqqətlə baxınız camalınıza. (Memmedquluzade [1906–1931] 1996–2014, 2:4)

Memmedquluzade defines his readership as both Muslim brothers and Turkic speakers, referring to their Turkic mother tongue: "while rocking you in the cradle your mothers sang you lullabies in the Turkic tongue" (2:4). He also uses the term "Muslim" to address the diverse communities of Muslims across the Russian empire, as well as internationally.[19] The particular figure of the Azeri Muslim participates in a series of relational ethnic, cultural, and linguistic discourses. He or she is both an insider and an outsider among other Muslims of the Russian empire such as Uzbeks and Tatars, the irrevocable outsider for the Russian, and yet a political insider as a subject of the empire. The term "my Muslim brothers," in turn, operates on multiple planes of speech. It refers at once to the everyman, the community of Muslim believers, and the populist cause of the workers in the Caucasus.

Writing after the workers' protests and the 1905 revolution during the final decade of Russian imperial control, Memmedquluzade addressed an Azeri audience that included both elite intellectuals and the working masses. In this way, the journal aimed to enlighten the same Muslim masses, who also served as the object of its critical gaze. Though literacy in the Caucasus among Muslims was only around 4–5 percent in 1905, the journal included a large selection of political cartoons, and Memmedquluzade was known to read selections aloud in local teahouses.[20] The journal thus played on the tension between elite and popular readership, not only as part of an aesthetic project to create a new genre of prose but as a political project to urge social reforms. This tension between the journal's functions as a work of literature and an agitator for political action is further emphasized in the final line of the passage, which recalls one of the most famous lines of Gogol's play *The Government Inspector*.[21] Memmedquluzade offers a symbolic mirror of social critique to his community of readers. He addresses his "Muslim brothers," in turn, as both readers of Gogol and objects of a Gogolian satire. Emphasizing the proximity between life and fiction, Memmedquluzade draws on Gogol's work to highlight the civic quality of literature to agitate as well as entertain.

The grotesque imagery and colloquial tone captured in the journal present folk culture as a source of entertainment, enlightenment, and agitation, which serve as the basis for Memmedquluzade's new literary genre. The style of the passage and *Molla Nesreddin*'s eponymous guide recall Gogol's experimentations with Ukrainian culture in his collection of short stories, *Evenings on a Farm near Dikanka* (*Vechera na khutore bliz Dikan'ki* [1831–1832]). Gogol's Rudy Panko, the fictional editor of the collection, performs the role of an exoticized "sly *khokhol*" or Ukrainian peasant for Gogol's Russian readership. Similarly, Memmedquluzade appropriates the legendary folk figure of Molla Nesreddin as both his pseudonym and the title of his literary journal. Panko and Nesreddin are storytellers linked to non-Russian popular Ukrainian and Muslim folk culture, although Molla Nesreddin is also a figure in Sufi philosophical teaching.[22]

Panko is the product of the author's divided persona as a native informant who is also a member of the Russian intelligentsia and contributes to the Russification of Ukrainian culture. However, at the same time, Gogol deconstructs the very notion of Russianness by charging a Ukrainian peasant with narrating his Russian language tales. Panko thus positions Gogol's work between Russian national discourses that contested Ukrainian otherness, viewing the history of Kievan Rus as evidence of its cultural ties to the modern Russian empire, as well as Ukrainian national discourses that insisted on Ukraine's unique cultural identity.[23] While for Gogol this struggle manifests internally when he is writing in Russian for a Russian readership, Memmedquluzade both presents an otherness through his work's implicit ties to a foreign literary legacy and cohesion through the sense of continuity shared by Nesreddin's popularity across the former Russian, Ottoman, and Persian empires.

The form of the archetypal Nesreddin story also makes up part of Memmedquluzade's play. The elliptical structure of the stories, while a common folk quality, is heightened by the transgressive force of its Sufist ethos, which informs Memmedquluzade's challenge to orthodox religious institutions and the moral objectives they formalize. Most stories hinge on a vision of Nesreddin as an idiot savant, whether emphasizing his inability to distinguish image from reality, word from action, or self from Other. This dynamic is most clearly illustrated in the stories themselves, such as the following example.

Molla Nesreddin was nailing a painting to a wall when suddenly his nail slipped and he punched a hole in the wall. Staring into the hole he noticed a herd of goats grazing, but didn't realize that he had broken through to his neighbor's yard. In a fit of excitement he called to his wife,

"Come, come, you will not believe what I have found!"
"What Molla?" his wife asked bemused.

Molla replied in astonishment:

"You will not believe it! I was standing here nailing in this picture and discovered an entire universe in this room—a universe of goats!"

The primacy of form is emphasized by the variability of the specifics, where the painting and goats could be replaced by a television and highway depending on the whims of the teller as well as the language in which the tale is told. Rather, the function of the tale illustrates both Molla's blindness, in his inability to distinguish the image from the real or copy from original, as well as his visionary capacity to reflect on the arbitrariness of the mimetic process itself. In the stories the cycle of laughter is always directed back at the meaninglessness of the teller's own tales as well as the specter of the teller himself. The details of the tale are, after all, as replaceable and universal as an Azeri Molla Nesreddin is interchangeable with his Turkic, Persian, and Arabic doubles Hoja, Efendi, Juha, or other iterations of the global archetype. While the Nesreddin story invites the search for meaning, it remains ultimately content to lead its listeners astray. In this regard, it does not necessarily *achieve* satire, although it may *function* as parody. Molla's power lies in highlighting the porousness of the boundaries between life and tale, just as this particular story emphasizes the fluidity between art and life.

Gogol and Russian literature more broadly are thus parodied through the satirical oral tradition embodied in Molla Nesreddin. In so doing, Memmedquluzade generates a literary language marked by a fusion of Turkic, Persian, and Russian cultural references as well as through literary elite and popular satire. Furthermore, if orality is somewhat lost for Gogol through his performance of Ukrainian otherness in Russian, it is at least partially recovered in Memmedquluzade's creation of *Molla Nesreddin*. Whereas Panko's stories were collected as texts, Nesreddin's literarity accompanied his emergence as a political-cultural icon for an image-based journal that was also regularly staged: that is, read aloud in public spaces. In this way, while the printing of the journal in 1906 at once shaped the ways in which it would be read, the journal's reliance on the forum of the coffeehouse oral performance generated a broader popular base for its civic function.

The vision of Gogol's work as the beginning of a genealogy of indigenous Russian literature as social critique was indebted to the work of Vissarion Belinsky and Nikolai Chernyshevsky.[24] Gogol's connection to an intertextual and social space of global exchange, however, owes its debt to the Russian formalists, including Yuri Tynyanov, Boris Eikhenbaum, and Dmitry Chizhevsky, as well as the work of Mikhail Bakhtin, who highlighted Gogol's literary appropriation of the oral tale. Eikhenbaum famously described Gogol's oral style as *skaz*, referring to "devices of verbal mimicry and gesture" whereby in a sort of "play-acting" "words and sentences are selected and ordered not according to the principle of mere logical speech, but more according to the principle of expressive speech, in which a special role is played by articulation, mimicry, sound gestures, etc."[25] For Eikhenbaum, meaning is governed by the rules of sound instead of signs. Both Eikhenbaum and Tynyanov highlight the performative aspect of *skaz*: that is, the way in which language exposes itself as a mask. While for the formalists *skaz* revealed the inner expressive quality of folk forms in literature, Bakhtin moved a step further from an account of the linguistic to that of the metalinguistic, arguing that *skaz* represented a double-voicedness, an "orientation toward someone else's discourse" (1984; 1997–2012, 6:217). Central to all these early Soviet critical formations was the notion that *skaz* revealed an inner otherness in language, in which otherness was constituted beyond the rational for the formalists or beyond the individual subject for Bakhtin.

Emphasizing the role of oral mimicry in transcending the rational individual subject, these formalist paradigms betray a strong debt to Nietzsche's parodic philosophy.[26] The influence of Russian Nietzscheanism on formalism offered a new vehicle for an old debate, the nineteenth-century polemic over whether the Russian writer's role was to *imitate* the literature and philosophy of Western Europe or to *innovate* unique Russian cultural products that reflected its status as a world empire. These discussions of Russia's cultural legacy, which informed Gogol's representations of Ukraine as both an exotic Other and an embodiment of the Herderean notion of the *Volksgeist* or spirit of the people, returned in the linguistic and metalinguistic theories of *skaz* and parody. In the 1830s Gogol provided details about Ukrainian life, while a century later the formalists employed Gogolian *skaz* to provide a linguistic ethnography of the internal otherness of the Russian language. However, before Gogolian *skaz* could become a talisman of Soviet internal otherness, it provided a form for articulating a colonial identity in the Caucasus.

Memmedquluzade's interest in Gogol in 1906, nearly a decade before his appropriation by the formalists, highlights the ways in which Russian prose not only internalized its own otherness but generated parodic discourses that contributed to the formation of an anti-imperial Azeri literary canon. That is, Memmedquluzade not only echoes Gogol's social satire and assimilation of (Ukrainian) folk culture but also generates a parody of the lexical-syntactic hybridity in Gogol's text. These resonances also reveal similar methodological and political challenges in thinking through the fragmented and relational discourses of identity, which emerge in Gogol's and Memmedquluzade's work, without either subordinating them to more institutionally established literatures (Russian, Polish, Persian, or Turkish) or projecting them onto ahistorical narratives of cohesive Ukrainian and Azerbaijani national identity.

Whereas Gogol's *Dikanka* cycle presents Ukrainian culture as part of a common Slavic yet non-Russian imperial identity, Memmedquluzade highlights the history of networks of cultural exchange present in Azeri speech, which include Russian, Persian, and Turkic syntax and vocabulary. The second issue of *Molla Nesreddin* includes an anecdote titled "Our Educated Ones" (Bizim 'obrazovannı'lar) about an Azeri youth who, after attaining a Russian education, returns home and scoffs at his "Tatar" mother tongue, reflecting his new Russified status.[27] Memmedquluzade writes:

> They say that while my friend was in Russian school, one day he says to his mother:
>
>> —Mother! Pojalusta svarit me something [that is, cook]!
>
> His mother answers:
>
>> —My child, what did you say?
>
> My friend answers:
>
>> Oh, Oh, you don't understand anything; I said cook something.
>> —My child, what shall I cook?
>> —*Chort ego iznaet.* I forgot . . . It's round; minced, and cooked in a [clay pot] or on a grill . . . It has some kind of name . . .
>> —My child, do you mean kufta?
>> —Yeah . . . yeah . . . qofta, qofta.

> Deyirlər ki, həmin mənim rəfiqim rus şkolunda oxuyan vaxt bir gün anasına deyib:
>
>> —Ana! Pajaluysta, mənə bir şey svarit elə! (yəni bişir!)
>
> Anası cavab verib:
>
>> —Bala, nə dedin?

Rəfiqim cavab verib:

—Ox ox! Siz heç bir zad qanmırsınız! Mən deyirəm: bir zad bişir.
—Bala, nə bişirim?
—Çort ego znaet! . . . Yadımdan çıxıb . . . Yumru olur, əti döyüb salırlar
çölməyə, ya qazana . . . Bir cür adı var . . .
—Bala, küftə deyirsən?
—Hə . . . hə . . . qofta, qofta! ([1906–1931] 1996–2014, 2:11–12)

The child's Russian inflected speech asking his mother to "please cook
something" (*pojalusta isvarit*) is reflected in the mutual unintelligibility
between the child and his mother, as well as his inability to remember
the classic Azeri dish. The episode recalls a passage in the *Dikanka* cycle
in which Gogol describes a boy who cannot remember the word "rake"
until it strikes him in the face. The boy's Latin education literally causes
him to lose his native tongue and culture, his Eastern Orthodox (*pravo-
slavnyi*) faith tied to his native language (*iazyk*) (Gogol' 2003, 1:70). The
boy's aphasia is connected both to a disappearance of his cultural identity—
his Orthodox faith—as well as physical injury—the blow to the face. Similarly for Memmedquluzade, the child's cultural assimilation, embodied in
his inability to remember the dish, is caused by his linguistic loss. In Gogolian fashion the gustatory register is connected to the domain of language. Indeed, in Azeri the word *dil* signifies both tongue and language,
like the Russian word *iazyk*. Memmedquluzade emphasizes the mater-
nal and nourishing elements of his native tongue, as well as its psychic
and material loss. The title of the short anecdote reveals the multiple linguistic registers interacting in this text, connecting the Azeri "our" to the
Russian term for education (*obrazovanie*), meaning cultural formation or
education. Creating a hybridized text of unknown or appropriated foreign
words, Memmedquluzade offers his parodic critique of the new generation's Russian acculturation in his fusion of multiple languages and registers of speech, which trace a cultural history of the imperial encounter in
the Caucasus.

In addition to the double register of Russian and Azeri, the journal also
plays on its reader's knowledge of Persian. In a recurring column in the
journal, Memmedquluzade includes a satirical Persian-Azeri dictionary.
The section uses the form of dictionary entries to confuse the relationship
between linguistic signs, their sound, and their meaning. For example, one

entry reads, "Ishtirak—that is to smoke opium during working hours. It is a Farsi word, but it is often used in Nakhchivan and Iran" (Memmedqulu-zade [1906–1931] 1996–2014, 1:6). Memmedquluzade plays on the sound of the Persian word *ishtirak* meaning to participate, but which to a Turkic reader would sound like *ish-tirak*—a portmanteau for "opiumwork," a combination of "to work" (*iş*) and "opium" (*tiyek*). As the Arabic or Persian word is used also in a socialist political context from the root *Sh-R-K*, meaning "to share," the dictionary links the notion of socialist labor to opium smoking.[28] On the one hand, the entry seems to submit to an orientalist cliché, that of the opium-smoking Persian. On the other hand, to a reader of Arabic or Persian, the line juxtaposes the idea of socialist participation against the practice of opium smoking, reflecting the failures of early Bolshevik revolutionary efforts. In a clever inversion of Marx, Mammedquluzade parodies a bourgeois vision of collective labor as the opium of the masses. In addition to the recognition of a certain *skaz* or sound meaning the joke hinges on a necessary bilingualism.

Drawing on the form of the dictionary, Memmedquluzade deconstructs the perceived rational order governing language. In this parodic dictionary, language provides a source of cultural and perhaps political knowledge, but one that can often betray its masters. Like Gogol, Memmedquluzade draws on both popular oral forms of speech and on the Russian and Persian languages to render his own language as if foreign. In so doing, he also traces a history of imperial cultural influences in the Caucasus from the Persian to the Russian empires, and finally to his new Turkic language journal. Building on Gogol's oral parody as a model, he complicates the vision of Ukrainian culture as an internal Other, by tracing the intersecting cultural legacies of the Russian and Persian empires. While Memmedquluzade at once externalizes these cultural influences as pretentious and backward, he does so self-consciously to produce a Turkic literary language that defines itself in relation to its hybrid constitution of Persian and Russian idioms. Like Gogol's work, Memmedquluzade's parody not only highlights the foreignness of these words but seeks to assimilate them into his literary world. For Gogol this process manifests as a struggle to reconcile Russian and Ukrainian identity and simultaneously to decenter the authority of both, albeit within the limited medium of Russian prose. While for Memmedquluzade the confusion of tongues lends itself not only to a satire of the history of overlapping empires but to a revolutionary parody of the very mechanism of cultural imperialism. Gogol's performance of Ukrainianness thus generated a language through which identity could be imagined on the periphery in 1906, preceding the emergence of the orientalist institution of the Soviet nationalities policies of the 1920s.

Modernization on the Periphery: Vehicles of Translation

One of Memmedquluzade's most sustained engagements with Gogol's wordplay occurs in a 1906 story "Qurbaneli Bey," which offers a translation and adaptation of a lesser known work, Gogol's short story "The Carriage"(Koliaska [1836]).[29] "The Carriage," like Gogol's play *The Government Inspector* and his novel *Dead Souls* (*Mertvye dushi* [1842]) highlights the foolishness and corruption of the landowning gentry. Memmedquluzade attacks the imperial bureaucracy by focusing on the complicity of the Russified Muslim landowning class. While Memmedquluzade sets his story in the South Caucasus, he translates Gogol's poetics—namely, his use of sound repetitions and metonymy—creating a literary Azeri marked by stylistic allusions to Gogol's Russian text. Drawing on the formal devices in Gogol's text, Memmedquluzade remaps Gogol's representations of the Russian imperial provinces onto the geopoetic space of the Caucasus, making visible the materiality of the imperial encounter through the use of sound, repetition, and interlingual wordplay. The materiality of language in the text recalls the history of Russian officials in the colonial setting. Aiming his critique at the Russification of the landowning class, Memmedquluzade parodies the very act of verbal mimicry and with it the practice of cultural assimilation.

"Qurbaneli Bey," like "The Carriage," satirizes the class pretensions of two provincial landowners who fail to impress a group of Russian officers with the status and wealth of their estates (Gogol' 2003, 3:177–89).[30] Both texts situate discussions of identity in the context of the relationships between hosts and guests in the bourgeois imperial space, where issues of class and ethnic identity, in particular, become manifest. The figure of the westernized landowner Chertokutsky in "The Carriage" finds a parallel in the figure of the Azeri Muslim landowner Qurbaneli in "Qurbaneli Bey," who is westernized *à la russe*. The nearly identical plots of the two stories follow the landowners who attend feasts held by groups of visiting Russian officers. The landowners boast about their modes of transport (in Gogol's text—his carriages and in Memmedquluzade's text—his horses), become intoxicated at the party, and return home, forgetting that they have invited the officers to visit their estates the next day. When the landowners awaken and find their guests at the gates, they hide in a carriage and barn, respectively, only to be discovered and humiliated by the officers. The objects of both Gogol's and Memmedquluzade's critiques are figures of class and imperial power—the landowning westernized or Russified elite and the Russian imperial authorities. In Memmedquluzade's text, these institutional critiques are particularly marked by class and by ethnic and civic identity.

While the action of "The Carriage" remains within Russia, Gogol highlights the marginal position of the provinces in relation to the imperial metropole through his parody of the alienating forces of modernization. Gogol represents the arrival of the imperial officials to the provincial town by exaggerating his descriptions of objects in a metonymic play that confounds people with animals and inanimate things. As critics have noted, while Gogol often attacks the French, his wordplay suggests an interest in Honoré de Balzac's poetics, particularly his fetishization of objects.[31] Gogol parodies Balzac's prose in order to critique the forces of westernization. His staging of Russia's ambivalent geopolitical relationship to Western modernity through an engagement with Balzacian metonymic play frames a geopoetics that in turn served as inspiration for Memmedquluzade's own parodic prose. Gogol contrasts the quiet provincial town with the liveliness of the officers' arrival, which introduces an estranging effect on his language as it alters the social space of the town. Mocking the pretension of the officers, Gogol describes their hats as "plumes" (*sultan*), which like the English cognate also signifies an "eastern monarch" (179). The officer's mustaches serve as metonyms, emphasizing their intrusions into the daily lives of the townspeople: "If the tradespeople gathered at the market with their scoops, there were sure to be mustaches peering over their shoulders" (179). While Gogol draws attention to the officers' arrival, he also mocks their authority by reducing them to their most recognizable features. Their entrance fosters a state of linguistic disorder whereby objects suddenly take on a central focus in the text.

Confusing his nouns in this absurdist play, Gogol draws a parallel between the arrival of the officials and French culture, both through the French phrase and the evocation of Balzac's style, lodging a critique of the Russian administration's policies of westernization and the force of imperial policing and control. For example, confusing animals with people, Gogol elicits his reader's laughter at the military officers' expense. Treating the word "Frenchmen" as a derogatory term for pigs, the narrator describes how the streets of the town "fill up with those burly animals, which the local mayor calls Frenchmen" (179). The mayor's confusion of the animal and the nation superficially satirizes the French people even as it unhinges a chain of signification. The sentence forms a structure of sound meaning, linking the "burly animals" (*dorodnye zhivotnye*) and the "local mayor" (*tamoshnii gorodnichii*), whereby root pairs are formed from the repetition of the sounds of the first and last words *dorod/gorod* and *zhivot/tamosh*. The word pairs also outline a relationship of proximity and distance, the second syllable *rod* in *dorod/gorod* signifying the homely and native, while *tam*, "there," in *tamosh* emphasizes distance. As Gogol suggests connections through these aural correspondences between the encroaching forces of westernization and imperial authority, he also disorients his reader's relationship to language itself.

Gogol describes the drunkenness that ensues at the feast through a reference to Napoleon's invasion of 1812, similarly eliding sound and sense. He writes, "A long conversation continued around the table, but somehow it was conducted strangely. One landowner who served in the campaign of 1812 recounted a battle that had never been and later for completely unknown reasons removed the stopper from a decanter and stuck it into a pastry" (Разговор затянулся за столом предлинный, но, впрочем, как-то странно он был веден. Один помещик, служивший еще в кампанию 1812 года, рассказал такую баталию, какой никогда не было, и потом, совершенно неизвестно по каким причинам, взял пробку из графина и воткнул ее в пирожное) (185). The battle of 1812, marking Napoleon's campaign in Russia and one of the pivotal historical moments in Russian intellectuals' rejection of French cultural influence, here forms a turning point in the order of the party and the narrative. The landowner's story is displaced from the historical record only to be replaced by the logic of sound repetition. The landowner places the bottle stopper inside a pastry combining the *p* sound of *probka* or stopper with that of the *pirozhnoe* or pastry. Gogol deconstructs the meaning of these signs by generating a semantic order of alliteration. In so doing, he undermines the authority of the narrative of westernization by creating a new logic of sound meaning. The "strangeness" of the conversation, which locates its historical authority in a battle that never occurred, both presents and subverts Petrine modernization as haunted by the influence of French westernization.

The use of the title figure of the carriage is a persistent theme in Gogol's work that serves as an ambivalent symbol of both the force of modernization and Russia's destiny. Gogol presents this struggle to envision Russia's future through his emphasis on the native and foreign quality of the carriage. Two words are used to signify "carriage"—*ekipazh* from a French borrowing and *koliaska* from the Russian root. Gogol uses the French *équipage*, which more generally signifies a team or crew, to highlight pivotal moments in the story. The arrival of the main character, the provincial landowner Pifagor Pifagorovich Chertokutsky, is announced by the foreign *mot de transport*. This arrival, Gogol notes, generates "more noise than anyone at the elections and arriving there in a dandy équipage" (более всех шумевший на выборах и приезжавший туда в щегольском экипаже) (179). Indeed, his own name evokes both order—Pythagoras—and chaos—Chertokutsky, being a combination of the word devil (*chert*) and dock-tailed or short (*kutsy*). The *ekipazh* emphasizes the artificiality of Chertokutsky's appearance, his inelegant and noisy presence. Again at the end of the story Chertokutsky's wife recognizes the arrival of the unexpected guests through their *ekipazh*, foreshadowing the confusion that will soon ensue. The disorder that follows the *ekipazh*, whether semantic—in the case of Chertokutsky's name—or narrative—in the case of the unexpected guests—emphasizes the confused destiny of the empire or, perhaps more literally, a sense of ambivalence toward the French word and the Western technology.

The appropriation of the Balzacian synecdoche produces an inverted vision of the town in which the part or fragment decenters the whole. The arrival of Western modernity as a distortion or disorder of sound and sense generates a new optic. Memmedquluzade foregrounds the peripheral setting of Gogol's story, rendering it central to his portrait of Azeri modernization. In so doing, he also positions language at the center of his critique of the artifice of Western modernity *à la russe*, rendering language as a material force shaping Russian colonialism. His use of wordplay and foreign borrowings highlights the forms of exchange that underlie his act of translation. His use of sound repetitions and lists similarly exposes the materiality of his prose. In his description of the police chief's wife's name-day celebrations, he underlines the excessive consumption and labor required to amuse the Russian officers. The feast preparations require the procurement of an almost grotesque number of four or five hundred eggs (Memmedquluzade 2004, 1:175). Paralleling Gogol's subversion of bureaucratic and semantic orders, Memmedquluzade represents a state of chaos that undermines the authority of both the Russian officers and the Russian language. He describes the noise and commotion at the police chief's house, "In the police chief's yard a dog wouldn't recognize its master" (Pristavın heyetinde it yiyesini tanımırdı) (175). Memmedquluzade compares the police chief's estate to ineffectual dogs' masters, highlighting the state of semantic and political upheaval at this public celebration.

In his rewriting, Memmedquluzade parodies Gogol's description of the feast preparations by exaggerating his use of onomatopoeia, littering his portrait of the town with the sounds of the feast preparations. In "The Carriage" the cooking is described through the "stook of cooks' knives," which could be heard from the gates of the town (Gogol' 2003, 3:179). In "Qurbaneli Bey," the sound of men's voices and meat cleavers is conveyed through the same "tap-tap," while the sounds of the Russian officers mimic the chickens, producing the same "howls." This description of the yard noise is repeated several times, "Again the tack-ing of the meat [mincing] knives, the tack-ing of people, the neighing of horses, the howling of chicks, hens, and [Russian] officers, as well as the haff-ing of hounds mixed with one another" (Genə katlet bıçaqlarının taqqıltısı, adamların tappıltısı, atların kişnəməsi, cücə-toyuqların və qlavaların bağırtısı və tulaların hafıltısı qarışdı bir-birinə) (Memmedquluzade 2004, 1:175).[32] As Memmedquluzade confuses the sounds of people and objects to represent the state of commotion in the yard he also subversively compares the arrival of the Russian officers to the noise of animals coming to slaughter. Indeed, the word used to signify the officers is a Russified invention. The word *qlavalar* combines the Russian word for head (*glava*) with the Turkic plural form. Thus the strangeness of the word in Azeri, which gestures toward the figure of the sovereign militarized head of state, renders it indistinguishable from the other objects and animals listed in the paragraph. Memmedquluzade blends the officers into the background noise of the bustling scene. Drawing on the setting of "The Carriage," he contests the authority of the Russian officers by offering sound as an alternative source of meaning.

Memmedquluzade's portrait of the Russian officers also emphasizes the artificiality of their appearance. When the Russian party travels to the Azeri landowner Qurbaneli's estate, its members' arrival is announced according to their clothing accessories, which function as signifiers for their Otherness. Like the officers who are introduced at the name-day celebration in a grocery list, these guests are similarly recognized at Qurbaneli's estate as inanimate objects. When his servant spots the riders from the kitchen rooftop he notes that from within a group of horses he "clearly recognized the officer's and police chief's buttons and the wives' hats" (naçalnik və pristavların düymələri və xanımların şlyapaları) (191). The focus on the minute elements of their dress from the servant's distant rooftop vantage point highlights the prominence of these features in the text. The markings visually distinguish the Russians' clothing from local styles of dress. A Russified term is used to refer to the womens' hats (*şlyapaları*), again creating a parallel between the semantic and narrative functions in the text. Memmedquluzade's translation of this Gogolian technique renders the Russified terms as if they were foreign or strange accessories, much like the otherness of the Russians themselves. Indeed, Memmedquluzade uses a similar strategy to illustrate the Russians' vision of Qurbaneli's alterity. When Qurbaneli invites the officers to dine at his house, the officer's wives agree, if only so that they can see what the bey's wife will wear (185). Memmedquluzade reverses the orientalist gaze of the officer's wives, who are interested in the dress of their Muslim hostess, when he marks their arrival by focusing on their Russified hats and military buttons. Like Gogol, Memmedquluzade emphasizes the materiality of language, alienating the Russian officials by bringing the reader's attention to the artificiality of their appearance. Drawing on Gogol's parody of French westernization, Memmedquluzade highlights the estranging process of Russification.

In "Qurbaneli Bey," shifts between Azeri and Russian words inform the negotiations of Azeri and Russian identity in the story. The reciprocal gaze of the Azeris and Russians is framed through the poetic space of the apartments. The view of the street is described from inside the Russian police chief's apartment "from an open window a horse's whinny rose from the street" (küçədən açıq akoşkalardan bir at kişnəməyə qalxdı) (177). While facing the same windows from the street side, the townspeople observe the police chief's apartment: "The villagers arranged themselves in front of the window(s) to look at the police chief's windows" (Akoşkanın qabağında kəndlilər düzülüb pristavın akoşkalarına baxırdılar) (177). The window provides the frame through which both the Russian officials and local villagers are connected in a reciprocal gaze. The word used for window is a transcription of the diminutive form of the Russian word (*akoshka*). Memmedquluzade's use of the Russian word emphasizes the Russian cultural space of the apartment. The function of the Russian word in its diminutive form also indicates a mocking tone, belittling the Russian gaze through which the village street enters the narrative. Memmedquluzade plays on the Pushkinian image of Petersburg as "window onto Europe" by offering a westernizing gaze through his Russified lexicon. Similarly, the arrival of the Russian party is announced when Qurbaneli's wife looks out her window: "The lady ran inside and from the window looked out onto the street and saw that the street was filled with horsemen" (Xanim qaçdi içəri və pəncərədən küçəyə baxıb gördü ki, küçə doludur atlılarla) (191). When the wife recognizes the Russian horsemen, the Azeri word for window (*pencere*) is preferred. Furthermore, once the drinking begins, Azeri and Russian words are used interchangeably to refer to drinking vessels including "a shot glass" (*rumka*), "a bottle" (*butulka*), and "matches" (*spiçka*). Presented with his first drink, the bey refuses the Russian shot glass, insisting that "for us," representing his identity as an Azeri Muslim, it would be considered a thimble for sewing (178). He instead drinks from a tea glass, although here he fills it with vodka. Memmedquluzade offers a fusion of the two cultural traditions, albeit not without a spirited layer of irony.

Memmedquluzade's choice to set Gogol's narrative about the Russian provinces in the context of the imperial Caucasus undermines the authority of the Russian imperial bureaucracy, while it offers a metacommentary on the unequal processes of linguistic and literary exchange that occur in translation. Written in 1906, Memmedquluzade's story describes the specific moment of transition from an ethnically Russian literature to imagining a diverse comedic space of literary production and contagion within the revolutionary space of the Russian empire. Memmedquluzade's text at once critiques Russian acculturation and seeks to highlight a new cultural space for his Turkic Muslim reading public. Gogol's poetics expose French and Ukrainian semantic play as mimicry through the processes of translation and poetic innovation. Building on this vision of the dynamism of literary language, Memmedquluzade's repetition of Gogol frames this process through the context of the colonial encounter and its effects on the Azeri historical inscription. While it might be tempting to read Memmedquluzade's engagement with Gogol through an interest in promoting Pan-Turkic, Russian revolutionary, or Muslim modernist discourses, the text at once inscribes and erases cohesive ideological positions. Memmedquluzade instead prefers an elliptical refusal of institutional power indeed characteristic of his penname and journal's namesake the folk trickster and holy fool Molla Nesreddin. The mimetic process is similarly exposed through doubles: Nesreddin's function as penname and journal, teller and tale, as well as Gogol's play of mirrors in *The Government Inspector*. Memmedquluzade's parody shifts the focus of "Qurbaneli Bey" onto the arrival of a form of social critique that is embodied not only in the revelation of a new form of transport in the Gogolian intertext of "The Carriage" but also in the revelation of the figure of Gogol himself.

Intoxicated Words: Revealing the Mask of Muslim Otherness

The trope of drunkenness in Memmedquluzade's work highlights the structures of power that inscribe both economic and cultural spheres through class inequality and religious corruption. Intoxication functions as a poetic device—as a space of shifting meaning in which signs are disordered (deconstructed) and reconfigured.[33] Indeed, this connection between the trope of drunkenness and verbal disorder also played a role in the intellectual history of Azeri/Persian literature and thought. For Memmedquluzade and his contemporaries, as one of his insightful critics, Takhira Mamed, argues, Sufi philosophy served an important although understated influence. Indeed, the paucity of scholarship on this topic can be attributed to a secular vision of Azerbaijani literature that emerged in Soviet historiography during the 1930s. Sufi philosophy manifests, as Mamed explains following a historical poetics model, in Memmedquluzade's vision of the past "as a memory formed in the (work's) poetic structure" (2001, 117).

A tension between reality and mysticism, as well as esoteric and exoteric knowledge, is captured in suspended states of madness and intoxication. For example, the ninth-century Sufi philosopher Abū Yazīd al-Bisṭāmī, or simply Bāyazīd, expressed an openness and oneness with God through a state of intoxication or drunkenness. In this space of the openness of spiritual intoxication Bāyazīd expressed his communion with the divine: "beneath my cloak there is nothing but God" (Sells 1996, 212–32; Zarrinkoob 1970, 169). Indeed, states of hallucination and intoxication have served as symbols of spiritual enlightenment in the Christian tradition of the Eucharist and the work of the Greek philosopher Plotinus in his conception of "sober intoxication" (*sobria ebrietas*). Reinvisioning this spiritual trope of divine revelation in his semiotic model, Mikhail Bakhtin described a search for meaning in disordered speech in Dostoevsky's work as a "crisis in consciousness": that is, a turning point that connects the hero with his or her other selves and in so doing reveals the "truth" of his self-consciousness (Bakhtin 1997–2012, 6:56–88). These hermeneutic games thus inhabit the trope of intoxication, revealing a tension between a search for spiritual truth and concerns for class inequality beneath the drunken ravings of Memmedquluzade's characters and the linguistic play that stumbles out of their slurred speech.

In his state of drunkenness, Qurbaneli performs a Russian orientalist trope, embodying an abusive and aggressive Muslim patriarch. He subsequently further alienates his own household by abusing his social status as a landowner. As Qurbaneli experiences a crisis in consciousness, he dons a series of masks of Otherness, revealing economic and cultural structures of power that inscribe the male Muslim body in late imperial revolutionary Russia.

Qurbaneli's intoxication at once facilitates and inhibits his performance of Russian acculturation. Noting his abstinence from the toasting festivities, a Russian officer taunts him, "unless you're a Muslim fanatic and that's why you don't drink" (Yoxsa sən də fanatik müsəlmanlardansan, üçün içmirsən?) (Memmedquluzade 2004, 1:178). In attempt to belie the allegation connecting his sobriety, Muslim identity, and perceived savagery, Qurbaneli proceeds to drink from increasingly larger glasses. Indeed, his intoxication seems to facilitate his communication with the Russian guests until it results in his fulfillment of the party's orientalist expectations, performing the fanatic Muslim patriarch by threatening to stab his servant, and then, performing the feminized body of the colonial subject, he hides from his guests wrapped in a sheet.

Although both "The Carriage" and "Qurbaneli Bey" critique the land-owning gentry, Memmedquluzade reflects the imperial as well as class dimensions of hospitality by reimagining his hero as both a colonial sub-ject and a beneficiary of Russian imperial policies in the Caucasus. In an attempt to foster a Russophile landowning elite among the empire's Muslim subjects, the December Rescript of 1846 privatized historically state-owned lands by granting them to locals of so-called "noble birth" and, in turn, contributing to a feudal infrastructure (Swietochowski 1995, 12–13). Thus the implied noble birth and economic status of the bey, or *agha,* was linked to Russian efforts to generate new systems of power in the Caucasus that increasingly relied on co-optation as a device to "tame" the Other. Qurbaneli's liminal social status stems from his otherness as a Muslim in the company of his Russian hosts and as a colonial agent within the local community. This class dynamic becomes evident when the intoxicated bey returns to his estate from the celebration at the offi-cial's house and, dagger in hand, harasses his doorman and then his wife's domestic servant. The servant responds to his threats, "As you will it, lord!" (İxtiyar sənindi, ağa!), exposing the bey's abuse of his newfound lordship (Memmedquluzade 2004 1:187). Confronted with the simple words of the domestic servant, Qurbaneli is dethroned as a drunken fool.

The series of drinking bouts in the form of lengthy toasts covers almost a third of the short story. At the height of his inebriation after a series of toasts to the Russian officials, Qurbaneli makes a final toast to the enemy of the Russian state, marking himself as an outsider. Indeed, Rus-sian writings imagined the figure of the Muslim as a radical combination of freedom fighter and ruthless and bloodthirsty barbarian. Orientalist works identified provincial Muslim groups such as the Naqshbandi Sufi order, which challenged the urban *ulema,* as freedom fighters.[34] However, as an encyclopedic entry in *The Nature and People of the Caucasus and Transcaucasus* attests, this description envisions a Muslim vagabond or banditas as an "Abrek, a word invented by Kabardians, means sworn foe . . . And the abrek in truth is the most terrible mountain beast, dan-gerous to his own and others. Blood is his poetry, the knife—his insepa-rable friend; he himself is the true and eternal servant of Satan" (Semenov 1869, 115–16).[35] The idea of the Muslim as a radical embodiment of an anti-imperial crusade for freedom, in turn, both appealed to many Decembrist sympathizers in the Caucasus and incited fear among members of the imperial administration.

Qurbaneli's drunken toast at once honors and undermines the power of the Russian police force. He boasts: "Thanks to your state, I fear no one" (Sizin dövlətinizdən mən heç bir kəsdən qorxmuram") (Memmedquluzade 2004 1:184). Indeed, it is also thanks to the Russian police force that the bey has acquired his drunken fearlessness. He declares proudly, "No matter what bravery an enemy shows, would he be dare cross me?! I'll plunge this dagger into his side!" (Hansi düşmən cürət eləyib mənim qabağıma çıxa bilər?! Bu xəncəli mən soxaram onun qarnına!) (181). Memmedquluzade emphasizes the blade, placing it at the foreground of the sentence. In Russian literary and ethnographic work, the body of the Circassian freedom fighter was envisioned as an extension of the same curved dagger (*kinzhal*) that was popular in the Caucasus (Azeri: *xenceli*, *xencer*).[36] Memmedquluzade offers a parody of the clichéd fanatical Muslim patriarch that was made infamous by the likes of Mikhail Lermontov's famous poem "Kinzhal" (1838). Lermontov writes, "I love you, my Damascene dagger / Cold and glowing comrade / Forged for vengeance by a brooding Georgian / Sharpened in deadly battle by a free Circassian" (Люблю тебя, булатный мой кинжал, / Товарищ светлый и холодный. / Задумивый грузин на месть тебя ковал, / На грозный бой точил черкес свободный [1958–1962, 1:392]). A similar image appears in his "Cossack Lullaby" (*Kazach'ia kolybel'naia pesnia* [1840]): "The cruel Chechen crawls onto the shore, / Sharpens his dagger" (zloi chechen polzet na bereg Злой чечен ползет на берег, / Tochit svoi kinzhal Точит свой кинжал [1:470]). Lermontov here imagines himself, a Decembrist supporter, as the freedom-fighting Muslim as he narrates the story of the dagger through the history of its linguistic evolution. Despite being forged by a Georgian, crucially in Lermontov's verse as in Memmequluzade's story, the *khanjali/kinzhal* is wielded by the Muslim whose aggressive fighting literally sharpens its blade.

Qurbaneli continues to bare his blade and repeat his drunken threat on more than five occasions in the story: once to an unnamed foe, once in reference to his own self-sacrifice, repeatedly to his servant on the way home, once to his doorman, once to the household servant, and finally—in a phallic gesture—to his sleeping wife as he stands above her before collapsing from intoxication. While Qurbaneli, a South Caucasian Azeri, is neither a Georgian nor a Circassian, at the height of his drunkenness he performs the very character that his hosts expect from a Muslim from the Caucasus—the fanatic sharpening his sword. Qurbaneli's performance of his Russian affectation is here conceived as a self-orientalizing gesture. The bey's devotion to the curved dagger and the Russian state are but drunken masks that bare the inhospitable relationship between colonizer and colonized masquerading as host and guest.

Unmasking Gogol: False Pretenders and Revolutionary Literary Genealogies

New historical and literary genealogies often begin with a sacrificial death. Memmedquluzade opens "Qurbaneli Bey" by announcing his debt to Gogol's literary legacy. However, his epigraph, which is also an epitaph, is addressed to neither "Gogol" nor "Hohol" according to his Russian or Ukrainian appellations but rather provides a new linguistic identity for the famous writer as "Qoqol"—that is, a transliteration of the Russian name into the Arabic-Persian-Ottoman script. Further estranging the author's name, the dedication/memorial is accompanied by a common Islamic expression recited in the name of the dead: "Gogol, May Allah have mercy on you!" (*Qoqol, Allah sene rehmet elesin!*) (Memmedquluzade 2004, 1:174). With this gesture, Memmedquluzade memorializes the writer in a Turkic Islamic idiom and in so doing anticipates a new Azeri literary genealogy inscribed in Gogol's death. Unlike Gogol's attempts to assimilate a Ukrainian history and culture for his Russian audiences, Memmedquluzade disseminates Gogol's story through his translation across the transnational spaces of the Turkic-speaking Russian, Persian, and Ottoman empires. In dedicating his work to Gogol's death, Memmedquluzade highlights the complex discourses of identity that pervade the writer's work and personal biography as a point of departure for his story's discussion of Azeri identity. The reader begins the epigraph as an epitaph in prayer, only to be met with the surprise ghostly appearance of a Russian writer hidden beneath the phonetic rendering of the word "Qoqol."

Memmedquluzade not only memorializes Gogol in his dedication but furthermore performs his death at the end of the story. The day after the party, Qurbaneli is woken from his drunken stupor to his guests' arrival and, realizing he has not made any preparations, hides in a bed sheet. In a gesture of self-sacrifice to his Russian guests, Qurbaneli's act of feigning dead anticipates the symbolic death of the colonial bourgeoisie. Indeed, Memmedquluzade plays on Qurbaneli's name, which in Azeri means "the greatest sacrifice." In the sheet, Qurbaneli disguises himself first as if in a *charshaf* or chador, feminizing himself, and then as if in a burial shroud (191, 193). Both masks present relationships of otherness and opposition— male and female, as well as life and death.

When the Russian officer discovers Qurbaneli lying in the stable in a burial shroud, he curses in Russian. The juxtaposition of the image of Qurbaneli wrapped in a sheet and the Russian curse echoes the epitaph to Gogol's death. Qurbaneli rests in the manger of the stable as a symbolic sacrifice to Russian imperialism. The unveiling of the mask of the bed sheet elicits surprise from the Russian officer who utters a most Gogolian curse, "Devil take it" (*çort vozmi*) (193). The common Russian exclamation of surprise or annoyance expressed at this pivotal moment in the story recalls Gogol's figure of chaos par excellence—the devil—as well as Qurbaneli's double, the "Dock-tailed Devil"—Chertokutsky. The reader indeed finally uncovers Chertokutsky, and by extension Gogol hiding beneath Qurbaneli's sacrificial shroud. In this final gesture, Memmedquluzade unveils his text's Gogolian mask, revealing the tensions between ethnic and class identity in the colonial space of the Russian empire that are hidden beneath the folds of his parody. His work simultaneously creates a space for Gogol's work in Azeri, as he draws on Gogol's work to critique the influence of Russification. These Gogolian masks at once introduce the work of Gogol to his reader and problematize the relationship between appearance and reality, the original and the translation, as well as Russian literature and its colonial politics.

Memmedquluzade's interest in the mimetic function of literature extends to his discussion of *The Government Inspector*. In an article titled "Qoqol" printed in a 1909 issue of *Molla Nesreddin*, Memmedquluzade frames Gogol's work as a civics lesson for his local readers. He writes:

> That is to say, our critics have forgotten something, all at once forgotten that the headline written concerning Gogol will carry this "warning": hey, Muslim brothers, a hundred years ago in Russia a man was born who wrote a

comedy against the Russian officials, such that the man, after reading it also believes that a 'revisor' [inspector] is coming on behalf of the government to Nachivan, Susha, and to all the Caucasian villages and small cities.

Demək, məqalə sahiblərimiz bircə şeyi yaddan çıxardiblar, bircə bunu yaddan çixardiblar ki, Qogqolun barəsində yazdıqları məqalənin başında gərək bir belə "xəbərdarlıq" eləyədilər ki, ey müsəlman qardaşlar, yüz il bundan qabaq Rusiyada bir şəxs anadan olub və rus məmurlarının barəsində bir elə komediya yazıb ki, onu də adam oxuyanda elə bilir ki, Naxçıvana Şuşaya və bütün Qafqaz kəndlərinə və balaca şəhərlərə hökumət tərəfindən 'revizor' gəlir. (1906–1931] 1996–2014, 4:183–84)

Mocking the population's ignorance of the Russian writer, Memmedquluzade evokes the hysteria of a local reader of *The Government Inspector* awaiting the imminent arrival of a Russian official. In so doing, he emphasizes both the consistent social reality of a corrupt authority that transcends the metropole into the "Caucasian villages and small cities," as well as the translatability of Gogol's text. While the play is set outside the imperial center, it is haunted by the symbolic ordering function of the imperial bureaucracy. Indeed, the character of the government inspector, like many of Gogol's central characters, recalls the ordering system instituted through Peter the Great's westernizing reforms. The play thus stages a critique of both the capital and the provinces, as well as the corrupting rather than civilizing effect of the former on the latter.[37] The Petersburg dandy Khlestakov is mistaken for the real inspector, exposing the emptiness of this modern order of imperial authority. The confusion of Gogol's text with an actual imperial bureaucrat also extends Gogol's critique of authority to the subject of the mimetic force of the Russian play itself.

Memmedquluzade's revelation of the resemblance between Gogol's text and the real inspector parodies the pretensions of both the Russian official and the literary canon itself. As Memmedquluzade seems to author a sense of continuity with the Russian tradition, he also marks a rupture in this genealogy. His representation of Gogol's death at the beginning of the story and his recasting of another overcoat as a site of regeneration in Qurbaneli's burial shroud anticipate a new literary canon. The false inspector in Gogol's work indeed recalls the series of illegitimate heirs to Ivan the Terrible's throne, linking literary production to the broken filial lines of the Russian monarchy.[38] For Memmedquluzade, however, neither the filial bonds of the monarchy nor the affilial bonds of Gogol's literary tradition survive their transport to the Caucasus completely.[39] Memmedquluzade instead asks us to read Gogol/Qoqol both *elsewhere* and *otherwise*.

In his calls to read "Qoqol" Memmedquluzade offers a moment of respite from the cyclical returns of Russian imperial history and its reflexive acts of colonization when he reverses the mimetic relationship between literature and life. Memmedquluzade's portrait of the revolutionary Caucasus in this way seems to repeat Gogol's fiction, and yet it not only mimics but challenges the location of literary social critique within a nineteenth-century Russian aesthetic canon. That is, Memmedquluzade raises the notion that art could produce life, not only by indebting himself to a Russian aesthetic genealogy but by staging its encounter with local forms of socially engaged traditions, such as through the folk figure Molla Nesreddin. While Memmedquluzade continues to offer an invitation to reread Russian imperial history, he alerts his readers to the dangers of the false authority of the Gogolian text. His prose reveals hidden Gogols, which instead serve a greater purpose of raising the self-critical mirror to his own readers and their vices. This Qoqol, read strangely, contributes to the creation of a new tradition of Azeri literature that decenters the metropolitan vision of the revolutionary moment. Memmedquluzade invites the reader to remain attentive to the dimensions of ethno-linguistic, national, and imperial identity within the literary text as he exposes its mutual imbrication with literature, politics, and experience underlying the imperial encounter and its literary legacy. In so doing, he renders legible a form of critique that not only chronicles the arrival of Russian culture and forms of knowledge but implicates Turkic Muslim culture in the production of new revolutionary literary genealogies.

Resurrection as Revolution: Theater as Messianic Ritual

Memmedquluzade's translation of Gogolian linguistic play generated a self-estranging Azeri that contributed to the creation of a new literary canon. However, this was not the only innovation marked by Qoqol's arrival in the Caucasus. That eternally mocking reflexive gaze, which has become the touchtone of both the Gogolian tragicomedy and the exploits of the folk character Molla Nesreddin, formulated a particular type of elliptical narrative, which in the public sphere generated tales without a moral and politics without a program. One of Memmedquluzade's most notable Azerbaijani critics, Aziz Sharif (1937), argued that Memmedquluzade's departure from Gogol centered around the structure of his narrative, preferring the cruel affect of mockery to more generative forms of tragicomedy.[40] In particular, Sharif bases his claim on Memmedquluzade's exacting critique of the clergy, which he juxtaposes to Gogol's faithfulness. On the one hand, such a claim highlights the important historical contexts in which the writers penned their works—Gogol amid a strong Russian Orthodox environment during the nineteenth century and Memmedquluzade on the eve of a cultural transformation to a new form of Bolshevik theology and its various local (national) incarnations. On the other hand, Sharif's claim perhaps confers too much fixity on Memmedquluzade's intentionally evasive vision of futurity, which instead prefers the impending temporality of the apocalyptic force of revolution. Indeed, a claim for historicizing the ethos of Molla Nesreddin is, in many ways, quite beside the point. Rather, I would suggest that the emphasis on resurrection as both a thematic and structural element in Memmedquluzade's work foregrounds his vision of revolutionary politics or, more precisely, a politics predicated on an almost anarchical commitment to the chaotic and destructive principles of revolution as such.

In Gogol's work, the mimetic tension between the structure of *The Government Inspector* and the imperial bureaucracy it critiqued was blurred by its function as a force of revolutionary agitation. Performances of the play during the early twentieth century commemorated a series of revolutions across the empire (Moeller-Sally 2002, 126–28). As Katerina Clark writes in her account of Vsevolod Meyerhold's production, the first rehearsal of the play in 1925 heralded "the new official genealogy" in which the Bolshevik revolution of 1917 was "the third and culminating moment in a series of revolutions, first the Decembrist uprising against the tsar in 1825—an aristocratic revolution—and the proletarian revolutions of 1905" (1998, 27–33, 29). The figure of the inspector not only challenged the authority of the existing order but promised the arrival of the *real* inspector, and with him a new system of order. Similarly, in the Caucasus the play gained popularity after the 1905 revolution and inspired Memmedquluzade's 1909 adaptation *The Dead* (*Ölürler*), which tells the story of the arrival of an Isfahani (southern Azeri or Persian) religious figure in the revolutionary Caucasus. Like "Qurbaneli Bey," *The Dead* links the arrival of a figure of authority, also marked as foreign, to a critique of language and power in a space characterized by its temporal and geographical tensions, as well as the transience of a revolution staged between crumbling imperial centers.

Adapting *The Government Inspector* to the context of the South Caucasus, Memmedquluzade highlights the tensions between spiritual and political authority across the empire more broadly. Beyond the specific objects of social and institutional critique in Gogol's play, Memmedquluzade draws on Gogol's vision of theater as a space for mobilizing collective agency. In particular, the dénouement of *The Government Inspector*, which invites the participation of the audience, engages with an Eastern Orthodox notion of *sobornost'*, or the union of individual believers in a unanimous whole. Similarly, *The Dead* alludes to the Shi'i apocalyptic tradition of passion plays, or *ta'ziyeh*, which call for an expression of collective union in the mourning of the death of Imam Huseyn.[41] As Memmedquluzade's translations recast an old literary genealogy in a new linguistic and political context, the arrival of *The Government Inspector* to the Caucasus also inspired a critique of the corruption of the religious bureaucracy. For Memmedquluzade, Gogol's play thus provides an opportunity to develop a strategy for public catharsis by reenvisioning collective rituals as triggers for audience response. In so doing, he creates a new form of collective action authorized by both a sacred ritual and its translation through a secular theatrical tradition. Reading *The Dead* alongside *The Government Inspector* reveals the ways in which the trope of mistaken identity contributed to the creation of a messianic political discourse.

The association between theater and religious ritual was established in the early twentieth-century Azeri press. The literary journal *Enlightenment* devoted its fifth issue from December 18, 1906, to the work of Friedrich Schiller and his theory of theater as ritual. The author of the essay—who was also the journal's editor, the Azeri writer Ali bey Hüseynzade—emphasized the need for a local Turkic language theater to raise the ethical consciousness of the common people. He writes by contrast that Schiller's "theatrical works in particular brought the ideals of freedom to the German people" (ələlxüsus teatra aid asarı ilə də ümumi-Cermən qövrinə

əfkari-hürriyyəti ilqa edib) (Hüseynzade [1906–1907] 2007, 77). Hüseynzade concedes that because there is not enough local talent to meet the
civic need, the translation and staging of European works into Azeri is
necessary. In addition to Schiller's work, Hüseynzade makes particular
note of Gogol's *The Government Inspector* as a successful example of
these translations (76–77).

Analyzing Schiller and Goethe's theoretical writings on theater,
Hüseynzade highlights the importance of the institution of the Church
in influencing the enlightenment function of theater. He writes, "Schiller wanted to first become a monk in order to secure the salvation of his
nation through church preaching and moral sermons" (76–77). According to Hüseynzade, the association between the space of the Church and
the theater was elaborated in Goethe's writings. To support this claim,
he quotes an apocryphal conversation between Goethe and "a monk,"
in which the former defends the performance of church rites in Schiller's
1800 play *Maria Stuart*. According to Hüseynzade, "Goethe says to the
monk: 'My dear sir, when the celebrant of the theater is a valuable religious preacher, the theater turns into a temple, whereas a church without
a suitable celebrant turns into a theater . . .' Because 'the place of honor
is the place of knowledge'" (Gete rahibə deyir ki: 'əfəndim, teatrın xad-
imi həqiqi bir vaizi-ruhani olduqca teatr mə bədə münqəlib olacağı kibi,
layiq bir xadimdən mərhum olan kəlisa da teatroya dönə bilir . . .' Çünki
'şərəfülməkan bilməkin' dir) (78). The quote refers to the confession scene
in act 5, scene 7, of *Maria Stuart*, in which Schiller's characters transform
a prison into a church, declaring that a layman can become a priest and a
common vessel—a celestial substance.[42]

The mimetic structure of the translation of the quotation into Azeri is
echoed in the transformation of the prison into a church and the generation
of social enlightenment in the context of theatrical entertainment. Both the
script and the staging of this scene in Schiller's play expose the relationship
between representation and reality, the original and the translation/perfor-
mance, as well as the creation of a space for social and political action in
art. Hüseynzade's article concludes that knowledge provides an effective
foundation for uniting the power of sermon with the rational clarity of secular thought. The creationist impulse of the church ritual is placed within
a secular frame in which the representation of reality generates knowledge. This connection between the role of theater, moral enlightenment,

and spiritual ritual provides a direct example of the ways in which Gogol's staging might have been read in the turn-of-the-century Caucasus. These allusions to church ritual were, in turn, mirrored in Memmedquluzade's interest in the messianic ritual of resurrection in *The Dead*.

The Dead imagined the arrival of a religious official in the Caucasus— a sheikh who claims the power to defy the laws of Islam and reanimate the dead. While at once drawing on the power of ritual performance, Memmedquluzade's play critiques the false authority of Islamic clerics and the lack of education and civic engagement of the Muslim peasants in the Caucasus. Indeed, his criticism of the clergy also recalls Molière's *Tartuffe* (1664). Gogol's inspector is transformed into the corrupt Sheikh Nesrullah, who like Khlestakov, takes advantage of the hospitality of a provincial town whose residents believe him to be an extension of the divine authority of the Shi'i clergy because of his professed power to raise the dead. Only the youth Iskender, who has recently returned from studying in France, recognizes the sheikh's scam. However, Iskender's perpetual drunkenness, which renders him an outsider and thus a symbol for the relative marginalization of Western thought, cripples him with the same social immobility as the town. Finally, exposing the sheikh for the fraud that he is, Iskender also denounces the townpeople, who in their complicity are the true dead.

The imperial context of Gogol's play is embedded within Memmedquluzade's critique of the corruption of Islamic institutions. Muslim religious officials in the Caucasus were recognized by local elites as conspirators in tsarist efforts to maintain imperial authority, while their reformist opponents in many cases allied themselves (albeit briefly) with Bolshevik revolutionaries.[43] In this way, Sheikh Nesrullah serves as both a representative of the spiritual and imperial bureaucracy. His role as a pretender to sacred authority and the supernatural power of resurrection echo the figure of the government inspector's connection to divine judgment. In "The Denouement of the Government Inspector" (Razviazka revizora), Gogol charges the inspector with the responsibility of the judgment of the town as well as the human soul. He writes, "The government inspector— this is our awakening consciousness . . . for he is sent by the command of the almighty" (Revizor etot—nasha prosnuvshaiasia sovest' . . . potomu chto po imennomu vysshemu povelen'iu on poslan) (Gogol 2003, 4:351). Gogol's play announces the return of a true inspector, who would renew the authority of both God and the tsar or the tsar as God's first servant, according to Orthodox convention. However, Nesrullah's revelation as a false prophet does not promise the arrival of a new prophet but rather the necessity of a new type of resurrection.

The central symbol of the resurrection of the dead in Memmedqulu-zade's play is connected to social and religious reform efforts in the Caucasus. Indeed, the works of the late nineteenth- and early twentieth-century Muslim modernist reformers highlighted the image of the corrupt clergy as vampires. Like Hüseynzade's call to translate theater, the reformers empha-sized the necessary function of Russian and European literature in awak-ening Muslims from sleep, as both an intellectual and spiritual revival.[44] In his 1881 essay *Russian Islam* (*Russkoe musul'manstvo*) the Crimean reformer Ismail Gasprinsky urged Muslims to translate Russian literature as a means of seeking enlightenment (Gasprinskii 1881, 74). Indeed, Gasprin-sky juxtaposes the technology of translation to biological assimilation as a deeper, spiritual form of assimilation. Gasprinsky writes, "The paths are twofold: either the pursuit of blood, so to speak, to the chemical (biologi-cal) unity of the people with the state—out of this the system of the assimi-lation (of the Russian Muslims), Russification, or an aspiration toward a unified ethics, so to speak, to the principle of spiritual assimilation on the basis of national individuality, freedom, and self-government" (Пути к тому двоякие: или стремление к кровному, так сказать, к химическому единению данной народности с господствующей—отсюда система ассимиляционная, русификационная, или стремление к единению нравственному, так сказать, к нравственной духовной ассимиляции на принципах национальной индивидуальности, свободу и самоуправления) (39).

The Azeri writer and statesman Nariman Narimanov, who translated *The Government Inspector*, extolled the play's "revolutionary idea." He wrote, "this drama, written with the highest mastery, with content taken directly from our lives, and with a revolutionary idea will play a major role in the lives of Muslims, clearing the rusty brain and giving life to departed souls" (Эта драма, написанная с высочайшим мастерством, с содержанием, взятым точно из нашей жизни, с революционной идеей сыграет огромную роль в жизни, с революционной идеей сыграет огромную роль в жизни мусульман, очистит заржавевшие мозги, придаст жизнь ушедшим душам) (1988, 1:186).[45] Narimanov's description of the play outlined the moral function of Gogol's work as prophetic pedagogy for enlightening the "dead" masses. Gogol's arrival in the Caucasus thus not only signaled a critique of the defunct imperial bureaucracy and the corruption of the westernized elite but exposed the influence of Russian messianism on the formation of discourses of Muslim modernism.

The application of messianic apocalyptic discourses to a modernist rhetoric of sociopolitical reform can also be contextualized within the cultural tradition of Shiʻi messianism. Like *The Government Inspector*, *The Dead* opens with the town leader's recitation of a letter announcing the arrival of Sheikh Nesrullah. The sheikh is described as having a voice endowed with the power of Allah, a long green face and black eyes, emphasizing his otherworldly presence. The speech given by the town's leader, Meshedi Oruc, blends Azeri and Persian when he describes the sheikh's appearance: his "black-eyed, blessed colored countenance with a green/earthly desire" (siyəh-çəşm və rəngi-ruhi-mubarəkeş bəsəbzə mail) (Memmedquluzade 2004?, 1:391). The phrase "green or earthly desire" (*be sebze meyl*) offers a poetic description of the slightly olive tinge of the sheikh's face, a reference both to his connection to earthly beauty and his involvement in the dark arts of necromancy. An Azeri audience may have understood this Persian expression to varying degrees. However, Memmedquluzade employs Persian and Arabic throughout the play to highlight and simultaneously mock the villager's belief in the sheikh's supreme authority over the domains of exotic, ancient, religious knowledge and particularly the dark arts. In this way, the effect of the Persian text on the townspeople and Azeri audience would have recalled a romantic, mystical incantation akin to the use of Latin for an English speaker.

The people's belief in the sheikh's authority to raise the dead also recalls the end of time invoked in the Shiʻi vision of the return of the Mahdi as the Twelfth Imam and redeemer of Islam. In particular, the Bábīs, who famously staged a revolution against the Persian Islamic clergy in 1844 (only to be put down in 1852), emphasized the symbolic value of the resurrection of the dead as seminal to the revelation of a new teaching. Indeed, it is noteworthy that Sheikh Nesrullah Isfahani's name evokes the prominent Muslim reformist figure and (secret) Bábī thinker Haj Mirza Nasrallah al-Isfahani, also known as Malik al-Mutakallimin, who served as a leader in the Constitutional Revolution of 1906.[46] This allusion more generally emphasizes the revolutionary character of the messianic trope of the return of the Shiʻi Mahdi. Historically, resurrection and messianic return were applied to broad political agendas in Eurasia. For example, the belief in the Mahdi activated in the Bábī rebellions was notably exploited by the Bolsheviks, who spread legends that Lenin was the reincarnation of 'Ali (Arjomand 1993, 223). The revelation of the sheikh's false prophecy in the final scene, like the arrival of the real inspector general, exposes the townspeople and audience as the true dead who are in need of not only moral resurrection but a revolution.

Both *The Government Inspector* and *The Dead* climax with the revelation of the pretender. In Gogol's work this turning point is notably marked by a mute scene, which mobilizes the audience in collective action. Critics have highlighted the influence of Christian theology on the staging of this mute scene, particularly the Orthodox concept of *sobornost'*, which invites the synthesis of individual believers in a unanimous whole without the loss of identity or diversity.[47] To this end scholars juxtapose the relationship between the mute scene and Gogol's writings on Karl Briullov's painting *The Last Day of Pompeii*.[48] Collective action is made visible in Pompeii through the apocalyptic force of the volcanic eruption, just as the painting itself requires illumination in order to be recognized by its viewer. Similarly, in *The Government Inspector* the revelation of the real inspector, like a volcanic eruption, incites collective action by exposing the role of the townspeople and audience in legitimizing the authority of the false inspector.

Gogol's use of *parabasis*, breaking the fourth wall, implicates the audience in his critical gaze. Structurally, the mute scene is preceded by the mayor's speech, reflecting the mayor's pivotal role in the plot as well as his symbolic position as the social and civic leader of the town. Gogol writes:

> (*In a frenzy.*) So look you all, look, the whole world, all Christendom, all of you look how the mayor has been made a fool! [Call] him a fool, a fool, the old scoundrel! (*Threatens himself with his fist.*) And you fat nosed [idiot]! Taking that insignificant scrap for an important person! And now he's rushing down the road with bells! He's spreading the story around all of society. At the very least he'll make you a laughing stock, [but worse] some hack writer will put you into a comedy. That's what's offensive! He won't even respect your rank, and everyone will grin and clap their hands. What are you laughing at? You are laughing at yourselves!

> (*В исступлении*) Вот смотрите, смотрите, весь мир, все христианство, все смотрите, как одурачен городничий! Дурака ему, дурака, старому подлецу!

(*Грозит самому себе кулаком.*) Эх ту, тостоносый! Сосульку, тряпку принял за важного человека! Вон он теперь по всей дороге заливает, колокольчиком! Разнесет по всему свету историю; мало того что пойдешь в посмешище— найдется щелкопер, бумагомарака, в комедию тебя вставит. Вот что обидно! чина, званья не пощадит, и будут все скалить зубы и бить в ладоши. Чему смеетесь? Над собою смеетесь! (Gogol 2003, 4:88)

The mayor's speech marks the plot's climax, emphasizing a rhetoric of visibility. The world, literally "all of Christendom" (*vse khristianstvo*), is asked to bear witness to his foolishness as a mayor. His self-abuse— threatening himself with his fist and mocking his physical appearance— embodies the reflection of the play's epigraph, "There is no blaming the mirror if your face is crooked" (na zerkalo necha peniat', koli rozha kriva) (6). Moving from society to self-reflection, the mayor then places himself within the metatextual matrices of Gogol's text, which he notes "will be spread throughout all of world history." The light of truth, like film, emphasizes this moment of exposure. The mayor casts himself as the author's fool and pawn through the writing and dissemination of the text. Gogol specifies that the mayor's reputation "raznset"—not only "spreads" but "breaks up" or even "detonates" like Vesuvius—a transgressive force that collapses the fourth wall of the play and with it the boundary between the text and history. Transcending the image of the civic leader and exposing his inner comic buffoon, he orchestrates the metatextual and audience- response movements in the play, bringing the story into the light (*svet*) of both civil society and world literature.

In the final scene of *The Dead*, Iskender resorts to a similar mode of self-deprecation when he likens his own as well as the townspeople's inaction to the stasis of death. Memmedquluzade ends the play with Isk- ender's speech, evoking the explosive intertext of Gogol's mute scene. He writes:

If I were something, I would have taken a bomb out of my pocket (*takes a bottle of vodka out of his pocket*), blown this house sky-high in a second, and buried the Isfahani scoundrel alive under the bricks . . . No, no, that's not something I can do. Only a hero can do that. People like you deserve a hero like me. My name is Drunkard Iskender and what should we call you? . . . I'll gather all the nations here and ask them to look at Sheikh Nes- rullah's harem, and then all the tribes of the world will call to you in unison:

"The Dead!" And those who will come after us will speak in unison for years and years, every time they recall you: *The Dead*

Əgər mən bir şey olsaydim, cibimdən bir bomba çixarıb (*əlini uzadıb cibindən araq şüşəsini çixardır*) bu evi bir saniyənin içində havaya dağıdıb, İsfahan lotusunu kərpiclərin altında diri-diri dəfn edəridim . . . Yox, yox, o, mənim işim deyil. O, igid işidir. Siz tək camaatın da igidi mənim tək olar. Mənim adım kefli İskəndərdir; bə sizin adınızı nə qoyaq? . . . Mən cəmi millətləri bur yığıb təvəqqe edərəm ki, Şeyx Nəsrullahın hərəmxanasına tamaşa eləsinlər; o vədə bütün yer üzünün tayfaları sizi bir səslə adlandırarlar: "Ölürlər!" Və bizdən sonra gələnlər illər uzunu sizi yada salıb bir səslə deyəcəklər. "Ölürlər" (Memmedquluzade 2004?, 1:428)

Iskender's speech generates a new revolutionary theatrical genealogy as it writes a history of the provincial town. Like Gogol's mayor, Iskender emphasizes that the town's story will also be retold by "all the tribes of the world . . . for years and years." The township's ignorance is reflected in Iskender's signifying act, which names them "the dead." With this action, he also raises the Gogolian mirror to contemporary and future readers of the play. Like the mayor's speech, Iskender's monologue deconstructs the space between the town in the Caucasus and the play's audience, as well as the intertextual relationship between *The Dead* and *The Government Inspector*. Iskender's failure as a hero, evidenced throughout the play by his constant drunkenness, is placed in the explicit context of revolution in the final scene as he mimics the loading of a bomb with his bottle of vodka.

It is noteworthy that the tragicomic tone of the final scene also evokes the tradition of mass mourning orchestrated through the passion plays. This theater tradition, popular in the Caucasus and the Persian empire, commemorated the life and death of the Shi'i martyr Husayn, as well as the messianic promise of a new Mahdi. In the more esoteric reading, the Mahdi symbolized the revelation of a new doctrine, as in the case of the Bábī revolution. Thus Iskender's speech attempts to move the audience to action, rehearsing a messianic trope through the revelation of the false prophesy of the "Isfahani scoundrel" (*İsfahan lotusu*). Indeed, the word *lotu*, if it is indeed a perversion of the Persian *luti*, referred both to a gangster/rowdy as well as a play actor. The rowdy serves as a double for the Sufi, or more generally folk figure of the holy fool, revealing truth in madness and drunkenness. Indeed, this character, who Memmedquluzade embraced so closely in his aforementioned penname, Molla Nesreddin, is in *The Dead* embodied in the disorder caused by the rowdy (*lotu/luti*) sheikh's arrival as well as his very unmasking in Iskender's drunken raving. The exposure of the corruption of the Isfahani sheikh through Iskender's intoxication is thus but a rehearsal for the revelation of new order, or perhaps the disruption of order altogether.

As Gogol's mute scene resurrects the final moments of Pompeii, Memmedquluzade similarly juxtaposes the spiritual failure of the sheikh and the civic failure of Iskender as he calls on the Muslims of the Caucasus to createa new social order. The collective impulse that unites the shock of the town with that of the audience is placed in motion by the deconstruction of the frame of the stage through the practice of *parabasis*. In this deconstruction, these plays not only disrupt the geopolitical boundaries between the imperial metropole and the periphery, but they also confound the relationship between revelation and revolution, poetics and politics on the discursive threshold of this literary encounter.

Memmedquluzade's translations of Gogol's poetics of alterity and theater as social critique establish both a linkage with and a rupture from a Russian imperial literary genealogy. In this way, the historical force of parody places the Eurasian imaginary on the threshold of a self-effacing otherness. Memmedquluzade's contribution to the creation of a supranational literary exchange between Russian and Azeri engages a project of mutual linguistic approximation or contagion. In so doing, it challenges both the official literary canon and the authority of the colonial administration, exposing the foundations of a connection between art and social polity in the revolutionary imperial space. Indeed, the foundation of a revolutionary literary poetics and its connection to material forces of disruption trace a line of continuity between these late imperial translations and the Marxist-Leninist aesthetics of the 1920s, which I discuss in part 2.

Parody and mimesis were central to the consolidation of a geopoetics of the southern peripheries of Gogol's and Memmedquluzade's literary imaginations. However, as the Turkic archive illustrates, Memmedquluzade's appropriation of these rhetorical and performative devices illustrates the function of this intertextual contact in the mobilization of civic reform in the Caucasus and abroad, following the wide distribution of his journal across the Turkic and Muslim world. Memmedquluzade's influential literary contributions thus not only follow in the footsteps of his namesake, the Azeri-Persian-Turkic folk character Molla Nesreddin, or his Gogolian doubles but more crucially sketch the contours of a chaotic and often cyclical politics that characterized the first years of the Bolshevik revolution in the Caucasus. Gogol's journey to the Caucasus tells a story of the role of nineteenth-century literature in shaping a vision of theater and literature as a public product and practice, even as it reveals the underwritten history of the non-Russian periphery and its role in setting the stage for the 1905 and 1917 revolutions. As the mayor's speech in *The Government Inspector* enters the light of the spiritual and social world of the Russian empire, Memmedquluzade's Caucasian towns generate a new poetic and political genealogy, as Iskender proclaims in the final scene of the *The Dead*, for "those who come after us" (bizdən sonra gələnlər).

2

Aesthetics of Empathy

The Azeri Subject in Translations of Pushkin

He left his native threshold
And flew to a far corner
With the happy ghost of freedom.
Freedom! Still only you
He sought in the desert world.

Покинул он родной предел
И в край далекий полетел
С веселым призраком свободы.
Свобода! Он одной тебя
Еще искал в пустынном мире.

> Pushkin, "The Prisoner of the
> Caucasus" (Kavkazskii plennik)
> (1979, 4:93–94)

The old white-haired Caucasus answers your howling in the songs of Sabukhi's verses.

Старец седовлавый Кавказ ответствует на песни твои стоном в стихах Сабухия.

Axundov, "On the Death of Pushkin"
(Na smert′ Pushkina) (1837, 297–304)

The figure of the romantic exile in the Russian empire was suspended between the ideological poles of Europe and Asia. At its apex Pushkin remains, as the Soviet literary critic and historian Lidiia Ginzburg wrote, "the pivot on which Russian culture turns, he connects the past to the future. Take away the pivot and the connections will disintegrate."[1] As a literary scholar traveling to Azerbaijan, I also encountered the national narrative through a game of "six degrees of separation" from Pushkin. The beginning of a "modern" tradition of Azeri prose, I was told, can be traced to these short lines by the Azeri poet, philosopher, and playwright Mirze Feteli Axundov responding to Pushkin's Caucasus imaginary.[2] Written amid the Russian conquest, these short lines indeed frame the creation of an intertextual dialogue between Russia's imperial periphery and its metropolitan center. The works furthermore establish romantic poetry as the ground for negotiating the cultural politics of the Russian conquest of the Caucasus and for the civic role of the author in the emerging empire. Like Gogol's prose for Memmedquluzade, Pushkin's poetry provided a counterpoint through which Axundov envisioned his homeland, divided along the Araz River into the Persian and Russian empires after the Treaty of Turkmenchay concluded the Russo-Persian war between 1826 and 1828.[3]

The bifurcation of Azeri Muslims across the new border with Persia and the introduction of Russian cultural and political hegemony changed both the intellectual and the physical geography of the Caucasus. The disembarkation of Pushkin's speaker onto this "desert world" is shrouded in the discursive trappings of an orientalist fantasy—a freedom achieved in the boundlessness of the desert topography. His poem "The Prisoner of the Caucasus" recounts the story of a young Russian soldier who finds himself a prisoner of war in the Caucasus Mountains where he is cared for by a beautiful young Circassian woman. In classical romantic fashion, after helping the captive escape she is stricken by a broken heart and drowns herself. Pushkin represents his speaker as at once an agent in

Russia's conquest and a captive, trapped between the geopolitical borders of Russia and Persia and the ideological binaries of Occident and Orient.[4] The prisoner mirrors the ambivalent geopolitical and ideological position of the Russian empire—on the threshold of Europe and Asia. However, this formation also obscures Russian orientalism's role in the domination and restructuring of its colonial territories. Pushkin's search for freedom in the "desert world" of Russia's Orient liberates only the Russian soldier, abandoning the Circassian woman to drown in a river.

It is in this spirit that Axundov answers Pushkin's "howling." Axundov commemorates Pushkin's death by calling for the creation of a new literary tradition in the Caucasus built on the form of dialogue. In so doing, he offers a voice to the "white-haired Caucasus" held captive in Pushkin's verse. Axundov's Caucasus signals the beginning of a series of intertextual encounters between Russian and Azeri verse. Like Pushkin, he is often considered the father of Azeri literature for his efforts to popularize literature written in the vernacular, beginning with his plays penned in the mid-nineteenth century.[5] Although, according to poetic conventions of the day, Axundov wrote this poem and much of his philosophy originally in Persian, due to his location within the imperial space his work was instead published largely in Russian.

Three-quarters of a century later, Axundov's "howling" was echoed by the poet Abbas Sehhet. Sehhet's translations and adaptations were generated during a period of relative freedom in the press during which growing unrest against authoritarian power resulted in a series of revolutions across Eurasia: the 1905 revolution in Russia, the 1906 Persian Constitutional Revolution, and the 1908 Young Turk Revolution. On the literary plane, Sehhet's poetry was also framed by Axundov's inaugural engagement with Russian orientalism in his commemoration of Pushkin's death. Sehhet's 1912 translations of Pushkin and Lermontov build on both this nineteenth-century literary tradition and his twentieth-century political context, negotiating the intertwining influences of Russian, Ottoman, and Persian poetics into an ethos of empathy, staged in a sublime Caucasus imaginary on the threshold of revolution.

Axundov's poem could be considered one of the first Muslim Russophone works printed in the Russian press during the nineteenth century, following two short stories by the North Caucasus writer Kazy-Girei.[6] Negotiating the intertwining cultural influences of the Russian, Persian, and Ottoman empires in the Caucasus, the poem generated a Russophone poetry marked by the heterology of diverse registers of speech. Sehhet's translations of Pushkin and Lermontov's poetry into an Azeri poetics marked by Persian and Ottoman aesthetic and lexigraphic continuities instead generated a vision of the romantic sublime that emphasized the influence of Islamic literary culture. In this way, the translations not only trace an Azeri literary history but also highlight the role of religious thought in the creation of a modern Azeri lyric subject.[7] Axundov's verses and Sehhet's translations framed a set of political concerns that shaped the shifts in Azeri civic identity under the late period of the Russian empire. On the one hand, they expanded the cultural and linguistic capacities of Russophone poetry, and on the other, they responded to the Russian poetics of the sublime and Ottoman modernization in fashioning a new style of twentieth-century Azeri verse.

This chapter traces this transitional revolutionary period through aesthetic shifts in the Azeri poetic landscape and through them the creation of a new civic identity and modern subjectivity. The nineteenth-century Russian orientalist imagination of the Caucasus served as a major catalyst to these poetic imaginaries, inspiring both Axundov's theatre and verse and Sehhet's translations. The renewed popularity of the Russian romantic canon in early twentieth-century Azeri poetry exposes the influence of the Caucasian imaginary on the construction of an Azeri literary language, as well as on the discourses of Turkic supranational identity that emerged from them. The romantic turn was accompanied by a political interest in the Muslim cultural sphere. In particular, the formal and symbolic connections of verse forms to a search for esoteric knowledge provided a foundation for poetic and political connections between forms of Islamic spirituality and a new modern subjectivity. Drawing on the ethics of romantic aesthetics, the poems highlight the power of the word to shape the new revolutionary society. The *translatio imperii* and foundations of a future Azerbaijani nationalism were thus again realized through translations of orientalist poetry.[8]

The process of translation not only creates multilingual texts but also generates a linguistic transformation from within the text itself. The act of translation thus describes the ways in which the text creates an outside referent, a connection to an "original" and its author, and in this way generates meaning through the relationship among the text, the translation, and its others. In this way, it also produces a new work of literature with an independent legal status. In *On Translation*, Paul Ricoeur defines translation as both a linguistic and ontological paradigm. According to Ricoeur, translation occurs both interlingually, within and between languages, as well as intralingually, as "the interpretation of any meaningful whole within the same speech community" (2004, 11). Intralingual translation reveals relationships between the self and another, as well as within the self—that is, between the conscious and unconscious. Providing a model of translation as a relational ontology, Ricoeur renounces the search for an original language or a priori codes and instead embraces the proliferation of polysemy and the creative fullness of interpretation: that is, the very act of translation replaces the notion of a singular linguistic origin. In this way, linguistic diversity and the reflexive process of the mediation between the author and reader form the basis of his theoretical, practical, and ethical act of translation.[9]

Ricoeur's theory of translation relies on a broader understanding of his hermeneutical phenomenology. In his three-volume opus *Time and Narrative* (1984–1988), Ricoeur offers an account of narrative as the human experience of time through the codetermined activities of the author and reader. He calls this temporal nature of human existence common to author and reader mimesis. He writes, "Generalizing beyond Aristotle, I shall say that mimesis marks the intersection of the world of the text with that of the hearer or reader; the intersection, therefore, of the world unfolded by fiction and the world wherein actual action unfolds" (1:71). Ricoeur's discussion of mimesis shares a strong affinity with Mikhail Bakhtin's analysis of narrative discourse and the figure of the *chronotope*, which he develops in *Problems in Dostoevsky's Work/Poetics*, "Forms of Time and Chronotope in the Novel," and "Discourse in the Novel."[10] Ricoeur's theory of narrative temporality shares with Bakhtin's work both a critique of structuralism and an emphasis on the importance of historicity and temporality.[11] In particular, poetics often bear the weight of this critique against structuralism. For Bakhtin poetics are confined only to an analysis of the linguistic and grammatical aspects of language, relating to material and formal characterization. His discussion of the chronotope and the relationship between the author and hero instead privilege the vision of history revealed in the connection among the author, the text, and the world.[12]

The figure of the threshold in *Problems of Dostoevsky's Poetics*, which I discuss in the introduction, serves as a chronotopic site that exposes the boundaries and dialogic meeting between one's own and someone else's consciousness. Furthermore, as Bakhtin develops in his earlier text "The Author and the Hero in Aesthetic Activity," the author generates an image of the human being in its totality and establishes a unique relationship of interiority and exteriority among him-/herself, the characters, and the reader. Indeed, in Bakhtin's notebooks he explicitly describes this relationship among character, text, and author as chronotopic (1997–2012, 6:393). Ricoeur similarly argues that "the fictive experience of time," can be defined as the "temporal aspect of this virtual experience of being-in-the-world proposed by the text" (1984–88, 2:100).[13] Ricoeur's understanding of narrative time through the experience of being in the world generated in the text thus evokes Bakhtin's definition of the chronotope as "the image of the human in literature."

Ricoeur's and Bakhtin's theories of narrative time situate the visibility of the human experience at the center of the intersubjective dimension of the processes of writing and translation. As Ricoeur thus seems to suggest, translation in particular highlights the spatio-temporality or chronotope of authorship by exposing a multiplicity of authors, characters, texts, and readers staged in the encounter between the "original" and its translation. Drawing on this hermeneutical phenomenology of authorship, I frame these translations produced in the Russian empire through the intercultural, interlinguistic, and intersubjective exchanges between nineteenth-century Russian and the twentieth-century Azeri works that they generated. The century-long time span separating many of these encounters (except for Axundov) is noteworthy as the evocation of the nineteenth century generated an archive through which the imperial past could be reimagined on the eve of revolution. In this way, the Russian romantic canon provided a point of dialogue for the twentieth-century Azeri poetic vision of revolution and the author's role in its agitation.

Susan Layton and Harsha Ram have convincingly argued that Russian orientalist representations of the Caucasus, which highlighted the sublimity of the landscape and the bravery of its inhabitants, became a vehicle for discussions of Russia's status as a world empire. This approach entailed a description of Russia's European, Asian, or Eurasian character, as well as literary efforts to individualize this imperial history by reconceptualizing it in aesthetic and spiritual terms. As an object of orientalist scholarship, the Caucasus set off Russia's Europeanness, serving as Russia's contribution to the West's *Renaissance Orientale,* as Layton (1994) writes, alluding to Raymond Schwab's foundational text. Furthermore, for Pushkin it formed the eastern boundary of Western Europe, recalling the sublime beauty of Byron's Parnassus and serving as a buffer between Christian Europe and "wild Asia." For Bestuzhev-Marlinsky and Lermontov, the Caucasus represented a space of hybrid mixing, defining Russia's success through its Eurasian character. In terms of their aesthetic value, as Ram argues, Pushkin and Lermontov's representations draw on an "oriental style" (*vostochnyi stil'*) that depends on the "topos of prophesy" (2003, 172). The romantic sublime thus contributed to the reconceptualization of imperial history by highlighting the individualized aesthetic and spiritual experience of the poet as prophet (172).

Azeri translations beginning with Axundov engaged with the romantic forms and symbols of the Caucasian sublime and the figure of the poet as prophet to generate a series of works that blended revolutionary politics with classical forms of mystical poetry. These translations and interpretations of Russian poetry embody Ricoeur's reciprocal model of translation in their displacement of the notion of poetic origins. Instead, fusing Russian romanticism with Azeri, Ottoman, and Persian poetic forms, symbols, and languages, they reimagined the Russian "oriental style" through a new spiritual and political power. While Pushkin's and Lermontov's verse draws on an orientalist imaginary to sublimate the prophetic power of the poet and promote an antitsarist political agenda, Axundov and Sehhet return the poem to the civic and spiritual space of dialogue. They also generate a new type of cultural identity based in part on Russian romantic poetics but oriented toward pan-Turkic and pan-Islamic forms of cultural and civic identity.

Reclaiming Russia's Orient: Pushkin and Axundov's Dialogue in Verse

Though Axundov wrote more than half a century before Sehhet, his work signals the opening of an intertextual, intercultural, and intersubjective dialogue with Russian orientalism. Axundov's biography, like those of his contemporaries the poet Mirze Şefi Vazeh and the poet, linguist, and historian Abbasqulu ağa Bakıxanov Qüdsi, embodies the divided homeland of a generation that was forced to reconcile itself to the repartition of the lands of Tabriz from the territories north of the Araz River. Under the Safavid dynasty, particularly from the sixteenth through the eighteenth centuries, Persian language and culture played an integral role in the poetic tradition in the Caucasus. However, in the nineteenth century Russian began to gain currency as a dimension of civic identity among intellectuals who sought to gain access to Russian and European ideas and literature. Vazeh and Bakıxanov carried on their classical training in the Safavid poetic and philosophical traditions, writing largely in Persian. Axundov instead began to write in modern Azeri, as well as to translate and publish his work in Russian.[14]

The contemporary historian Ali Abasov describes this movement of writers and reformers during the early nineteenth century as the "Azerbaijani Enlightenment" (2008, 60). For Abasov, the movement is defined by a commitment to critical thought and reform, which arose in response to the "socio-cultural shock" of the collision of Azeri and Russian culture. Axundov's interest in Russian and European literature as well as his engagement with Islamic philosophy and the classical Persian poetic tradition thus grew out of the diverse cultural environment of the Caucasus during the nineteenth century. Axundov's public attention to civic issues of reform also characterized this new generation of Azeri intellectuals in the Caucasus. His writings critique the domains of education and women's rights and launched the first alphabet reform campaign.[15] He also contributed to the establishment of an influential educational institution—the Transcaucasian Gori Teacher's Seminary—and the staging of professional theatrical productions.[16]

Axundov was born in 1812 in Nukha (today Sheki), a historic trading post located in the northern region of the South Caucasus.[17] Family conflict led to his mother's decision to take young Axundov to live with his uncle, under whose tutelage he studied the Qur'an, Islamic law (*fiqh*), as well as Arabic and Persian languages in preparation for a religious career.[18] While studying in Ganja, he met Vazeh, who introduced him to European thought, most notably the works of the French Enlightenment as well as German and Russian romanticism. This friendship changed the course of Axundov's career, and in 1834 he moved to Tiflis to work as an assistant translator in the office of the Russian viceroy of the Caucasus. There he joined Vazeh's literary salon known as the "Court" or "House of Wisdom" (*Divanı Hikmet, Hikmet Evi*), where he met with a diverse group of international writers and thinkers including the Russian orientalist Adolf Berzhe, the German orientalist Friedrich von Bodenstedt, and the Russian writer Alexander Bestuzhev-Marlinsky.[19] In particular, he developed a relationship with Bestuzhev-Marlinsky, whom he tutored in Turkish and with whom he would later collaborate on the translation of his poem into Russian. These interactions with European orientalists coupled with his administrative work as a translator shaped Axundov's encounter with Russian literature.

The conquest of the Caucasus also spurred an expansion of Russian orientalist scholarship, which had begun to a certain extent under Catherine the Great and then more systematically in the early 1800s under the directives of Alexander I and the creation of oriental languages departments in Kazan, Tiflis, and Irkutsk.[20] As an object of study, the Caucasus affirmed Russia's status as an emerging world empire. In his 1810 essay "Projet d'une Académie Asiatique," the future minister of education Sergei Uvarov outlined Russia's advantageous geographical position as the decisive factor in its future contributions to "the renaissance of oriental studies" (1810, 8).[21] He writes:

> With her back to Asia and dominating the entire northern part of this continent, Russia shares with the other powers a moral interest that guides them in their noble enterprise; but furthermore she retains a political interest so clear, so substantive that a glance at the map suffices to convince one of it. Russia, one might say, relies upon Asia. An immensely long land border puts her in contact with practically all of the peoples of the Orient, such that it is difficult to believe that of all of the states of Europe, Russia finds itself the one which has engaged the least in the study of Asia. (8)

Uvarov emphasizes Russia's proximity to and "dominion" over Asia as evidence of its unique capability to produce knowledge about the "orient." Indeed, Russia's contiguous imperial geography and its geographical proximity to the "Orient" through its southern and eastern borders determined its discourses of Eurasian imperial identity (Hokanson 2008). Furthermore, Uvarov argues, Russia's reliance on Asia (*La Russie repose, pour ainsi dire, sur l'Asie*) authorizes its place among the European states.

Russia's status as a European empire is thus established not only through its imperial expansion but through its production of knowledge about its southern and eastern borderlands. Similarly, in a short article published in the popular newspaper *The Caucasus* (*Kavkaz*) in 1868, Berzhe speci-fies the Caucasus's role in Russia's contribution to European oriental stud-ies. The Caucasus, he wrote, "would fulfill one of the most visible gaps in the field of the study of the East" ([1868] 1987, 87–88). Berzhe was not only responsible for outlining the theoretical importance of the Caucasus but also for playing a major role in introducing the figure of Axundov to a Russian audience.

Although Axundov was best known for his Turkic plays written in the 1850s, he made his literary debut in the Russian press in 1837 with a poem commemorating Pushkin's death in the same year. While manu-scripts attest to a Persian-language original, the work was published only in Russian translations under the title "On the Death of Pushkin."[22] Indeed, the history of the poem's translation and circulation exposes the intertwining linguistic and cultural influences that contributed to its com-position. Axundov's exposure to Russian culture through his work as a translator in the Russian imperial administration and acquaintance with Russian writers and orientalists not only piqued his interest in Pushkin's poetry but facilitated his poem's publication. The poem was first pub-lished in Axundov's own prose translation in the journal *The Moscow Observer* (*Moskovskii nabliudatel'*), with the aid of the Russian oriental-ist Ivan Klementev.[23] The publication carried an additional subtitle "A Composition in Verse by a Contemporary Persian poet" (Sochinenie v stikhakh sovremennogo persidskogo poeta) and was accompanied by an analysis of the poem's literary significance in Persian culture. The intro-duction cites Klementev's praise for the work as an example of the gifts of the Russian civilizing mission on "a tribe, still oppressed by the yoke of wild passions" (*plemen', eshche geneshomykh iarmom strastei dikikh*) (Sharif and Kurbanov, 1979, 299). He excuses the "savagery and wildness of expression" (*zhestkost' i dikost' vyrazheniia*) of Axundov's text in the spirit of preserving the "bright local color of Iran" (*iarkii kolorit Irana*) (298). Axundov is here further distanced from Russia. Although the poem was penned in Tiflis, the language of the poem's composition contributes to its exotic allure. Indeed, for Klementev the power of this "wild" lan-guage is so strong it transcends the Russian translation.

Similarly, in an accompanying introduction to a revised prose translation by Bestuzhev-Marlinsky published in 1874 in the journal *Russian Antiquities* (*Russkaia starina*), Berzhe also praised Axundov's positive "impression on her [Russia's] Muslim population in one of the remote outskirts of Great Russia" (1874, 76–78).[24] This version also boasted a revised title "An Eastern Poem on the Death of A. S. Pushkin" (Vostochnaia poema na smert' A. S. Pushkina) (76–78). While the translations offer a rare example of the publication of works by Muslims from the Caucasus in the nineteenth-century Russian press, the accompanying commentary relegates them to the "remote outskirts" of the imperial periphery. Stripped of their rhythmic and metrical structure, Axundov's Russophone translations, however, create a new space for the absent verse in Russian prose. Framed by its commentary, the poem at once becomes an object of orientalist scholarship—an "eastern poem"—and exposes a delicate interplay between Axundov's self-translation of the affected "oriental style" of the romantic canon.

The original composition, available through photographs and transcriptions, can be classified according to the Persian tradition of the *marsiya*, or elegy, often rooted in religious martyrological tradition. Its form follows the *qaṣīda*, a form of panegyric ode intended to honor a prophet or king, which was popular across Arabic, Persian, Ottoman, and Urdu poetic traditions.[25] The original is composed of fifty lines, or *baits,* of fourteen syllables each and concluding in a consistent rhyme ending with the *rawiyy* or rhymed letter *r* (*rā'*). Following an architectural metaphor, the *bait*—meaning house or tent—is a complete syntactic unit composed of two rhymed half-lines—or *miṣrā'*—meaning door or tent flap.[26] Rhetorically the *qaṣīda* follows a bipartite or tripartite non-narrative structure either presenting a metaphorical transformation from the physical to the metaphysical world or tracing the ascent of the speaker from a state of ignorance to understanding and from despair to hope (Andrews 1985; Sperl and Shackle 1996, 63–70).

Despite the loss of its verse structure, Axundov's prose translation preserves symbols and themes from the classical tradition. The translation also contains fifty lines and follows the speaker's ascent from his despair over Pushkin's death to his hope for the continuation of Pushkin's legacy. The opening verse describes the speaker-poet struggling to find inspiration in the obscurity of night, "Not surrendering my eyes to a dream, I sat in the night and spoke to my heart: Oh, spring of the pearls of mystery!" (Ne predavaia ochei snu, sidel ia v noch' i govoril serdtsu: O rodnik zhemchuga tainy! Не предавая очей сну, сидел я в ночи и говорил седцу: О родник жемчуга тайны!) (1837, 297). The image of the speaker caught in a liminal state between sleep and wakeful meditation associates the spiritual or metaphysical states of prayer or trance with the poet's existential crisis of creation. He expresses his grief to his heart, which he refers to through both the symbolic natural riches of the fountain and the pearl. Axundov also draws on the image of the garden as a symbol for a community of spiritual and cultural texts in order to memorialize the significance of Pushkin's death. Indeed, the figure of the Caucasian garden served as the central metaphor in Bakıxanov's history of the Caucasus *The Heavenly Rose Garden (Gulistan-e Eram* [1845]).[27] Following the Persian tradition, natural imagery is often used in Azeri poetry to function as a mirror reflecting the internal strivings of the poet (Esgerli 2005, 21). Nature, depicted in the form of a rose garden, reflects social life and the humanistic ideals that surround the figure of the poet (13). In Axundov's verse, the image of Pushkin awakens the speaker from his physical sleep and creative inertia. The inspiration for the poem is thus linked to Russian literature's spiritual and creative enlightenment.

Turning away from loss and stagnation, the second movement develops the symbols of the cathedral and garden alongside a brief genealogy of the luminaries of Russian literature, weaving together a new cultural lineage. Axundov writes thus in praise of Pushkin,

Are you really unaware of this world! Have you really never heard of Pushkin, head of the pantheon of Poets.

Of that Pushkin, for whom a hundredfold praise thundered from the ends (of the earth) when he playfully poured out his dreams.

Of that Pushkin, for whom paper thirsted to lose its whiteness, if only his plume would drive the line along its face.

In his dreams, like in the movements of a peacock, there appeared a thousand marvelous colors of Literature.

Lomonosov adorned the abode of Poetry with the beauty of genius, but his [Pushkin's] dream was validated through it.

Though Derzhavin conquered the orb of literature, he [Pushkin] was elected for its direction and organization.

Karamzin filled the cup with the wine of knowledge, and he [Pushkin] drank the wine of this overflowing cup.

The glory of his genius traveled throughout Europe, just as the might and
majesty of Nicholas did from China to Tatary.

His luminous mind made him a model dear to the North, just like the crescent moon, which is so dear to the East.

Разве ты, не ведающий мира! Разве не слышал о Пушкине главе собора Поэтов.

О том Пушкине, которому стократно гремела хвала со всех концов когда он
    игриво изливал свои мечтания.

О том Пушкине, от которого бумага жаждала потерять белизну свою, чтобы
    только перо его проводило черты по лицу ее?

В мечтах, его, как в движениях павлина являлись тысячи дивных цветов
    Литературы.

Ломоносов красою гения украшал обитель Поэзии, но, его мечта в ней
    утвердилась.

Хотя Державин завоевал державу Литературы, но для управления и
    устройства ея избран бы он

Карамзин наполнил чашу вином знания, он выпил вино сей наполненной
    чаши.

Распостранилась слава его гения по Европе, ка могущество и величие
    Николая от Китая до Татарии.

        По светлому уму своему был образцом на Севере, подобно
        молодой луне, которой вид дорог Востоку. (1837, 300–301)

In this passage, Axundov recounts the major figures who contributed to
the creation of the Russian panegyric ode, including Lomonosov, Derzhavin, and Karamzin—presenting Pushkin as the culmination of the
Russian literary tradition. Invoking the theological rhetoric of unity, he
describes the poets' membership in a pantheon or *sobor,* a term that draws
on the space of the cathedral as a metonymy for a great assembly or council. This religious signification is, however, unique to the Russian version.
Its Persian pair reads, "of Pushkin ruler of the army/masses of poets" (*az
Puŝkin be kheyl-e sokhanvarân-e sâlâr*) (Âdamiyat 1970, 275). Again in
the Russian, Axundov places this Orthodox concept alongside symbols
from the Persian mystical poetic and folk traditions such as the overflowing cup of wine and the multicolored peacock. Placing Pushkin within a
figurative garden, Axundov compares his death to the felling of a young
tree. He writes: "with the merciless axe the gardener cut the height of
that young tree from the surface of the garden" (Сей старый садовник

секирою безжалостно срубил его стан, как молодую ветвь с террасы сего цветника) (1837, 300–301). The image of the garden presents Russian literature as the social bed from which both Pushkin and Axundov's verse springs. Although Axundov seems to root his poetic inspiration in the spiritual-cultural unity of Lomonosov, Derzhavin, Karamzin, and Pushkin, the symbol of the garden itself supplies the foundation for his introduction to Russian literature. Inverting the imperial narrative of progress from enlightened Russia to wild Caucasia, the garden signifies the ordered and cultured space of the Azeri/Persian tradition that does not emanate from but rather coexists with Russian literature.[28]

The poem's grounding in Russian and Persian renders the work a multilingual object. The Russian text relies on an understanding of Azeri/Persian symbols, while its Persian original bases its praise upon the history of a foreign literary tradition. Drawing on the poetic structure of the *qaṣīda*, Axundov generates a series of similes in Russian that seem to replicate the *bait* structure, building on overlapping sequences of meaning in the text. Describing Pushkin's fame, he writes: "The glory of his genius traveled through Europe, just as the might and majesty of Nicholas from China to Tatary." Here Axundov compares Pushkin's poetic legacy to the expansion of the Russian empire.[29] Appropriating the orientalist term "Tatary" to describe the Muslim regions of the empire, Axundov places Pushkin within a lineage of European orientalists whose literature about empire generated a hegemonic Western literary canon. Axundov continues: "his luminous mind made him a model dear to the North, just like the crescent moon, which is so dear to the East." Invoking the classical poetic structure, which articulates a parallel between the earthly and the celestial realms, Axundov compares Pushkin to the moon. As a model for Russian literature, Pushkin provides both physical and spiritual illumination like the crescent, which both emits moonlight and refers to the international community of Islamic believers, the *umma*. In this way, Axundov portrays Pushkin as the spiritual leader of Russian literature.

In the final lines of the poem, Axundov relates Pushkin's work to his own role as an initiator of a new poetic tradition in the Caucasus. He calls to the ancient lands of the Caucasus and Crimea to answer the writings of Pushkin. In this verse, the lands of Crimea and the Caucasus assert their existence before Pushkin's poetic discovery and endurance after his death. He writes: "The fountain of Bachisarai sends your ashes with a spring zephyr of two roses. The old white-haired Caucasus answers your howling in the songs of Sabukhi's verses" (Фонтан из Бахчисарая посылает праху твоему с весенним зефиром благоухание двух роз твоих. Старец седовлавый, Кавказ, отвечает на песни твои стоном в стихах Сабугия) (1837, 302). The roses refer to two of Pushkin's most famous orientalist works about the Muslim territories of the Russian empire—"The Fountain of Bakhchisarai" (Bakhchisaraiskii fontan) and "Prisoner of the Caucasus"— which describe the landscapes of the Russia's southern colonies in Crimea and the Caucasus. Anthropomorphizing the landscape, Axundov emphasizes the active role of the Caucasus in answering Pushkin's verse, as well as its wisdom symbolized by the snowcaps of the "white-haired" mountains. While in Axundov's Russian translation, the figurative image of the Caucasus responds (*otvetstvuet*) to Pushkin's poetry, the Persian version of the final stanza differs. Axundov writes that the Caucasus is mourning (*mātam dar*) Pushkin (Âdamiyat 1970, 276). Axundov's emphasis on the active role of the Caucasus engaging in dialogue with Pushkin is thus particular to the context of its Russian publication. Notably, when the poem was republished in 1880 in the journal *The Petersburg Leaflet* (*Peterburgskii listok*) to commemorate the erection of the Pushkin monument in Moscow, a free-verse translation by A. A. Sokolov did not include this image of the Caucasus's response.[30] The omission of this final line, perhaps the most crucial turning point in the tone of the poem, silences Axundov's response to imperial Russia's conquest of the South Caucasus.

The final couplet exposes the mutual imbrication of the Russian and Persian versions of the text, as if generating a dialogue between the versions through the figure of Pushkin. In a gesture common to Azeri and Persian poets, Axundov marks the beginning of a new literary tradition by designating himself, through his pen name, as the storyteller of the Caucasus, *Sabuhi* (transliterated into Russian as *Sabugi*). The word in Persian means "one who awakens early," and in Azeri "the man of tomorrow." The form of the title reflects a traditional type of Azeri/Persian pseudonym; however, its meaning also emphasizes a rupture or break, the creation of a new movement of literature and ideas—that is, a vision of literary modernity. While the body of the poem describes the speaker's literal awakening and spiritual/cultural enlightenment through Pushkin's verses, the final line designates a new beginning inaugurated by Pushkin's death and charges the poet to revitalize the literature of the Caucasus. For Axundov, the subject of Pushkin's death becomes an occasion to give a new voice to the same Caucasian landscape that had been the object of Pushkin's orientalist imagination. Translating his elegy into Russian, Axundov draws on the literary legacy of the Russian ode to create a space for a multilingual and multivocal text. The symbolic death of Pushkin, remembered as the father of the literature of the North, gives birth to a new literary genealogy in the verse of the "old white-haired Caucasus." Here Axundov also generates an intertwining vision of literary modernity as at once bound by traditional poetic convention and liberated by the new layers of meaning acquired in translation.

Axundov's Heterodoxy: Authorship and Islam

Axundov's self-styled westernized persona, perhaps most famously immortalized in a photograph of him dressed in a Russian imperial officer's uniform, lends support to the frequent denunciations and celebrations of his work as an apology for atheism.[31] At the center of this debate is his famous philosophical treatise *Three Letters from the Indian Prince Kamal od-Dowle to the Persian Prince Jalal-od-Dowle* (1860–1864).[32] The text, Axundov insists, is a translation of a Persian epistolary correspondence between historical princes, the Indian prince Kamal-od-Dowle and the Persian Prince Jalal-od-Dowle.[33] Whether or not original Persian-language exemplars of the manuscript exist, Axundov's claims to providing an authentic record frames his work in dialogue with an Enlightenment genre of pseudotranslations, or alleged translations, often of philosophical epistolary correspondences, such as Montesquieu's *Persian Letters* (1721).[34] Ironically, Axundov's emphasis on historical authority has encouraged autobiographical readings of the text as a personal confession of his atheism. In particular, the voice of the character Kamal-od-Dowle and his denunciation of the backwardness of Qajar monarchy and Shi'i religious hierarchy are cited as a primary example of Axundov's rejection of religion.[35] Highlighting this disjuncture, Axundov poignantly responds, "Look I do not say these words, Kemaludovle says them" (1953, 1:279). This complex internal and external function of the author-hero relationship is precisely the point Bakhtin raises when he describes Dostoevsky's characters as "*free* people, capable of standing *alongside* their creator, capable of not agreeing with him and even of rebelling against him . . . *not only objects of authorial discourse but also subjects of their own directly signifying discourse*" (1997–2012, 6:6–7). Axundov's Kemal-od-Dowle is both a historical personage and a character whose discourse has its own coexistent space and time within the literary text. *Three Letters* should not be read only biographically or historically but rather, like his theatrical works, through the dialogic interplay between the characters' speech.

Axundov's work generally critiques religious figures, teachings, and institutions; however, he also recommends a reformation of Islam, which he calls "Islamic protestantism." In his autobiography, Axundov expressed an interest in "protestant Islam" as he penned *Three Letters*. He explains: "I began to write 'Kemaluddovle' with an overwhelming desire to undermine the foundations of this faith, deal a blow to fanaticism, and awaken the peoples of Asia from slumber, and, on the other hand, to demonstrate the necessity of Protestantism in Islam."[36] Indeed Axundov's critique focuses specifically on the corruption of the social institution of religion (Abasov 2008, 64). Axundov's interest in "protestant Islam" can thus be understood as a confession of religious belief mediated by science (64). However, Axundov does not elaborate this religious philosophy. He describes his interest in the concept of Protestantism only in terms of the historical example of North American and European Protestants in order to emphasize the corrupt authority of clericalism (64–65).[37]

Axundov's discussion of "protestant Islam" provides an example of the coexistence of multiple planes of secular and religious thought in his work and introduces a reformist Islamic critique. Kamal-od-Dowle argues that the social and cultural backwardness of the Persian people results from the loss of their ancient national characteristics of truth, bravery, and democracy. In this way, the statement idealizes the pre-Islamic Sassanid empire as a utopian society and a model for rational and efficient institutions that fell under corrupt leadership after the conversion to Islam. Axundov presents a vision of the recovery of pre-Islamic wisdom and hence engages with an intellectual tradition that became popular among both European orientalists and Islamic modernist reformers during the nineteenth century.[38] It is thus possible to think of Axundov's engagement with Islam as a precursor to similar concepts underpinning Islamic reformist movements. In particular, the jadid cultural reform movement relied on Qur'anic scripture to legitimize the use of European technology and harnessed the critical faculties of *ijtihad* to prove the compatibility of Islam with European thought.[39]

Axundov's simultaneous critique of religious institutions and engagement with Islamic thought served as an inspiration to twentieth-century Azeri thinkers, especially Memmedquluzade. In a 1928 article, published during the liberal Soviet period of the New Economic Policy (NEP), which I discuss in the final chapter, Memmedquluzade points out that Axundov's work was not considered atheistic until Soviet critics appropriated an excerpt from *Three Letters* for their own ideological purposes.[40] In an elliptical argument typical of Memmedquluzade's rhetorical style, he traces Axundov's correspondence in order to illustrate the internal incongruities within it. In his letters, Axundov recounts his denunciation by a Sheikh Mohsun for his character Kemal-od-Dowle's statements. Impassioned, Axundov responds that Sheikh Mohsun will be charged for his slander on the Day of Judgment. Axundov's reliance on the existence of the Day of Judgment as an arbiter of final justice, Memmedquluzade argues, illustrates Axundov's personal investment in his faith. Tracing such inconsistencies in Axundov's work, Memmedquluzade argues that atheism poses a far too absolute or transcendental notion of truth to encompass Axundov's critical process.

In *Three Letters*, Kamal-od-Dowle discredits Sufi, Sunni, and Shi'i religious leaders, the sayings of the Prophet, and various selections from the Qur'an. Finally, he makes a famous declaration that all religions are an empty fiction (Axundov 1953, 107). Kamal-od-Dowle says, "Hey, Jalal od-Dowle! Don't assume from these words that maybe I prefer some other religion and sect to Islam. *I regard all religions to be empty and legends*" (279). Memmedquluzade contextualizes this statement within the work as a whole by citing the second letter in the collection. In this selection, Kamal-od-Dowle argues that his philosophy of religion is based on the works of the Persian scholar and Sufi poet Nur al-Dīn Abd al-Rahmān Jāmī (1414–1492), the Persian Sufi poet Mahmūd Shabistarī (1288–1340), the Italian scholar and poet Francesco Petrarch (1304–1374), and the French thinker Voltaire (1694–1778). Kamal-od-Dowle addresses his Muslim readers through his response to Jalal-od-Dowle:

> Until you become informed about astronomy and the natural sciences, you will always believe in extraordinary miracles, angels, and these sorts of

superstitions. You will not know that the whole universe is one perfect unity
of energy . . . and its law that individuals appear and that the seed of the
tree that is underground becomes a tree after sun, air, and water lend it their
care and all in heaven and earth that is visible and invisible to you with your
five senses, and all sorts of objects are just fragments and pieces comparing
to the being-whole [*vücudi-vahid*], and all of those fragments are whole and
that wholeness is the being-whole. And it is this whole-being which is itself
creator and itself creation. (279)[41]

The passage can be divided into three major arguments: (1) a critique of
superstition—miracles, and other ritualized practices; (2) an emphasis
on the study of natural sciences and particularly materialist philosophy;
and (3) a reference to the concept of the wholeness of being that is central to conceptions of esoteric knoweldge rooted in Arabo-Persian philosophical traditions. These three points can be extended more broadly to
Axundov's work as a whole. The critique of superstitions is a common
point throughout *Three Letters* and a central thematic in his first play,
*The Story of Monsieur Jordan the Botanist, and the Famous Dervish Mes-
tali Shah (Hekayeti-müsyö Jordan hekimi-nebatat Derviş Mesteli şah caduküni-meshur)* (2005, 1:45–68). The analysis of the universe as a unity of
energy, the references to the five senses of perception, and the growth cycle
of the tree clearly emphasize Axundov's interest in materialist philosophy.
The passage also equates the wholeness of the natural world with a unity
of being, literally a "being-one." The Azeri *vücud* is taken from the Arabic *wajūd,* "being" or "existence," while *vahid* is a taken from the Arabic
wahid, "one" or "oneness." *Vücudi-vahid,* thus, literally translates as
"being-one," and is a form of the Arabic *wahdat al-wujūd,* also called simply the *tawḥīd,* the Sufi metaphysical concept of the Unity of Being most
often attributed to the thirteenth-century Islamic philosophers Ibn Sab'īn
and Ibn 'Arabī.[42] The concept in Islamic philosophy refers to the unity of
truth and existence within God. It is noteworthy that even though Axundov
does not embrace any religious institutions, his work contains many references to Islamic philosophy and culture. His pen name in "On the Death of
Pushkin" is the word *Sabuhi,* which derives from the root *S-B-H,* or sunrise but can refer to a short form for *sālāt al sub,* or the morning prayer
(Wehr 1980, 500). Although these examples do not prove Axundov's piety,
crucially they inform a layer of signification in his rich discourse.

Directly following this quotation, Kamal-od-Dowle addresses his inter-locutor's skepticism. This aside to the reader emphasizes the importance of the form of dialogue to the process of critique. It also provides Axun-dov with the opportunity to expand on the concept of unity. Axundov writes: "Here you address me 'Dear Kamal-od-Dowle! From where does the human embryo or the seed of the tree emanate?'" (1953, 107). Kamal-od-Dowle answers by describing the perfect unity of the universe. Indeed, he alludes to the Qur'anic sura 112, *al-Ikhlās* or *al-Tawḥīd*, replacing the figure of God with the natural world.[43] Axundov continues: "This universe is one being, powerful and perfect. In the beginning he was not preceded and in the end he did not follow" (107). Particularly the fourth verse of the sura is relevant, declaring that God is the one, eternal and perfect one "who neither begetteth nor is begotten" (*The Holy Qur'an* 112). This sense of unity is expressed both in the wholeness of God as a transcendent noncorporeal being, as well as through the wholeness of time, which here extends beyond the concept of human reproduction or ancestry.

In these passages, Axundov resignifies the concept of divine unity in the context of his discussion of a materialist philosophy of the universe by working through the internal logic of the text. Although he does not argue explicitly for the compatibility of Islam and materialism, he intertwines these discourses in his treatise. Axundov writes that the world is revealed to the human through the five senses, though the things that are sensed are only fragments in comparison with the *unity of being*. If the *unity of being* could also be understood as truth, then this truth can signify both the discussion of the natural world that Kamal-od-Dowle outlined in the previous lines, or perhaps a new genealogy of Islamic philosophy. Axundov's heteroglossia, to appropriate Bakhtin's term, generates his hetero-dox vision of Islam and approach to literary modernity.

All Roads Lead to Parnassus: Sehhet's Translations of the Russian Sublime

Axundov's invocation of Pushkin was indeed ahead of its time. As I discussed in the first chapter, it was only after the boom in the Muslim press follow-ing the 1905 revolution that Russian literature began to receive a substan-tial engagement in the Azeri press. Of course, this was in part because local language outlets had been censored during the nineteenth century. The new journals aimed to educate the local population about advances in science, technology, and culture. In particular, the journal *Enlightenment* (1906–1907) served a foundational role in the formation of a new literary and aesthetic canon for its twentieth century Ottoman and Azeri readership. The journal, which was edited by Ali bey Hüseynzade, was often considered the most Western-leaning Azeri journal of its time. *Enlightenment* printed articles on a broad range of topics, from discussions of the contemporary politics of the region to the masterworks of European literature. Its politics was oriented toward constitutional reform. For example, it discussed the historical Ottoman constitutional reforms of 1876 of Ahmed Midhat Pasha as well as the contemporary Persian Constitutional Revolution.[44] In the realm of scientific and technological innovations, it devoted many pages to the creation of the telegraph and the work of the Russian chemist Dmitry Mendeleyev.

With the prominent pan-Turkic thinker Hüseynzade as its editor, *Enlightenment* fostered a common ethno-linguistic identity among the journal's international Turkic readership. In his poem "Turan" Hüseynzade refers to the community of pan-Turkic peoples across Hungary, the Ottoman empire, and Central Asia.[45] He writes:

> Hey, you nation of the Magyars (Hungarians), you are our brothers
> Turan is our common origin
> All of us, God-lovers are of one religion
> Could the Gospel and Qur'an divide us?
> They made the Chinggisids tremble
> And subdued the Timurids to the shahs of the shahs
> And the kingdom of the tsars moved to conquer them all.

> Sizlərsiniz ey qövmi-macar bizlərə ixvan
> Əcdadımızın müştərəkən mənşəyi Turan
> Bir dindəyiz biz, həpimiz həqqpərəstan
> Mümkünmü ayırsın bizi İncil ilə Quran?
> Cingizləri titrətdi şu afaqı sərasər
> Teymurları hökm etdi şəhinşahlara yeksər
> Fatihlərinə keçdi bütün kişvəri-qeysər.

> (2007, 32)

In this model, the shared Turkic linguistic origin of Turanians offers a united front against the common enemy of Russian imperial rule. Tracing the linguistic and cultural ties of Turan, Hüseynzade outlines the journal's reformist objectives to "Turkify, Islamicize, and Europeanize," elaborating that "It follows that our system of thought seeks guidance from Turkic life and from the worship of Islam. It also calls for acquiring the benefits of civilization from contemporary Europe" ([1906–1907] 2007, 23).[46] From this point of view, *Enlightenment*'s efforts to translate European romanticism into a common Turkic tongue and poetic canon emerged from both an interest in religious reform and a pan-Turkic linguistic and cultural project.

Enlightenment's most enduring contribution in the cultural sphere was its cultivation of a new aesthetic tradition in Azeri poetry. To this end, it published a series of translations and discussions of the most prominent figures of classical Persian poetry—including Ferdowsi, Rumi, and Hafiz—and European and Russian romanticism—including Goethe, Schiller, Byron, and Karamzin—as well as the Turkish New Literature movement (*Edebiyat-i Cedide*), led by the poet Tevfik Fikret.[47] For example, the first issues included an article on Schiller's plays (which I discuss in chapter 1), a translation of Goethe's *Faust*, and a comparison of the works of Shakespeare to Homer and Ferdowsi. *Enlightenment* highlighted the Turkish New Literature movement's interest in the French Parnassians as well as Russian and German poetic and philosophical engagements with neoclassicism. The journal thus laid out two routes to Parnassus, so to speak. *Enlightenment*'s world literary pantheon proposed the creation of a new aesthetic tradition. It blended Ottoman and Persian poetics rooted in Islamic culture with European romanticism's reverence for a vision of the spiritual power of nature, in the famous words of the French poet Charles Baudelaire as "a temple where the living pillars / Sometimes give voice to confused words" (1974).

In 1912 the poet Abbas Sehhet—one of *Enlightenment*'s contributors who was also inspired by its Ottoman counterparts, the New Literature and the Dawn of the New Age movements—published an anthology of translations of European and Russian classics. The son of an Islamic cleric who came to literature after studying medicine in Tehran, Sehhet remained critical of the secularization of Azeri culture while promoting educational and civic reform. The collection, *The Suns of the West* (*Meğrib güneşleri*), included works by Hugo, Musset, Prudhomme, Pushkin, and Lermontov, returning verses from the west as if to announce a new dawn in the east. Sehhet includes in this selection some of the most famous Russian orientalist poetic works depicting the Caucasus, including Pushkin's "The Caucasus" (Qafqaz), "The Prophet" (Peyğember), "The Gypsies" (Qaraçılar), and Lermontov's "Mtsyri" (Mtsıri), "The Circassians" (Çerkeşler), "The Prophet," "The Argument" (Mübahise), "The Gift of the Terek" (Terekin sövqatı), and "Hadji Abrek" (Hacı Abrek) (2005, 450–51).

Sehhet's selection of texts not only highlights his interest in Russian portraits of the Caucasian landscape but also the figure of the Muslim hero as a prophetic poet. Like Axundov, his translations seize the voice of the Russian orientalist and render the figure of the Muslim Other with dignity and heroism in his native tongue. The process of translation provides Sehhet with a textual space for working through an emerging form of Azeri literary modernity marked by the cultural influences of nineteenth-century European literature and classical Ottoman and Persian poetics. The poems develop the form and topoi of the romantic sublime of Pushkin's and Lermontov's orientalist narratives, clearing a space for an image of the human in the literary space and constructing a more inhabitable and hospitable vision of the Caucasus.

Perhaps the most distinguishing feature of Pushkin's and Lermontov's imagined Caucasus is the poetics of the sublime. Susan Layton discusses the sublime as the topoi of a Byronic "doom and gloom" embodied in the image of the Caucasian mountains. In this imagined geography wrecked by violent storms, the mountainous climes both physically and spiritually entrap their wayward Russian heroes. Nature becomes an actor in which rivers and ravines are anthropomorphized as savage, angry beasts and the mountains as proud yet dreadful giants (1997, 36–53). Harsha Ram argues that the sublime is constituted through the development of the formal features of the Russian ode. By tracing the ways in which "the *thematics* of empire became complexly imbricated in questions of *poetics* and *rhetoric*," Ram illustrates how modern Russian poetry developed as "a response to and effect of the imperial state" (2003, 4). The Decembrists' ideological opposition to the tsar, which found literary expression in a civic-minded romantic trend known as the "oriental style," served as the groundwork for Pushkin's and Lermontov's negotiation of the politics and poetics of empire.[48] The fusion elements from diverse sources from the Bible to Persian poetry and folklore, which characterize this "oriental style," formed one of the central features of Russian orientalism. Thus for Ram, Pushkin's and Lermontov's poetry constitutes an "oppositional imperialism," in which representations of the Caucasus are marked by an ambivalence as a space of both resistance and conquest.[49] Ram's analysis accounts for the ways in which poetic inspiration parallels the power it describes. However, the "oriental style" operates exclusively from within a self-concealed vision of the wholeness of the Russian poetic system. Oppositional imperialism thus cannot attend to the value of meaning outside the hermetic world of Russian poetry. That is, if the effects of the sublime are relative to the formal conventions of Russian poetry, the agency of the speaker is confined within the structures of that system.

The hermeneutical phenomenology of translation offers a more generative model for envisioning the poetic encounter between Sehhet and Pushkin. Placing Sehhet's verse in dialogue with Pushkin's and Lermontov's exposes the ways in which the agency of the lyric subject and the power of the word are negotiated through the translation and transformation of the imperial sublime into neo-classical Persian and Ottoman forms. Both Pushkin's works and their translations share the theme of the poet's reflection on nature, and in this way they constitute the sublime experience through the relationship between the poet's subjectivity and the Caucasian landscape. While for Pushkin the topos of the Caucasus *endows* his creative power as a poet, for Sehhet it instead generates a bridge through which the poet makes contact with the celestial realm.

This distinction centers on the difference between Pushkin's *inspiration* and Sehhet's *intuition* (even if Pushkin's verse employs poetic intuition and the "oriental style" as its inspiration). Sehhet's translations draw upon the intuitive traditions of the *ghazal, qaṣīda,* and related forms in Persian and Ottoman poetry, which are indebted to a pattern of symbols from forms of esoteric Islamic thought.[50] In this sense, poetry provides a medium of communion and embrace of the full spiritual consequences of God's oneness acting as a bridge between the material and spiritual worlds.[51] The poetic structure replicates the existence of two worlds, the earthly world of the senses and decay and the celestial realm, which as the Ottoman scholar Walter G. Andrews contends, is "accessible only through the powers of intuition or insight" (1985, 66). Reason alone does not provide a gateway to knowing the world but rather, Andrews continues, "the power to perceive the world of reality manifests itself in those states that our this-worldly judgment deems most un-reasonable" (67). In this tradition, the terrestrial object has an otherworldly counterpart that transcends a metaphorical relationship and draws a bond between the human and God (69–70).

The landscapes of poetic reflection also diverge. Sehhet transforms Pushkin's and Lermontov's Caucasus with figures from classical Persian and Ottoman poetry, such as the gazelle and the Simurgh. Sehhet's translations thus provide a vision of poetic intuition, which reinscribes the search for esoteric knowledge onto the sublime poetic topography of the Russian orientalist canon. Sehhet's translation of Pushkin's "The Caucasus" shifts the relationship from the subjectivity of the poet and the earthly, natural world. The opening lines of both poems begin with the image of an isolated poet gazing down at a mountain from its summit. The reader follows the poet's eye down the mountain, describing the scenery. Structurally, Pushkin's poem is divided into verse stanzas while Sehhet shifts most of the rhyme scheme to accommodate the poetic convention of the *bait*. This formal shift is significant as the structural relationship of the aforementioned *bait* and *miṣrā'*, the poetic whole and part or home and threshold, parallels the relationship of the poet to spiritual intuition. In this way, the structure of the *bait* generates a passageway between the physical and celestial worlds, transforming the structural and conceptual framework of Pushkin's verse.

Pushkin's work is organized into four stanzas, each of which describes a stratum of life on the mountain, following the movement of the poet's gaze from the heights of the tranquil clouds and plunging into the fierce waters of the Terek beating against the rocks. The movement of the text from the lofty heights where both the eagle and poet reside to the waters of the river reflect the topos of the sublime. The anthropomorphism of the river, which as Pushkin notes in the final stanza "Plays and howls, like a young beast" (*Igraet i voet, kak zver' molodoi*) and whose "Hungry waters lick the cliffs" (*lizhet utesy golodnoi vodnoi*) echoes the doom and gloom of the orientalist canon. As the reader follows this sublime descent, sheltered by the distance of the author's viewpoint from the heavens, the poem creates a sense of wonder in its portrait of the wildness and animalism of nature. The opening stanza marks this distance:

> The Caucasus lies beneath me. Alone at a height
> I stand above the snows at the edge of a precipice;
> An eagle, rising from a distant peak,
> Hovers motionless at my vantage point.

From here I see the birth of streams
And the first movements of terrible avalanches.

Кавказ подо мною. Один в вышине
Стою над снегами у края стремнины;
Орел, с отдаленной поднявшись вершины,
Парит неподвижно со мной наравне.
Отселе я вижу потоков рожденье
И первое грозных обвалов движенье.

(II. 266)

Pushkin here notably deemphasizes the presence of his hero in the poem. The speaker notes his position, standing above the snows; however, it is rather his gaze along which the reader must travel to reach the valley beneath. The lyric gaze thus traces a movement from the site of poetic inspiration, the mountain's precipice, to the creative capacities of the poet to anthropomorphize the landscape. While Pushkin's poem provides a vision of the ungraspable powers of nature as an analogue to Russia's orient, he secures the safety of his reader from the wildness of nature emphasizing the distance between the poet, hovering with the eagle above, and nature roaring below.

Sehhet instead highlights the power of the poem to transcend these two spheres. While some variation occurs at the beginning and ending of the poem, the greater part of Sehhet's verse employs the *bait* form to create moments that parallel the experience of the poet and the natural world. His first three *baits* recreate a similar sequence of images:

The Caucasus lies beneath me, at the greatest summit I—
Alone grasped resolve upon the precipice of the snowy mountain.
If the blackbird [hawk] flying high from a distant peak,
No matter how high it flies, it flies anew in my orbit.
From here I see in the bubbling of the springs,
The first sign of dubious, terrible avalanches.

Qafqaz altımdadır, ən müdhiş olan zirvədə mən—
Tutmuşam tək uçurum, qarlı dağ üstündə qərər.
Qaraquş uçmağa qalxarsa uzaq bir təpədən,
Nə qədər yüksək uçarsa, yenə dövrəmdə uçar.
Buradan mən görürəm çəşmələri qaynamada,
Şübhəli, qorxulu uçqunları ilk oynamada.

(2005, 342)

Most notably, while Sehhet also positions his lyric subject's gaze from the top of a snowy mountain, he foregrounds the cognitive efforts of his speaker to grasp his purpose or perhaps his faculties of judgment (*qerer tutmuşam*). While Pushkin's speaker marks his position standing above the snows (*stoiu nad snegami*), Sehhet locates his speaker instead in the *desire to comprehend* the mountain view, as if emphasizing the distance between his translation and Pushkin's original portrait of the mountain-scape. The first *misrā'* presents two positions within the earthly world, the Caucasus and the summit, while the second highlights the speaker's path to cognition and intuition. Indeed, Sehhet's word order stresses the distance between the speaker's act of grasping—the first word in the line—and the judgment or purpose—the last word in the line—which are separated by the description of the speaker's solitude and the snowy mountain peak. This syntactical arrangement dramatizes the path from the earthly world of the mountain, which can be grasped or obtained, and the conceptual realm of purpose, judgment, or resolve. The circular motion generated through the speaker's path to understanding via his contact with the landscape is further echoed in the orbital or turning motion of the hawk or blackbird around the speaker in comparison to Pushkin's eagle, whose position hovering motionless at the speaker's vantage point is marked by verticality, recalling the imperial motif of the double-headed eagle.

While the position of Pushkin's speaker is static, his dynamism resides in his poetic power to animate the landscape. Sehhet instead attributes the changes in life on the mountain to the cycle of the seasons. Moving down the mountain, both speakers describe the stirring of avalanches. Sehhet writes, "From here I see in the bubbling of the springs, / The first sign of dubious, terrible avalanches." The water's boiling or bubbling signals the beginnings of avalanches, indeed proof of the spring's effects on the warming of ice. Pushkin's poem instead locates this movement in the poet's gaze. He writes, "From here I see the birth of streams / And the first movements of terrible avalanches." His image of the spring's "birth" prefers the spontaneous godlike power of creation and sense of awe to Sehhet's more holistic description. While both verses describe the terror of the beginnings of an avalanche, Pushkin's poem suggests divine involvement, while Sehhet's translation instead records this experience as part of the mountain's ecology.

Throughout the poem, Sehhet draws on the even pairings of the *bait* structure in order to narrow the distance between the poet and his setting. In the
middle of the poem, he links the shepherd's descent into the valley with the
poet's appreciation of nature through the structure of a single *bait*. It reads,
"The shepherd walks down from the mountains to the valley. / A man falls in
love with this beautiful scenery" (Yürüyür dağ aşağı orda çoban da dərəyə. / İştə
məftunlaşır insan bu gözəl mənzərəyə). Indeed, this second line, which completes Sehhet's couplet, does not appear in Pushkin's original and serves as
both a structural and conceptual keystone in Sehhet's description. The beautiful setting causes the man to "become a lover" (*meftunlaşır insan*), alluding
to a classical mystical symbol, the figure of the poet-lover, whose quest for
his beloved realizes his path to spiritual enlightenment. The movement down
the mountain, which mirrors the poet's descending gaze in Pushkin's work,
for Sehhet realizes the role of nature in man's path to enlightenment. While
Sehhet echoes the Pushkinian theme of the wonders and beauty of the Caucasus, he also distinguishes the observance of life as the path to enlightenment
from the creative power of the poet as a prophet of avalanches and storms.
While the inspiration of Pushkin's speaker lends him poetic power, for Sehhet
grasping the purpose of things requires observing the intricate balance of life
on the mountain. That is, while Sehhet's vision of the Caucasus presents a
cyclical network of interdependent movements of nature and forms of life,
Pushkin's Caucasus seems to emanate from the omnipotent gaze of the poet
hovering above the landscape. Pushkin's vision of poetic inspiration is centered around his evocation of an imperial sublime—from the poet's distant
location on the precipice alongside the eagle to his perception of the divine
"birth" of streams. Sehhet instead relocates the revolutionary energy of Pushkin's Caucasus in his series of *baits* that trace the poet's love of nature to his
observance of a hospitable, ecologically interdependent vision that includes
the warming of streams in spring in the Caucasus.

Two years after completing his translation of Pushkin's poem, Sehhet
returned to the landscape of the Caucasus in his "Homeland" (Veten
[2005, 81]). "Homeland" emphasizes the relationship of the poet to nature
and more specifically the Caucasus as a source of a collective identity. The
first *bait* describes the poetic and physical space of the Caucasus as the
poet's home: "The fragment of the Caucasus is my homeland, / Because
of the Simurgh it is my dwelling" (Qafqaz qitəsidir mənim vətənim, /
Simürğün sayəsində məskənim). The Caucasus is imagined through the

dual signification of *qite* as both a poetic fragment and a piece of land or a continent. The term implicitly connects the space of the Caucasus to the notion of a textual homeland. The Simurgh conjures the image of a giant bird of prey that features in both Persian and Turkic myths and is often depicted with the head of a dog and claws of a lion, such as in the tenth-century Persian poet Hakīm Abu'l-Qāsim Ferdowsi's *Book of Kings* (*Shahnama*), the twelfth-century Persian poet Farīd al-Dīn al-'Attar's *The Conference of the Birds*, and throughout Turkic folklore. As a benevolent or often divine force, the Simurgh here serves a similar role in granting the poet his homeland. The poet's indebtedness to the myth signifies at once his reverence for the divine force and his appreciation of the creature as a shared symbol of both *qites*—that is, as fragments of land as well as fragments of Persian and Turkic literary traditions. Sehhet thus dedicates this tribute to his homeland to his celestial and transcontinental "dwellings."

In the poem, each of the first three *baits* parallels the spiritual, mythic, and real spaces that form the poet's homeland:

> The fragment of the Caucasus is my homeland,
> Because of the Simurgh it is my dwelling.
> In that country I came into being,
> I surrendered myself [in prayer] to my people.
> In that place where the blackbird and hawk—
> The sultan of the Qaf mountains—was named.

> Qafqaz qitəsidir mənim vətənim,
> Simürğün sayəsində məskənim.
> O məmləkətdə mən vücüdə gəldim,
> Xalqıma qarşı sücüdə gəldim.
> O yerdə kim qaraquşu, tərlanı—
> Adlanmışdır Qaf dağının sultanı.

(2005, 81)

Sehhet's emphasis on fragmented space articulates the contested nature of his homeland. These linguistic and symbolic pieces tell the history of multiple imperial rules in the Caucasus. He describes his own birth and the lineage of sultans in spiritual and mythic terms. Invoking multiple mythic and literary traditions, he constructs a homeland that extends beyond the physicality of Pushkin's imaginary. His parallel spiritual transformations—coming into being and surrendering to prayer—are connected to his country and people. The parallel structure at once constructs a romantic narrative of civic identity as it establishes a mystical poetic connection between the celestial and terrestrial homeland. The mythic space of the Qaf Mountains becomes home to the Simurgh and through it articulates a transcontinental poetic continuity among the traditions of Ottoman Turkey, the Caucasus, the Persian empire, and Central Asia. This space at once represents a physical home to blackbirds, hawks, and the sultan as well as to the mythic space of the Simurgh. Crucially in Sehhet's vision it is also the Qaf Mountains, that very space of mythic and spiritual power, which endows the sultan with his authority.

The location or dislocation of Sehhet's homeland into fragmented mythic literatures not only articulates a connection between his homeland and this borderless space but provides a set of portable symbols in his work more broadly. The pieces of the homeland, particularly the divine symbols of the Simurgh and the gazelle appear both in this poem and in his translations of Pushkin's "The Caucasus" and Lermontov's "The Argument." In "The Caucasus" the gazelles (*ceyranlar*) roam in place of Pushkin's deer (*oleni*).[52] Sehhet's insistence on the figure of the gazelle, as *ceyran* specifically connotes the mystical animal, places the work within a distinct Ottoman/Persian classical poetic register, signifying the beloved incarnation of the divine. Similarly, his reference to the Simurgh in "The Argument" imports an entirely new landscape into Lermontov's work. Lermontov describes caravans of camels and a king eagle flying in the clouds: "The caravans are already passing through / Across your rocks, / Where only the clouds pass / The eagle tsar" (Уж проходят караваны / Через те скалы, / Где носились лишь туманы / Да цари-орлы [1958–1962, 1:526]). Sehhet embellishes this image, extending it to fill two *baits*:

Here is the Qaf Mountain, sultan of birds,
Only the rock-perching Simurghs—
Who the thick black clouds envelop,
Through here the caravans now pass.

Qaf dağıdır bura, quşlar soltanı,
Ancaq simürğlər qonan qayanı—
Kim çulğayır qalın qara dumanlar,
İndi burdan gəlib keçir karvanlar.

(2005, 312)

In the first *bait*, the local Simurghs replace the imperial/tsarist eagle, reinstated as sultans of the mythic Qaf Mountains. The second *bait* conveys the parallel movement of the sky and earth. The celestial clouds surround the Simurghs as terrestrial time passes with the caravans. Sehhet imagines a poetic and mythic space from within Lermontov's description of the Caucasus. While these symbols serve as foreign additions to Pushkin and Lermontov's works, they remain reminders for Sehhet of his ever-present and portable textual home, as well as the complex and contested history of his homeland. Sehhet's translations provide a hermeneutical detour through the symbolic structures of the mythical fragment. In this way, the lyric subject is mediated through the spiritual, folk, and high literary aesthetic registers at play. In turn, the soaring heights of the Pushkinian and Lermontovian sublime are transformed into a space of interlingual, intercultural, and intersubjective dialogue. Indeed, many of these works have been alternatively read as integral to a static vision of an Azerbaijani nationalism. However, by placing Sehhet's and Axundov's works on the threshold of an intertextual encounter with the Russian imperial sublime, they acquire a new plasticity and political force, in turn, framing Azeri literary modernity through spaces of critical dialogue.

The Poet as Prophet: Rewriting the Pushkinian Word

The connection between the figures of the poet and prophet in Russian literature developed in the eighteenth-century ode. It was marked by a shift from the panegyric to a prophetic form of the "psalmodic or sacred ode" inspired by translations of the Bible and Qur'an.[53] In the nineteenth century, the notion of the prophetic power of the poet informed the civically engaged poetry of the Decembrists and shaped Pushkin's role as the father of modern Russian literature. The prophetic theme at once attends to the secularization of poetry in post-Petrine Russia and the politicization of the figure of the poet in the work of the Decembrists. The poet-prophet embodied the codetermined yet seemingly paradoxical discourses of Russian imperial messianism and the moral and political character of the Russian word (or its creator the poet).[54] However, in so doing it derived both moral and political authority from spiritual rhetoric, transforming this religious power into claims for political justice and personal liberty. In turn, the prophetic theme was explored in Azeri-Russian literary encounters, shaping the conception of the poet in the revolutionary milieu in the South Caucasus. Sehhet's translations attend to the highly politicized orientalist image of the Russian poet as prophet and open a dialogue about the role of literature in shaping the relationship between religion and politics.

Pushkin develops the prophetic theme in his 1826 poem "The Prophet" (Prorok), which describes a spiritual crisis through a poet's violent transfiguration by a six-winged seraphim. Gouging his eyes and replacing his heart with coal, the angel resurrects him from a half-dead state, endows him with prophetic vision, and charges him with spreading the word of God. Written following the Decembrist uprising of 1825, Pushkin's lofty, stylized, and graphic verse passionately urges for the poet's role as defender of the moral and political rights of the people. Pushkin describes his journey:

> Tormented by a spiritual thirst,
> I dragged myself through the gloomy desert,
> And a six-winged seraphim
> Appeared to me at the crossroads.
> With fingers light as a dream
> He touched the pupils of my eyes.
> Which opened wide in prophesy,
> Just as a frightened eagle.
> . . . .
> Like a corpse in the desert I lay,
> And God's voice called to me:
> "Rise up, prophet, and see and hear,
> And wander sea and earth
> Be filled with my will,
> And crossing sea and land,
> Burn the hearts of people with the word"

> Духовной жаждою томим,
> В пустыне мрачной я влачился,
> И шестикрылый серафим
> На перепутье мне явился.
> Перстами легкими как сон
> Моих зениц коснулся он.

Отверзлись вещие зеницы,
Как у испуганной орлицы.

. . . .

Как труп в пустыне я лежал,
И Бога глас ко мне воззвал:
"Восстань, пророк,
и виждь, и внемли,
Исполнись волею моей,
И обходя моря и земли,
Глаголом жги сердца людей."
(1979, 2:338–39)

The angel touches the pupils of the speaker's eyes, transforming a dream into a spiritual vision. The image of the dreamlike touch and the dilation of the speaker's pupils evoke the physical experience of hallucination, exposure to extreme light, and carnal excitement. Pushkin describes the spiritual experience of enlightenment through the physical awakening and resurrection of the speaker. The poem borrows its thematic from biblical images, such as the prophet's desert wandering, the speaker's resurrection from a corpselike state, and the image of the prophet as a vessel for God's will and word. The poet-prophet's transfiguration also echoes the trope of the captive in "Prisoner of the Caucasus." The immobility of the prisoner, which reflects his ambivalent position in relation to tsarist and imperial power, is echoed in the poet-prophet's liminal position between life and death, as well as mortality and divinity.

The figure of the prophet expressed the intelligentsia's civic role in contributing to the spiritual and moral values of Russian society.[55] Drawing on this connection between the public persona of the poet and his work, Pushkin identified himself as a prophet. In a letter to the poet Petr Viazemsky, Pushkin described the experience of leaving behind his cycle of poems "Imitations of the Qur'an" (*Podrazhanie koranu*) during his journey from Odessa to Mikhailovskoe as being analogous to the Prophet's journey from Mecca to Medina.[56] In so doing, he equated his own verse with the spiritual authority of the Qur'an. Similarly, Gogol and Belinsky's critical essays in the 1830s echo the image of Pushkin as the prophet of Russian literature.[57] Indeed, Gogol reasoned that Russian literature was poetic in spirit because "its poets were potential successors to the Hebrew prophets, filled with the 'spiritual nobility' [*dukhovnoe blagorodstvo*] that he (Gogol) regarded as the true hallmark of Russian writers" (2003, 8:504). Similarly, Lermontov takes up this theme to pay tribute to Pushkin's death.

Lermontov's 1837 poem "The Death of the Poet" accused the government not only of stripping the people of their liberty but of executing their prophet-poet Pushkin. Tsar Nicholas I's fear of the poem's call to revolution indeed sent Lermontov into exile in the Caucasus.[58] Critiquing tsarist autocracy, the poem compares the political and moral role of the intelligentsia to the figure of Christ. Here Pushkin is not described as a visionary but rather as Christ, sacrificed for the injustices of the tsar and the corruption of Russian society. Lermontov writes:

> And having removed the former wreath—a crown of thorns
> Entwined with laurels, set upon him:
> But the hidden needles sharply
> Pierced his glorious brow.
>
> И прежний сняв венок—они венец терновый,
> Увитый лаврами, надели на него:
> Но иглы тайные сурово
> Язвили славное чело.
>
> (1958–1962, 1:412–14)

The poetic crown of laurels is removed from Pushkin's head and replaced by a crown of thorns, whose upturned spines draw blood from the poet-prophet's fallen forehead as in the images of Christ's Passion. Lermontov highlights the moment of the immortalization of the prophet's death, emphasizing the injustice of tsarist society. The poem then concludes with a condemnation of the ruling elite. Lermontov marks the "illustrious fathers" (*proslavlennye ottsy*), the tsar, and his court of powerful nobles as the "executioners of Freedom, Genius, and Glory" (*Svobody, Geniia i Slavy palachi!*) (412–14). For Lermontov, Pushkin symbolizes the savior of the realms of the ideal and pure, whose poetic corpse embodies the execution of freedom. While Pushkin's prophet, like the work of the Decembrists, attempted to generate continuities between a stylized Judeo-Islamic fusion and a contemporary literary ethics, Lermontov instead casts Pushkin as a Christian sacrifice, embodying the political and moral corruption of society. In this way, Pushkin and Lermontov contributed to the politicization of both the poetic word and the figure of the poet, while emphasizing the connection between poetry and sacred testament.

Lermontov's vision of Pushkin accompanied him to the Caucasus, inspiring Axundov's rumination on Pushkin's death that same year, an exchange that was likely facilitated by Bestuzhev-Marlinsky. In his tribute to Pushkin, Axundov replicates the liminal dreamlike state and moment of awakening; however, he replaces the orientalist tropes of the desert wandering, sacrificial death, and prophecy with symbols common to classical Persian verse such as the night, dream, and poetic garden, generating both a heteroglossia and heterodoxy in his verse. Half a century later, Sehhet addresses the Russian orientalist tropes again in his transfiguration of Pushkin's prophet with the power of a new spiritual word. Sehhet's translations draw on the major works of Pushkin and Lermontov's Caucasian canon, staging an intervention into the poetics of Russian imperial politics. His transformation of their vision of the sublime "doom and gloom" of the Caucasian mountains and the creative power of the poet instead reclaim the subjectivity of the Caucasus and its Muslim inhabitants through his cultivation of poetic intuition. In this way, his translations foster a symbiotic relationship between the power of social critique and the classical Persian and Ottoman poetic tradition.

Mirroring the lofty style of Pushkin's poem, Sehhet's translation incorporates an elaborate Persian lexicon to describe the poet's spiritual encounter. Transforming Pushkin's verse into the *bait* structure, he expands Pushkin's description of heavenly space. The opening and closing section of the poem, comparable to the selections in Pushkin's text read:

> Wearied by a spiritual thirst
> I dragged myself across a gloomy desert.
> Suddenly the six king-feathered Israfil,
> Appeared in sublime mercifulness.
> With a gentle heavenly body,
> With a hand light as a dream
> Slowly he touched my eyelashes,
> The light of grace came to my eyes,
> I looked with premonition to the length of the heavens,
> I was aware of the truth of things
> . . . .

Like a corpse I fell upon the desert,
My body on the earth, my soul high on God's throne.
He preached to me God's command
I heard the sonance of the Lord-prophet
Rise up, o prophet, see, hear, incite!
Go inform the beings of my command!
The creatures of the desert and sea wake,
The hearts of the people burn with his word.

Ruhani təşnəliklə yorğun ikən
Zülmətli bir çöldə sürünürdüm mən.
Altı şahpərli İsrafil nagəhan,
Əsnayi-rahımda oldu nümayan.
Mələkuti cismi-lətifi ilə,
Röya kimi dəsti-xəfifi ilə
Toxundu çox yavaş kiriklərimə,
Kəramət nuru gədi gözlərimə,
Baxdım bəsirətlə ərzü səmayə,
Vaqif oldum həqaiqi-əşyayə.
. . . .
Meyit kimi düşmüşdüm ol səhradə,
Cismim yerdə, ruhum ərşi-əladə.
Təbliğ etdi mənə əmri-xudanı
Eşitdim sövti-həzrəti-sübhanı:
—Ey peyğəmbər! Dur, gör, eşit, qiyam et!
Get əmrimi məxluqata elam et!
Səhra, dərya müvcudatın oyandır,
Kəlamınla xalqın qülubun yandır.

(2005, 343–344)

Sehhet's translation evokes a similar setting: his speaker's spiritual thirst, the gloomy desert landscape, the transfiguration of the poet-prophet, and the awakening of society. However, he transforms Pushkin's image of the seraphim, which is drawn from Isaiah, and instead designates Israfil, one of the four Islamic archangels whose horn or trumpet announces the day of resurrection. Specifying an Islamic context for his audience, Sehhet highlights the apocalyptic tone of the poem and lends greater weight to the specificity of the theme. Indeed, the trope of Israfil or Israfil's horn became common in early Soviet-era propaganda as a revolutionary trope.[59]

Sehhet's translation evokes the *masnavi* poetic form, made famous by the thirteenth-century poet Jalāl ad-Dīn Rūmī and composed of independent rhymed *miṣrā'*. In adopting the *bait* structure, he expands Pushkin's description of the transfiguration. While Sehhet replicates the image of the speaker's deathlike state—lying like a corpse in the desert—the second half of the *bait* expands the imagined landscape of the poem, extending the poet's soul to God's throne. Indeed, the image of the distance from the earth to the throne of God is used in the Islamic tradition to express Israfil's sublime magnitude. However, it also recalls Isaiah's vision of God's throne in the Judeo-Christian tradition. Among Sehhet's most revealing word choices is his use of *kelam* from the Arabo-Persian tradition, referring to the word or speech of God as well as philosophical discourse or debate. While the semantics of the Russian word *glagol* is also used to express divine speech or more generally discourse, Sehhet's *kelam* unmistakably places his reader in an Islamic context.

Syntactically, the line also juxtaposes the terrestrial and the celestial, replicating the symbolic structure of classical verse in which poetic intuition serves as the bridge between the world of God and the world of things. Indeed, Sehhet and Pushkin's portraits of the delivery of the messages differ. Pushkin's God speaks directly to the poet, ordering him to "Be filled with my will" (*ispolnis' voleiu moei*), emphasizing the image of the poet as a vessel for the prophetic word. For Sehhet the speaker hears "the sonance of the prophet-Lord" (*sövti-hezreti-sübhanı*), a compound noun that fuses the texture of the sound of God's command with prophetic greatness. Although Sehhet's poet never possesses God's will, he encounters the divine through a sensory and synesthetic experience. The poet's agency is further emphasized by his charge to incite and deliver the message. While Pushkin's poet is instructed in the imperative to burn the hearts of people, Sehhet prefers a more passive construction. In this sense, the power of the poem for Sehhet is displaced from the individual figure of the poet to the prophetic word.

For Pushkin, the poet's transfiguration endows him with godlike power, a depiction that served a political purpose in lending purchase to the figure of the poet (and historically for Pushkin the Decembrist intelligentsia). Sehhet's poem instead draws a distinction between the civic role of the poet to awaken and incite the people to action and God's power to deliver the word. Pushkin thus employs these sacred allusions to realize an aesthetic and political project, to emphasize the civic role of the poet rather than his romantic genius. Transforming Pushkin's text, Sehhet highlights the role of both political action and religious thought in social transformation, reinvesting political value in the imprint of religious experience on the literary. This aim is clarified in the final line of the first quoted selection, which describes the poet's initial prophetic vision. Looking to the heavens, Sehhet's poet becomes "aware of the truth of things" (*Vaqif oldum heqaiqi-eşyaye*). Indeed, this line does not appear in the Russian original, which instead compares the dilation of the poet's pupils to the eyes of a frightened eagle. Pushkin draws a parallel between the physical manifestations of hallucination or spiritual ecstasy and the sublime symbol of the eagle's gaze, a classic Byronic image, while Sehhet draws on Pushkin to take a closer look at the spiritual and human world.

Sehhet describes the symbiotic passage between poetry and the world in one of his most notable essays, "How Should New Poetry Be?" Here he outlines his theory of poetic affect:

> The issue that we are talking about here is: how should new poetry be [written]? First of all, when we write something, we must submit ourselves to our feelings in order to make the word touch the heart of the reader and awaken feeling in another's heart. So in this way, it is necessary to understand feeling.
>
> Feeling has two types: evident and instinctual. Evident feeling cannot influence anyone. It is natural or instinctual feeling that influences another and the contents of the written poem as a tablet-mosaic reveals its complete, subtle nuances and precise essence. For example: a lovely summer evening, the sun is about to set; the sunset darkening slowly spreads behind the mountains and seas, and everywhere there is a calm and tranquil mood. The feeling presented by this evening reveals itself in every particle. A little later the sun sets, on the banks undulating steam escapes, but nevertheless the next moon follows the day's sunset. So we write and elaborate on our feelings and our dream-thoughts while watching this scene, and of course it will impress the hearts of readers and will awaken another's heart-feeling. (2005, 243–45)[60]

It is a description of the reciprocal transference of feeling from the natural world to poet and reader through the image of the sunset. The sun's transformation into the moon in the sky and the water's flight into steam from the sea draws an analogue between the writer's creative act and the awakening of sensations in the reader. Ultimately the movements of nature, embodied in the esoteric symbol of the moon, generate a bond linking the poem, the contemplative self, and empathy for an Other. It is in the poetic reflection of nature that Sehhet locates this series of emotional and empathetic responses connecting the world, the poet, and the heart of the Other.

His translation performs a poetic transfiguration of Pushkin's verse, transforming the politics of the sublime into an occasion for reinstating the spiritual power of Azeri poetry. Yet he does not glorify a singular image of the West or a revival of orthodox religious institutions. Indeed, as the title of his collection suggests, Sehhet's poetry looks to the *Meğrib güneşleri*, an eastern West evoked in his preference for the Arabic term *meğrib/al-maghrib* instead of the Turkic word *qerb*. His verse initiates a dialogue among the archetypes of Russian romanticism, classical mystical poetry, and the Turkic New Literature style in order to generate a more symbiotic vision of the sublime as both a spiritual and an aesthetic experience. If Sehhet imbued the poems with a new spiritual content, however, he did so without presuming a singular or monolingual vision of religious language or orthodox belief. As Axundov did with his vision of a heterodox materialist and spiritual *oneness of being*, Sehhet invokes wholeness through a multiplicity of meanings and references from Pushkin to classical Persian and new Ottoman traditions.

Whereas Sehhet's verse situates Azeri civic identity in the context of pan-Islamic and pan-Turkic aesthetics, other contemporary Azeri poets such as Mehemmed Hadi called more directly for a Romantic Marxism. Hadi's poetry reflects an enthusiasm for reform and commitment to class consciousness, embracing a pan-Islamic cultural worldview alongside a conscious appeal to the working masses. In the poem "The Voice of the Time and Sayings of Life" (Vaxtin sesi ve heyatın sözü [1909]), Hadi combines a series of aphorisms, many of which refer to Islamic philosophy or the teachings of the Qur'an. However, Hadi places these proverbs in the context of the need for education among the masses. Speaking of the blindness of ignorance, he writes, "You will not see what is free on this earth, / A beautiful woman is busying tongues" (Sən görməyəcəksən yerin üstündə nədir hur, / Bir nimnigəhlə ediyor dilləri məshur). Hadi contrasts the invisibility of the spirit of freedom with the banality of earthly physical beauty. He describes a preoccupation with earthly pleasures—praise given to earthly beauty—as a distraction from invisible freedom. Indeed, freedom refers both to the intangible realm of the divine or spiritual and to the political state of liberation. The couplet in the poem reveals the relationship between the divine and political—specifically Marxist—rhetoric. Hadi writes:

> Those masses have the right to live—
> To go out to the intellectual war, at the frontlines of ignorance.
> From now on the world wants a great, wise and brave man,
> So if you want to live, show your knowledge!
>
> İştə yaşamaq haqqına haizdir o kütlə—
> Bir hərbi-münəvvərlə çıxıb cəbheyi-cəhlə.
> Bundan belə dünya böyük ürfanlı ər istər,
> Sən də yaşamaq istər isən, bilgini göstər!
>
> (2005, 285)

The "rights" of "the masses" are won on the battleground of ignorance. However, read in the context of the poem as a whole, the spiritual and political state of freedom provides the cure for this ignorance. The life and rights of the masses are elevated to an important role in Hadi's compilation "Sayings of the Time." The life of these aphorisms, Hadi insists, is as relevant in this time of the awakening "masses" as their participation in transnational or supranational Islamic philosophic and cultural traditions.

Hadi's life of the masses, Sehhet's poetic homeland, and Axundov's howling propose a new civic identity in their acts of literary transgression of national boundaries. They generate a portrait of the transnational revolutionary movements across Eurasia during the first decade of the twentieth century. In so doing, they also create a space for the Azeri Muslim through the interlingual, intercultural, and intersubjective experience of being in the world of the text exposed at the threshold sites of intertextual dialogue. Sehhet's poems connect the mythical and modern-hybrid through the translation of a sublime poetics. His vision of the wholeness of being, like Axundov's, is rather dependent on his work's exposure of the heteroglossia and heterodoxy of intertwining cultural, linguistic, and political influences that come into contact in the Caucasus. The collection of symbols and forms present in Sehhet's translations in particular offers a portrait of a truly heterogeneous body of literature, one that transcends the boundaries of "rational" space and time and thus national difference. Beginning with Pushkin and Lermontov's legacy, he reimagines Pushkin's orientalist inspiration in the Caucasus through a worldly translation of Russian content and Ottoman forms.

While Sehhet's and Hadi's work can be understood as part of a broader Turkic New Literature movement blending the influence of the French Parnassians with neo-classical Persian and Ottoman poetics, their dialogue with Russian Orientalism emphasizes a connection between the emergence of a hermeneutical tradition and the emergence of a modern revolutionary Azeri subject. Nature was for Baudelaire, as for Hegel, not only a temple but an orientalist vision of eastern mysticism.[61] The sublimity of God's magnitude structures that experience, which exceeds the individual capacity to use language. Pushkin and Lermontov thus affirm the ineffable quality of the sublime Caucasus and the captivity of their lyric poets within it. However, following Sehhet, these reflections on nature expose a history of affect in the empathetic responses linking the world, the poet, and the heart of the reader.

The temporality of the text in Bakhtin's and Ricoeur's hermeneutical phenomenology of authorship, with which I framed my discussion of translation, offers a model for attending to the inseparability of ethics and aesthetics in this imperial encounter. Bakhtin, also fascinated by the figure of the romantic exile, cites Pushkin's 1830 poem "Parting" (Razluka) as support for his analysis of the creative role of the author.[62] The poem is not about prophesy in particular but rather exposes the tensions between spiritual and physical exile through the poet's separation from his beloved. Her desire is both individuated through the experience of exile and unified in their love. In the poem Pushkin writes:

> My cries prayed you not to break
> The terrible anguish of parting.
> But from that bitter kiss
> You tore away your face,
> Out of the bounds of gloomy exile
> You called me to another place.

You said: "When once again we meet
Beneath a sky forever blue,
In the shade of olive trees, the kiss of love
Shall, my friend, reunite us two."

Томленье страшное разлуки
Мой стон молил не прерывать.
Но ты от горького лобзанья
Свои уста оторвала;
Из края мрачного изгнанья
Ты в край иной меня звала.
Ты говорила: «В день свиданья
Под небом вечно голубым,
В тени олив, любви лобзанья
Мы вновь, мой друг, соединим».

(1979, 1:257)

The act of reading Bakhtin's reading of Pushkin's poem itself enacts an "aesthetic empathizing," or as Sehhet describes it, "the awakening of the heart-feeling of another." Bakhtin's model compels us to consider the ways in which literature not only represents but itself provides a space for the negotiations of the role of the human in society. For Axundov and Sehhet this space of dialogue and empathy is achieved in the act of translating Pushkin. Translation creates a space for envisioning the intersubjective encounter among subject, poet, and critic, as well as between Pushkin and Sehhet. Indeed, such an encounter generates a penetrating if not prophetic vision of the shifting image of the value of language in the imperial encounter. While Sehhet emphasizes the political tenor of the Azeri lyric subject through the active role of the poetic word to incite the people, his translations also reflect the concerns of the intuitive tradition and its codetermination of heteroglossic and heterodoxic sources. Prophecy for Sehhet does not entail the glorification of the poet as a political actor but rather the role of poetry in opening up the doors of the *bait* to offer the reader a glimpse onto the world.

Part II

Heterology and Utopian Futures

3

A WINDOW ONTO THE EAST

Baku's Avant-garde Poetics and the Translatio Imperii

The Soviet vision of its eastern frontier in 1920 resembled Paul Klee's *Angelus Novus*, which Walter Benjamin famously described as the angel of history, its gaze fixed on the wreckage of the past as it is propelled into the future by the storm of progress (1968, 257). When Bolshevik politicians and futurist poets immigrated to oil-rich Baku—a strategic eastern frontier during the Civil War—they too could not look away from the wreckage of Russian imperialism. Struggling to establish a sense of continuity with the imperial past and envision the future of a Soviet Eurasia, they also experimented with the formation of a new relationship between aesthetics and politics.

After the October revolution in 1917 and leading up to the invasion of the Red Army in the spring of 1920, a series of governments were set up and dismantled in Baku, including the Transcaucasian Federation (February–May 1918), the Baku Commune (April–June 1918), the Socialist-Revolutionary Central Caspian Dictatorship (June–September 1918), and the Azerbaijan Democratic Republic (May–September 1918 in Ganja, September 1918–April 1920 in Baku).[1] During the annexation from 1919 to 1920, Bolshevik politicians and avant-garde poets evading censorship and searching for employment during the war years immigrated to Baku, fleeing Menshevik-governed Tiflis and food shortages in war-ravaged Moscow and Leningrad. The city's distance from the central Soviet government provided poets and artists with a significant degree of artistic freedom at this moment, and thus avant-garde aesthetics continued to develop and transform in Baku. In this way, the literary production in Baku extended and sustained the utopian imaginary of the waning revolutionary Communist International to the southeastern corner of the empire. As a strategic location for Soviet imperial expansion, the propaganda division in Baku also offered many opportunities for Russians and Russophone Azeri writers and artists seeking employment during the war.

Baku's considerable oil resources—which flooded funds to the city during the first two decades of the twentieth century, contributing to the cultural transformations of the Azeri enlightenment—became an essential resource for funding the creation of the early Soviet state during the Civil War. Indeed, Lenin famously ordered that all war efforts focus on the seizure of Baku.[2] The revolution thus shifted the center of administrative control in the Caucasus from Russian imperial Tiflis to revolutionary Baku. Between 1919 and 1920 the Bolsheviks set up a local division of the Russian Telegraph Agency to print posters, an official journal *Art* (*Iskusstvo*), and theaters to advance the Soviet eastern propaganda campaign. These propaganda divisions, while directed by Russian poets and bureaucrats, were staffed with a few Azeri writers, artists, and actors. As perhaps their greatest work of artistic propaganda, in 1920 the Bolsheviks held the Congress of the Peoples of the East in Baku. During these early years poetry, art, and propaganda often shared a stage, furthering a vision of the creative charge of the proletarian poet to carry the revolution eastward.

During these years oil resources not only contributed to funding propaganda but served as a crucial commodity for Azeri politicians negotiating the terms of federation with the central Soviet government. However, these negotiations proved short-lived, for once Moscow centralized its control over the periphery in the mid-1920s, this leverage was lost. On the ideological front, the Baku oil workers were positioned as visible figures in early propaganda, both in attempts to generate solidarity with Persian social democratic groups, such as the Adalet, which supported Persian oil workers based in Baku, and more generally to internationalize the image of the eastern proletariat as part of a strategy to spread the revolution to Persia, India, and China.

Baku served as a pivotal location for the direction of the Eastern International, framed around Soviet efforts to expand their influence into Persia, India, and China. Obscuring the connection between this conception of an Eastern International as a network of proletarian anti-imperial solidarities and Soviet colonial designs, the Bolsheviks generated a call to revolution based on the fusion of avant-garde aesthetics and a nineteenth-century Russian orientalist imaginary. The poetry penned in Baku was thus central to the formation of the Soviet Eurasian threshold; no longer conceived as a savior of the European West, the Soviet Union now reimagined itself in Baku as the defender of the East. The Soviet orientalist imaginary that the Bolsheviks generated, like the Russian orientalism that preceded it, functioned as an institution that drew its discursive power from a reliance on the work of poets, ethnographers, geographers, linguists, and politicians and emphasized the central role of literature in the state-building project. In this way, while the image of the Caucasus as the center of the new Soviet Orient formally denounced the imperial imaginary, it simultaneously drew on its discursive power to instrumentalize Muslim support for the Bolshevik revolution, mapping imperial Eurasian geopolitics onto a Marxist-Leninist anti-imperial ideological platform.

In Baku, Soviet modernist poetics thus opened a "window onto the East," a gateway to envisioning a permanent revolution, which on the one hand competed with British imperial interests, while on the other consolidated Soviet power. This chapter explores the ways in which works by Russian avant-garde émigrés written in Baku expose the tension between Soviet colonialism and its paradoxical anti-imperialist rhetoric articulated through an orientalist vision of an Eastern International. Benjamin's (1968) description of Klee's art indeed shares more with the Russian and Soviet avant-garde than an obsession with the past. The Soviet imaginary of the Caucasus, as this chapter demonstrates, was animated by the fusion of a spiritual or messianic poetics with the historical materialist vision that Benjamin traced in Klee's avant-garde form. In this way, the Baku avant-garde highlights the mutual contagion between modernist aesthetics and Soviet political rhetoric that manifested through the uniquely belated reception of the avant-garde on the periphery, which in turn anticipated a vision of Soviet political aesthetics.[3]

The relationship between art, literature, and politics in Russia during the 1920s has been a source of much debate. Scholar Boris Groys traces a theoretical continuity in the aesthetic-political program of the early avant-garde to socialist realism through a connection between the will to power and the artistic will to master the material (2011, 7).[4] Critical of Groys's model of continuity, the historian Nina Gurianova instead highlights a historical rupture that she argues distinguished a prerevolutionary "aesthetics of anarchy" from a postrevolutionary movement, which was institutionalized by the Soviet state under the People's Commissariat of Enlightenment (Narkompros).[5] While the institutionalization of art under new state organizations marks a notable shift in the intentionality of the aesthetic agency of the postrevolutionary avant-garde, I argue that the aesthetic continuity between the pre- and postrevolutionary movements remains crucial for understanding the paradoxical codetermination of a discourse of anti-imperialism and the process of Soviet colonization on the former imperial periphery. The will to power that Groys describes indeed often intersected with a poetic militancy. This militarized rhetoric linked art to the politics of empire through a materialist vision of the pen as sword. The critique of the Russian imperial canon, an announcement of the destruction of the old world order, was in this way built on a rhetoric of violence that served the destructive ends of Soviet expansion.

The connection between avant-garde form and the construction of a material political reality is taken up in Jacques Rancière's *The Politics of Aesthetics* (2000). Rancière draws an analogy between the role of the aesthetic regimes of art in deconstructing the hierarchies separating arts. The process of breaking down these hierarchies exposes the redistribution of the sensible in language, which in turn breaks down and reshapes social and political hierarchies. While he concedes that ultimately the state of politics determines the political meaning of art, nonetheless art's impact on the redistribution of the sensible renders it a mode of reading, if not shaping, social and political structures. In his description of the avant-garde Rancière distinguishes the idea of the party and its capacity to read the signs of history from a more expansive vision of the "global political subjectivity" of avant-garde aesthetics and its "aesthetic anticipation of the future . . . [its] invention of sensible forms and material structures for a life to come" (2000, 28).[6] This distinction between political subjectivities allows Rancière to distinguish the organization of art by the state from the ways in which art redistributes the sensible material for the construction of political structures beyond the governing intentionality of the party.

While for Soviet artists the party served a practical function—that is, supplying funding—the adoption of avant-garde aesthetics generated a sense of both rupture and continuity with the cultural production of the imperial past. The political dimension of the avant-garde was linked to the state sponsorship of art, but as I argue following Rancière, it also tied the ways in which its anti-imperial ideological platform invented a new language and the material structures of the Soviet Eastern International. In the context of Baku, the invention of the sensible also accounts for the political necessity of communication with a multi-lingual population and the translation and dissemination of texts across transnational readerships. In this way, the vision of literary modernity cultivated in Baku in 1920 articulated a form of Soviet political modernity premised on infrastructural development campaigns, the mining of energy resources, and the region's strategic geopolitical position for the dissemination of international agitational propaganda campaigns, or agitprop.

This intimate relationship between literary production and political performance was shaped by the community of avant-garde Russian artists and writers in Baku and their contact with the fledgling state infrastructure. Many members of the avant-garde moved to the city in the summer of 1919, where under the newly independent government of the Azerbaijan Democratic Republic they both witnessed and participated in the Soviet annexation of the region. The most influential of these figures included the avant-garde poets and artists Iurii Degen, Sergei Gorodetsky, Velimir Khlebnikov, Alexei Kruchenykh, Vladimir Mayakovsky, Tatiana Vechorka, as well as the symbolist poet and philosopher Viacheslav Ivanov.[7] Between 1919 and 1923 Gorodetsky, Khlebnikov, Mayakovsky, and Vechorka produced work for the local Bolshevik propaganda division, the Baku Windows of the Russian Telegraph Agency (BakKavRosta), while Ivanov taught at the newly established Baku State University.[8] BakKavRosta orchestrated several cultural institutions leading up to and following the Soviet takeover. These included an artistic union that designed agitprop posters, a musical academy, and an agitprop theater by the name of the State Free Satirical Agitprop Theater or The Free Critique-Propaganda Theater.[9] Many of the artists, writers, musicians, and actors who participated in these projects were not newcomers to the Caucasus, having first moved to Tiflis after the October revolution for various reasons, including draft evasion and censorship, or because of difficult living conditions in Russia (Gurianova 2012, 212–14). Theaters were staffed with members from the touring Russian satirical cabaret revue group The Bat (La chauve-souris) and Red Army soldiers who had remained in the city.[10]

A select few local artists, composers, and playwrights—including Üzeyir Hacıbeyov, Abdurrahim bey Haqverdiev, and Azim Azimzade—who had published in the Turkic press and were involved in the local theater productions during the prerevolutionary years also played a significant role in shaping these Soviet cultural institutions.[11] The Tiflis-based avant-garde worked with Armenian and Georgian artists and writers, forming the Syndicate of Futurists (1917–1918) and the 41° (designating the latitude of Georgia).[12] The subsequent movement of many of these figures to Baku in 1919 can be explained, albeit only in part, by the promise of better living conditions and work opportunities in Bolshevik-dominated Baku. This included prerevolutionary figures evading censorship such as the symbolist Ivanov, avant-garde poets such as Gorodetsky seeking to climb the new ranks of the Soviet bureaucracy, and others such as Vladimir Mayakovsky, who was born in Baghdati, Georgia, and Tatiana Vechorka, who was born in Baku, for whom this marked a homecoming of sorts.

While in Baku, the émigré community continued to organize through the prerevolutionary forums of literary-salon-style gatherings, a culture that was kept alive in Tiflis through the revolution. During the fall and winter of 1919, they organized the Poets' Studios (Studii poetov), which became the Poets' Workshop (Tsekh poetov), and the cabaret theater The Merry Harlequin (Veselyi Arlekin).[13] The creation of public spaces such as these served as meeting spaces for the growing community of Russian émigré writers. The relative isolation of these groups from the Azeri community, unlike in Tiflis, fostered a nostalgia for the avant-garde experiments of the past decade. However, it is notable that at the first meeting of the Poets' Workshop, Gorodetsky sent greetings to the Blue Horns, the Georgian symbolists, as well as an unidentified "circle of Muslim poets in Baku" ("Tsekh poetov" 1919).

Displaced from Moscow and Petrograd, the Baku avant-garde confronted the state-building project in the Caucasus at the end of the Civil War with both the estrangement of an orientalist gaze and a persistent nostalgia for revolutionary forms. The application of avant-garde aesthetics to political ends during the formation of the new republics was thus also animated by the imagined geography of the Russian imperial Caucasus. The spatio-temporality of the Baku avant-garde, personified in Klee's *Angelus Novus*, manifested in a fascination with a romantic vision of the imperial past and utopian, universalist cultural topographies. Writers appropriated this spatio-temporality in their poetry (and art), at once representing Soviet anti-imperial ideology through orientalist discourses and simultaneously critiquing the tsarist imperial past. This paradox manifested in particular through the popularity of the revolutionary tropes of the carnival, expressed in the theme of the Commedia dell'arte, as well as the simultaneous fascination with and rejection of the figure of the Decembrist exile in the Caucasus. During this brief period between 1919 and 1921, writers and artists applied avant-garde form to the project of state building on the Soviet periphery. Indeed, the lack of centralized Soviet control during these early years also facilitated a brief period of experimentation. In this way, Gorodetsky's poems written at the end of the Civil War present the project of Soviet eastern expansion as part of an anti-imperialist campaign tied to both carnival aesthetics and anti-imperial propaganda.

The Baku Carnival and Gorodetsky's Anti-Imperialism

The text of the "Hymn of the Merry Harlequin Nightclub in Baku" (Gimn nochnogo teatra v Baku "Veselyi Arlekin"), written and sung by Gorodetsky during the winter of 1919–1920, captures a rare portrait of the interior world of the Russian émigré community in Baku months before the invasion of the Soviet army. It also illustrates the role that the émigré writers and artists played more broadly in shaping the politics of Soviet aesthetics after the revolution.

> I went to Volodia Lenin
> To chase his melancholy away,

And the windy weather
Carried me to Baku.

Everything here smells of kerosene
People, animals, and homes,
Even the sturgeon in the sea
And the jail outside of town.

The oil brings gloom to the people
And I alone laugh
Because by nature
I'm a merry harlequin.

I traded laughter for work
And bought a parcel of land
In a neutral zone
So that no one could strike a shot.

And I live, drilling
Among other riffraff like me
I praise the oily earth
Awaiting a fountain [to rise] to the sky

Every night without fail
I descend into the cellar,
Where ever in sorrow
Fat Momus slept peacefully.

If I must confess, my aim
Is to pierce melancholy's copper brow
To teach you to smile
And maybe even laugh.

All peoples are dear to me,
Except for those who love spleen,
Because by nature
I'm a merry harlequin

Пыл я к Ленину Володе
Расогнать его тоску,
Да по ветреной погоде
Занесло меня в Баку.

Все здесь пахнет керосином,
Люди, звери и дома

Даже в море осетрина
И за городом тюрьма.

В нефти хмурятся народы
И смеюсь лишь я один,
Потому что от природы
Я веселый Арлекин.

Разменял я смех на боны
И участочек купил
Посреди нейтральной зоны,
Чтоб никто не подстрелил.

И живу себе, буравлю
Средь таких, как я повес.
Нефтяную землю славлю,
Жду фонтана до небес.

Каждой ночью непременно
Опускаюсь я подвал,
Где в печали неизменной
Толстый Момус мирно спал.

Цель моя, если признаться,
Медный лоб тоски пробить
Научить вас улыбаться,
И смеяться, может быть.

Все мне дороги народы,
Кроме тех, кто любит сплин,
Потому что от природы
Я Веселый Арлекин.
(cited in Bowlt 1995, 83–85)[14]

Gorodetsky's hymn, written as the Red Army was battling on the southern front of the Civil War, seems to "merrily" welcome the Soviet colonization of Baku, which occurred only a few months later in the spring of 1920. The beginning of the citation refers to Gorodetsky's encounter with Lenin at the First Congress of the Communist International (Comintern) in March 1919, when before leaving for Baku, Gorodetsky began to voice support for the Bolshevik campaign.[15] This shift is marked, as his work produced while living in Tiflis only a few years earlier expressed strong anti-Bolshevik views.[16] Only a few months later when the Red Army conquered Azerbaijan, Gorodetsky further committed himself to the cause by taking on the leadership of the BakKavRosta alongside the Tiflis-born graphic artist and book designer Solomon Telingater.[17]

Assuming the mask of the Harlequin, albeit here in the guise of Lenin's court jester, Gorodetsky describes his move to Baku through political allegory and avant-garde tropes. The Civil War in the Caucasus is cast into the windy wake of Lenin's melancholy and the avant-garde tropes of the Commedia dell'arte serve a vision of a new Soviet eastern utopia. The aesthetics of Gorodetsky's hymn render legible the historical and political transformations in the Caucasus after the revolution, from the conquest of the former imperial territories through the formation of the Soviet republics.

Gorodetsky describes a shift in the appearance of the city through the development of the oil industry and perhaps more crucially, his own labor as a writer. Despite the hymn's reference to the environmental and ecological destruction of oil drilling, "Everything here smells of kerosene / People, animals, and homes, / Even the sturgeon in the sea / And the jail outside of town," the tone of the hymn remains cheerfully triumphal, emphasizing the laughter of the merry Harlequin as he drills for oil in Baku. He contrasts a place where "The oil brings gloom to the people" to the almost magical force of industrial revolution, which wrests oil from the earth like "a fountain to the sky." Rejecting the aesthetic mood of an older romantic order, he reproaches "those who love spleen" and instead promises to fulfill his goal to teach the audience to smile and laugh. Spleen, a trope characteristic of European romanticism and particularly French decadence, is associated with Europe earlier in the poem when he writes, "Let the empty steamships / Carry gloomy spleen to London." Gorodetsky connects a popular Bolshevik anti-British sentiment to a common avant-garde refrain rejecting the romantic image of melancholic spleen.[18]

Furthermore, "melancholy's copper brow" describes the stubbornness of Europe through a biblical allusion in which God addresses the idol worship of the "iron-necked" and "bronze-browed" Israelites (Isaiah 48:4). Assuming both the position of Harlequin and God, Gorodetsky generates a messianic vision, a promised land for the industrial and spiritual vitality of the new Soviet East. Like much of the work produced by the émigré writers, the hymn offers few details about life in Baku. The material reality of revolutionary Baku recedes into the background, while the aesthetic polemics of the avant-garde emerge instead from beneath its oily veneer. In this way, the hymn exposes a sense of play in Gorodetsky's work between prerevolutionary avant-garde themes and a growing interest in the connection between literature and political propaganda.

As its title indicates, the hymn was sung at the Merry Harlequin, a nightclub and theater organized by the director Nikolai Evreinov, the artist and set designer Sergei Sudeikin, and Gorodetsky. The theatre's allusion to the Commedia dell'arte and Gorodetsky's hymn written for its celebration were characteristic of a more general interest in prerevolutionary avant-garde aesthetics among the émigré community in Baku. The model for the theater was the tradition of the prerevolutionary cabarets of Moscow and St. Petersburg, The Bat (1908–1922) and the Stray Dog (Brodiachaia sobaka) (1911–1915), as well as the avant-garde revival cabaret in Tiflis known as the Fantastic Tavern (Fantasticheskii kabachok) (1917–1918).[19] The Merry Harlequin, however, most directly refers to Evreinov's play 1908 play *The Merry Death* (*Veselaia smert'*), which was first performed in St. Petersburg in 1909 and revived many times, including in Georgia in March 1919. Drawing on the famous love triangle from the Commedia dell'arte of Pierrot, Columbine, and Harlequin, the play recounts the story of Harlequin's attempts to cheat the hour of his death. Indeed, interpretations of this theme were common among the prerevolutionary avant-garde, such as Vsevolod Meyerhold's production of Alexander Blok's *The Fairground Booth* (*Balaganchik*) in 1906, Sergei Diaghilev's production of Igor Stravinsky's *Petroushka* in 1911, and the symbolist poetry of Andrei Bely, Elena Guro, and Viacheslav Ivanov.

In its avant-garde incarnation, *The Merry Death*, like *The Fairground Booth*, rejects a totalizing vision of authorship. Instead it highlights the role of the actors in challenging the authority of their author and the confines of the genre. As it dramatizes the dialogic relationship between the audience and the actors, it calls into question the form of the play itself. Indeed, the play ends in a monologue in which Pierrot declares the play itself a farce.[20] The play revolves around the question of fate through Harlequin's attempts to cheat death with laughter and Pierrot's manipulation of time by spinning the hands of a clock. Harlequin finally dies "merrily" as he is making love to Pierrot's wife, Columbine, while Pierrot looks on. Narrative time and the relationship between reality and representation are parodied by Harlequin's merry death, which is framed as part of a larger struggle to challenge the limits of the form of the play itself. Most avant-garde interpretations of this theme identify the figure of Pierrot as an alienated and effeminate double for the failing artist, while Harlequin, who always wins the love of Columbine, is associated with a primitive masculine character. For the prerevolutionary avant-garde the characters signaled a myth of European modernism in which the force of the primitive would sweep away European decadence.[21]

Many of the works, including theater sets and posters, produced under Gorodetsky's direction at the BakKavRosta also evoked the theme of the Commedia. One such example is a series of sketches for a poster in triptych form titled "Baku Help Starving Russia" drawn by Gorodetsky in 1921 as part of a campaign to render aid during the 1921 famine—here featuring Harlequin, Pierrot, and Columbine. The first frame depicts Harlequin merrily dancing at a ball with Columbine under glowing red and yellow orbs. In the second frame the dancers have vanished and Pierrot appears against a blue palette. Having dropped one of the yellow-red orbs, he looks on with anguish at a seemingly endless line of starving people. In the final frame Pierrot stands on the bones of the dead, the magnitude of which pile is captured in a black trail that extends beyond the page. Pierrot holds a tambourine and raises his hand appealing for help, under which an inscription reads, "If you are not blind, / To human suffering, / Lend a helping hand, / And we will kill hunger" (если не ослеп ты, / чтобы видеть людское горе, / помоги щедрою лептой, / и мы голод уморим) (*Tri ognia* 2000). The merriness of the revolution is captured in Harlequin's and Columbine's celebration at the ball, while Pierrot addresses the wartime consequences of the famine. While the images capture the duality of the characters of Harlequin and Pierrot as embodiments of the spirit of joy and sorrow, the artistic Pierrot, who is usually associated with pensive reflection, here exhibits a particularly political and philanthropic character as part of a propaganda campaign to render aid to Russia. The quick sketch renders the characters in simple geometric forms, expressive gestures, and simplified features. Gorodetsky thus employs prerevolutionary style and tropes to support a didactic social campaign.

Gorodetsky's hymn also evokes the tropes of the Commedia, while in many ways inverting its terms. His focus on the figure of Harlequin marks a shift from the avant-garde fascination with the pensive, artistic Pierrot to a new model for a more masculinist vision of the Bolshevik hero who "exchanged laughter for work" and lives by drilling. Indeed, this evo-lution of the heroic figure from the pensive writer to the active builder follows a similar trend in the postrevolutionary metropole. Gorodetsky's tribute to the Commedia and its echoes within the émigré circle signal a desperate attempt to maintain a sense of continuity with the aesthetics of the prerevolutionary period. It provides a way of, as the theme of *The Merry Death* suggests, extending the life of the avant-garde on the eve of the Soviet colonization of the periphery. However, Gorodetsky's emphasis on the figure of the Harlequin and a muscular, utilitarian aesthetic trans-forms the early avant-garde trope into a hymn that formulates a more direct connection to state power. In place of the author, Lenin's figure dominates the hymn. While the verse celebrates the theater of the Merry Harlequin as well as the avant-garde trope itself, the hymn emphasizes the Harlequin's charge to bring laughter to Baku and in so doing chase Lenin's melancholy away. The source of melancholy appears here as Lon-don, indeed referring to British competition for influence on the Civil War front. The will of Gorodetsky's Harlequin, despite his evocation of the anarchist spirit of the carnivalesque, remains in part subject to the whims of his newly pro-Bolshevik author. The hymn thus traces a transitional moment in the relationship between aesthetics and politics, recalling pre-revolutionary themes as it looks toward a new relationship between art and state power.

Gorodetsky's work during this period also addresses the Bolshevik rhetoric of anti-imperialism on a global scale. His poem "Coffee," written in Baku on December 13, 1919, reflects Bolshevik Civil War propaganda through a critique of the Dutch coffee market. The poem, which is set in Java, exemplifies the intersection of discourses of orientalism with Soviet anti-imperialism and anticapitalism.

That is why, when black coffee
Boils in porcelain with its golden sheen,
A sea of turbulent desires comes to mind
And suddenly the soul yearns for catastrophe.

Blow up Europe! For the native's freedom
Take away the shameless evil of buying and selling!
The magnolia flowers do not need whips,
The ocean's sun needs no guard!

Avenge the fury of belted lashes!
May the harbors recede into a bloody mist!
So that naked lovers can
Freely exult in the marshes of Java!

Вот отчего, когда кипит в фарфоре
С отливом золотистым черный кофе,
В мозгу встает желаний буйных море,
Душа тоскует вдруг по катастрофе.

Взорвать Европу! Снять с дикарской воли
Бесстыдство злое купли и продажи!
Плетей не надо для цветов магнолий,
Не надо солнцу океана—стражи!

Отмстить за бешенство бичей ременных!
Пусть гавани в туман уйдут кровавый
Чтобы можно было для нагих влюбленных
Свободно ликовать в болотах Ябы!
                    (cited in Bowlt 1995, 72)[22]

The poem evokes an exotic image of coffee production through an orientalist trope—naked lovers wandering freely in a tropical setting. However, instead of inspiring fantasy, the decadent beverage, boiled in porcelain and glowing golden, moves the soul toward catastrophe, and as the next verse suggests, leads to the destruction of Europe. These images of revolution animate Gorodetsky's otherwise romantic lexicon, which includes the "sea of turbulent desire" (*zhelanii buinykh more*) and the untranslatable verb form of *toska*, which can be likened to the brooding anxiety of the French *ennui*. The "shameless evil" of Europe contrasts the childlike (*kak deti*) quality and free will (*volia*) of the natives, recalling the biblical trope of original sin. However, here sin is associated with economic exploitation, "buying and selling," which strips the natives of their innocence and freedom. The directive to destroy Europe hopes to restore the paradise of the naked lovers in the marshes of Java, as well as oppressed peoples more globally. As a statement against imperialism, the poem projects the "sin" of the orientalist gaze onto Europe through its emphasis on economic oppression and modes of production over questions of race.

Notably the poem's publication a year later in the 1920 collection, *Crimson Oil* (*Alaia neft*), reveals a shifting emphasis from the exotic register and its attendant romantic imagery to the ideological power of the Soviet anticolonial project. In the 1920 edition the final stanza reads:

> May the predators recede into a bloody mist!
> Long live the freedom of the oppressed
> In every corner, as in the marshes of Java!

> Отмстить за бешенство бичей ременных!
> Пусть хищники в туман уйдут кровавый!
> Да здравствует свобода угнетенных
> Во всех краях, как на болотах Явы!
> (Gorodetsky 1920, 19–20)

In this version, the boundlessness of the orientalist imaginary is transformed into an anti-imperial political project, a play on the romantic connection between the cognition of open space as liberty or political will popular in the nineteenth-century narratives.

Gorodetsky's penchant for biblical allusions also extended to his descriptions of Soviet modernization. Drawing on the avant-garde trope of technology and industrialization, Gorodetsky's poem "Energon," from *Crimson Oil*, represents oil in the language of biblical apocalypse. "Energon" describes a fantastic political industrial entity, which embodies a spiritual power, and perhaps more specifically alludes to Ezekiel's vision of God as a whirling energy of creation. He writes: "It's time to blow it up, break forth the primeval earth. In the name of Energon, / Energon, energon!" (Пора им взорваться, / Землю дремучую бросит вперед. / Имш им энергон, энергон!) (1920, 13–14). He concludes: "Many still remain oppressed and sleeping. / The city sucks the juices of the colony, / London still drinks from India's shriveled breast" (Много еще угнетенных и спящих. / Сити сосет еще соки колоний, / Индия грудью иссохшей поет еще Лондон) (13–14).

For Gorodetsky, industry provides the spiritual and economic power, the "energon" of anti-imperial revolt. Indeed, the repetition of the word "energon" highlights its creationist power while recalling the style of folk poetry. Gorodetsky thus associates oil extraction with a spiritual energy that breaks up the "primeval earth." The poem, like *The Merry Harlequin*, emphasizes the role of drilling in Baku's modernization. However, in place of the everyman at the drill's command, an ambiguous powerful force of energon displaces the process of industrialization onto the plane of the fantastic.

In another poem from the same collection titled "Industry" (Promysla) Gorodetsky connects oil to the world revolution. The final stanza reads, "And like oil from beneath the sand / seething with desire / to instate under the red banner / a world revolution" (И, как нефть под песками, / Накипает желанье / Стать под красное знамя / Мирового восстанья) (17–18). The personification of oil as desire highlights its role as a creationist force endowed with both sexual energy and religious messianic rhetoric. Gorodetsky's vision of Baku shrouds it in a primeval space and in so doing departs from the discourse of scientific modernization, locating the authority and power of Soviet anti-imperial discourse in the language of romantic belief.

Soviet Anti-Imperialism: Theorizing the Soviet Muslim East

The application of Marxist economics to anti-imperial ideology was perhaps the Bolshevik's most important ideological tool. Lenin's treatise of 1916, *Imperialism: The Highest Stage of Capitalism*, argued for this elision between late capitalism and imperialism. Building on a Marxist notion of the global accumulation of capital, Lenin defines imperialism through the exploitation of capitalist empires. He argues that capitalism in a monopoly stage was forced to seek new markets through imperial expansion and thus generated an unequal structural relationship between the imperial metropole and the colonial periphery.[23] This understanding of imperialism in exclusively economic terms not only obscured race as a definitive feature of inequality but further expanded the geography of the revolution.

Building on this argument, in subsequent 1917 and 1919 addresses to the Russian Muslims and the Communist Organization of the Peoples of the East, Lenin urged the support of Muslims to overthrow imperialism.[24] Furthermore, he framed Russia's Eurasian character as the historical and geographical precedent for Soviet anti-imperialism. He writes, "Owing to a number of circumstances, among them the backwardness of Russia and her vast area, and the fact that she constitutes a frontier between

Europe and Asia, between the West and the East, we had to bear the whole brunt—and we regard that as a great honour of being the pioneers of the world struggle against imperialism" (1993, 253–65). Inverting the nineteenth-century trope of Russia as the defender of the West, Lenin represents Soviet Russia instead as the defender of an oppressed East. He distinguishes Russian from European imperialism by highlighting Russia's Eurasian geopolitics: that is, its location on the frontier or threshold of Europe and Asia. Politically, Lenin's anti-imperial campaign provided ideological support for competition with the British over control in Persia, Central Asia, and India. As the rallying cry of the Comintern, it also aimed to generate global networks with anticolonial movements across the tricontinent and thus to compete with other supranational discourses such as pan-Islamism.[25] Discursively, it created a global revolutionary aesthetic topography while obscuring the connection between Soviet expansion and imperialism.

Relying on this anticapitalist, anti-imperialist ideology, the revolutionary and early Soviet vision of the Orient extended beyond the former imperial territories. Defined exclusively in terms of imperial exploitation, the influence of the Soviet East thus extended to much of the tricontinent. The Comintern's creation of the Communist University of the Toilers of the East (KUTV) in the spring of 1921 offers an example of the global scope of this revolutionary anti-imperial ideology. The first years of the university's operations between 1921 and 1925 reflect this broad understanding of the communist East in its inclusion of African American and Latin American communists under the geopolitical designation of "easterners" alongside communists from the former imperial territories of the Russian empire (the Caucasus, Central Asia, and the Volga), as well as Asia and Africa.[26] The university thus realized the concept of a revolutionary Soviet East that was theorized by Soviet orientalists. Two figures stand out in these discussions—the Marxist propagandist Mikhail Pavlovich (Vel'tman) (1871–1927) and the former prerevolutionary orientalist Konstantin Troianovsky (Konstantin Mikhailovich Troianovskii) (1876–1951), both of whom contributed to the foundation of a Marxist-Leninist school of Soviet oriental studies and by extension its role in the creation and dissemination of Soviet propaganda.

Troianovsky's conception of the Eastern International (International Vostoka), which he developed in *The East and the Revolution: A New*

Political Program for the Countries of the East—India, Persia, and China (1918) outlined a theory for a united Eastern anti-imperial campaign that opposed a Western capitalist international (1918, 46). Troianovsky's Eastern International was predicated on a vision of Islam as the key to the liberation and transformation of a communist utopia on the Soviet frontier. Drawing on the work of the Hungarian orientalist Ignác Goldziher, Troianovsky argued that the "spiritual-cultural" basis of Muslim unity, its combination of "theology, ethics, justice and the supreme earthly power, that is, the state" rendered the Muslims a historically "political people."[27] Troianovsky and Goldziher's understanding of political Islam is particularly indebted to the mythic resistance of the North Caucasus freedom fighters against the tsar in the Russian orientalist imagination.

Soviet anti-imperialist representations of the North Caucasus can in part be traced to its nineteenth-century predecessors. One crucial text in this lineage is the 1859 article "Muridism and Shamil" (Muridizm i Shamil) written by the South Caucasus-born orientalist Mirza Kazim bey (also known as Aleksandr Kasimovich Kazembek), which characterized this interest in the historical and cultural politics of the Muslims of the Caucasus during the nineteenth century.[28] Kazembek's work, as well as his own biography as a South Caucasus-born Muslim convert to Christianity, focused on the orientalist trope of Caucasian bravery and valor. He traced Muridism, a Russian term to describe Sufi sectarians, to the idea of *davat* (*dawat*), which he defined as an "invitation to the people to revolt against hated authority and to protect laws or religious rights" (1985, 33).[29] He also highlighted the "strong spiritual sense" and the "cold, unshakable bravery" of the people of Daghestan (40). Suspected of supporting the revolutionary figure Imam Shamil, Kazembek was treated with apprehension by the tsarist government, repeatedly denied clearance to leave the Russian empire for fear that he would rally revolutionary support for the Muslim communities of the Caucasus in Europe (Schimmelpennick van der Oye 2008, 452).[30] Kazembek's censoring by the tsarist authorities made the circulation of his recollections of Shamil and more broadly the idea of revolutionary Islam crucial for Russian political exiles as well as Soviet orientalists such as Troianovsky.

Following Kazembek, Troianovsky cites the organized resistance under Shamil against Russian imperialism as proof of a united Muslim commitment to revolutionary politics. Troianovsky's emphasis on the political character of the Muslim people (*narod*) proposed an Eastern International as a state that would instrumentalize "the [pan-Islamic] cultural movement toward unity . . . in the name of national freedom, in which the last word is state independence" (1918, 42–43). Providing the foundation of state unity, Troianovsky envisioned Muslim Bolshevism through the Eastern International as an engaged form of cultural, spiritual, and political unity that would challenge capitalism.

Pavlovich offered a similar geopolitical mapping, while specifying the role of oriental studies in this transformation. In his 1921 inaugural description of the new Soviet orientalist association, the All-Russian Scientific Association of Oriental Studies (Vserossiiskoi nauchnoi assotsiiatsii vostokovedeniia), published in its official journal *The New East* (*Novyi Vostok*), Pavlovich describes the Soviet orientalist project as part of a global anti-imperialist revolution. He writes, "The East is the whole colonial world, the world of oppressed peoples, and not only Asia but Africa and South America—in one word, that whole world that rests under the exploitation of the power of the capitalist societies in Europe and in the United States" (1922, 9). The address not only resignified a "new East," as the title of the association's journal suggests, but redefined the role of the orientalist scholarship in its formation. The intention of the association, he argues, "alongside special scientific work can pursue the goals of the economic and spiritual [*dikhovnoe*] emancipation of the East" (5). Indeed, Pavlovich emphasizes a rupture with the imperial past. He writes,

> Everything changed from the moment Soviet power triumphed in Russia. Worker-peasant Russia—powerful, invincible in the face of her Red Army, and enchanting [*skazochno charuiuschaia*] in its new look—already in the eyes of the Asiatic peoples did not appear as a tormentor Bey from all the Muslim world, nor as an enemy—neither the conquerors England, Germany, or France in the fight to divide the yellow continent—but in reverse, as a guardian angel [*dobryi genii*], a sincere friend to all of the oppressed peoples of the East in the struggle against world imperialism. (4)

Pavlovich likens Soviet rule to a fairy tale in which the "enchanting" power of the worker-peasant transforms the relationship between Russia and the East from a tormentor to a friend and guardian. In distinguishing the objectives of the new Soviet orientalist science, he insists on the emancipatory function of Soviet oriental studies. However, his celebration of the Soviet project also romanticizes the anti-imperial revolution as a primordial battle to return spiritual freedom to the oppressed masses. Pavlovich's rhetoric of "spiritual emancipation" echoes Gorodetsky's vision of the recovery of the paradise of Java. Indeed, the enchanting powers of the Soviet liberation of the tricontinent lay in its mobilization of a poetic and scientific discourse that cloaked Soviet expansionism in anti-imperial ideology.

The anti-imperialist vision of the Muslim East and its role in forging the future of the global Soviet project was also championed by Muslim communist intellectuals, particularly the Tatar intellectual and head of the Muslim division of the Commissariat of Nationalities Mirsaid Sultan Galiev and the playwright and head of the Azerbaijan Soviet Socialist Republic Nariman Narimanov.[31] Leading the brief but influential Soviet Muslim communist campaign, they generated linkages among local reformist interests that had been championed by pan-Turkic Muslim thinkers at the turn of the century. Of these, perhaps the most influential was the Soviet appropriation of the unveiling campaigns based on contact with Central Asian jadids who joined the party during the Civil War (Baberovski 2010, 614).

Narimanov, like the Central Asian jadids, promoted educational reforms and in particular championed literature and theater as agents for the formation of a Muslim cultural consciousness.[32] Highlighting the strength of cultural institutions, he envisioned the humanistic role of theater on the enlightenment of Muslim youth. Written in 1899, Narimanov's essay "A Few Words about Theater" provides an early sketch of his argument for the central role of cultural institutions such as the theater in Muslim enlightenment. He writes: "Such human affairs cannot be implemented by the force of a single person. For this reason, theater establishes an educated, cultured [kul'turnyi] and conscious [soznatel'nyi] Muslim youth" (1988, 1:48). While this humanist political vision was the product of his education in tsarist-era schools, its leading figures such as the oil millionaire philanthropist Zeynalabdin Tağıyev would later become the object of Narimanov's class critique.[33] Indeed, Narimanov's poor upbringing and frequent struggles to pay for his schooling contributed to his radicalization at the turn of the century.[34] However, like Lenin, Narimanov's vision of modernity remained deeply rooted in a conviction in the power of literature and theater to drive the Bolshevik enlightenment project.

In meetings with Lenin in 1920 Narimanov negotiated access to Baku's oil for a political commitment to the liberalization of cultural policies in the Caucasus, as well as his own role as leader in Azerbaijan's Sovietization.[35] In this way, despite his denunciations of British and French imperialism, in many ways Narimanov played a major role in the incorporation of Azerbaijan into the Soviet Union. Narimanov's relationship with Lenin was central to his vision to make Azerbaijan the capital of the Soviet East, or as he wrote, the "window onto the East" (*okno na Vostok*) (1990, 29). Nerimanov's inversion of Peter the Great's famous adage of modernization, which hailed St. Petersburg as Russia's "window onto the West," exposes his vision of the consolidation of Soviet power in the Caucasus through the transformation of aesthetic-discursive forms of power centered around the *translatio imperii*.

Narimanov's modernization efforts were, at least theoretically, directed toward the integration of Azeri peasants in the countryside into the economic, political, and cultural space of Baku. In this way, he highlighted the role of Islam in the transformation of the countryside as central to what he believed was the most important objective of the party: that is, to spread the communist revolution eastward.[36] Narimanov emphasized the ways in which Islam could be useful to communist propaganda. In his closing remarks at the second congress of the Azerbaijan Communist Party in 1920, he argues that unlike imperial Russia, in which the clergy served the tsar, "Our mollas can be persuaded by references to the Qur'an, which does not contradict communism. If we approach a molla and tell him what communism means and explain to him how its ideas should be understood, he will believe us and say to himself: 'Yes, it's been written so long ago'" (1988, 2:392). In this way, Narimanov was a complex figure, at once keen on amassing his power and promoting the central role of Azerbaijan in Soviet Eastern International efforts, while also emphasizing the necessity of a Bolshevik appeal not only to the educated elite in Baku but also to the peasants in the countryside.

Sultan Galiev and Narimanov argued, following Lenin, that the oppressed eastern nations accounted for the major lines of production of imperialism, thus the efforts to galvanize Muslim communism would rob Western capitalism of its economic base (Galiev 1979, 132–36; Narimanov 1990, 28–29). In an article in *The Life of Nationalities* (*Zhizn' national'nostei*) published on August 9, 1920, Sultan Galiev describes

Soviet Azerbaijan as the center of the communist world revolution in the East. He writes: "The sovietization of Azerbaijan is a highly important step in the evolution of communism in the Near East . . . Soviet Azerbaijan, with its old and experienced proletariat and its already consolidated Communist Party—The Hümmet Party, will become the Red lighthouse for Persia, Arabia, and Turkey" (Galiev [1921] 1979, 154).

As both Anouar Abdel-Malek and Robert Young have noted, Sultan Galiev's ideas laid the foundation for tricontinental Marxism. Young writes, "Identifying with the revolutionary pan-Islamism of al-Afghānī, he [Sultan Galiev] also emphasized what was to become a fundamental political identification of tricontinental societies, dividing the world into the oppressors and the oppressed" (2001, 175; Abdel-Malek 1981, 84). While Sultan Galiev identifies the relationship between imperial and class politics, his detailed account of the "oppressed nations" falls instead within his designs for Soviet propaganda. He writes, "Thus, the particular position of Islam, which can be explained on the one hand by its greater vitality due to its late appearance and on the other hand by the psychological state of the oppressed or only lately liberated Muslim peoples, necessitates an approach and new methods of antireligious propaganda" (quoted in Bennigsen and Wimbush 1979, 148).

Sultan Galiev concludes that it is the role of Muslim communists to organize Soviet propaganda efforts, which emphasize the role of politics in transcending the division between the public and private spheres. He writes, "we must carry on the campaign in daily life, by our example and activities" (148). What is perhaps most distinctive about Sultan Galiev's vision of Muslim communism is not only his division of the world into the categories of the oppressors and the oppressed as Young notes, but rather his mapping of the "psychological state" of the oppressed, which forms the basis of his model of propaganda.

The Soviet orientalist enterprise, harnessing the contributions of Russian imperial orientalists, geographers, and poets, as well as Azeri writers and statesman, thus crafted a vision of the communist East to lead the internationalist anti-imperial charge, drawing on an interdisciplinary emphasis on poetic and scientific discourses as central to Soviet politics. In so doing, Soviet orientalism also designated a specifically political position for literature, not only as an instrument of revolution but increasingly as a tool of state building. Such militant artistic collaborations indeed extended beyond the page and onto the stage as the Congress of the Peoples of the East attempted to perform this Eastern International in the newly established Soviet Socialist Republic of Azerbaijan.

The Romantic Orientalist Intertext at the Congress of the Peoples of the East

Organized by Muslim, Jewish, and Russian Bolshevik politicians from Ukraine, the Volga region, and the Caucasus, the Congress of the Peoples of the East brought over two thousand delegates from more than twenty ethno-national groups to Baku in September 1920.[37] The organizers included Narimanov and Sultan Galiev. Despite its lofty ambitions to unite the oppressed colonized people of the world against the evils of capitalist imperialism, the congress proved to be more theater than politics. As Narimanov would later lament in his 1923 pamphlet "Toward a History of Our Revolution in the Borderlands" (K istorii nashei revoliutsii v okrainakh), the congress was no more than "leftist play." In this controversial tract, which contributed to his marginalization from the party and exile from Azerbaijan, Narimanov accuses the Soviet government of withdrawing support for resistance movements, such as the one in Iran, while promoting the spectacle of anti-imperialism. The Soviet politicians, he complains, sent photographs of representatives to British Prime Minister David Lloyd George so that he could laugh at the image of delegates with their naked blades (*kinzhaly*), revolvers, clubs, and knives threatening European capital.[38]

While the Congress of the People of the East indeed proved to have little impact on shaping Soviet policy in the republics, its legacy extends beyond an empty diplomatic gesture punctuating the end of the Civil War. Read alongside the work of the Russian avant-garde in Baku, the congress reveals the ways in which Soviet anti-imperial discourse relied on both the politicization of poetry and the circulation of poetics in political rhetoric. The congress sought to realize the theoretical concept of the Eastern International, using the location of Baku and the congress's international representation to highlight the Soviet Union's Eurasian hybridity. The congress authorized an anti-imperial political subjectivity through its performance of multilingualism, while it simultaneously promoted the hegemonic status of Russian. In its construction of a vision of the Caucasus and, more broadly, the Soviet East, it relied on romantic poetic intertexts. However, these representations were themselves indebted to a Russian romantic orientalist imaginary of the Caucasus. Such contradictory politics contributed both to the unique expression of Soviet antiimperialism and to its ultimate failure.

One of the most striking features of the congress was its attempt, however unsuccessful, to translate communism into the native languages of the delegates. The introductory remarks delivered by Grigory Zinoviev (Grigorii Evseevich Zinov'ev), chairman of the Comintern, emphasized the importance of multilingualism, proclaiming that "the Communist International wants to unite under its banners speakers of all the languages of the world" (Riddell 1993, 55). The increasing importance attributed to translation for the success of the Soviet Union was championed by Lenin in his "Address to the Second All-Russia Congress of Communist Organizations of the Peoples of the East" only a year preceding the congress in 1919. Lenin described the central role of translation in mobilizing the peoples of the East in the Soviet battle against the united imperialism of Germany, France, Britain, and the United States.[39] He argues that translations of the Russian Soviet constitution served as the strongest weapon in the war, because instead of defeating the imperial troops it won them over and converted them to the Soviet cause (1993, 263; 1958–1965, 39:329). In Lenin's vision, armed with a universally translatable ideology, the Soviet Union was undefeatable. The power of the Soviet Union, he writes, is realized in the fact that "the word *soviet* is now understood by everybody, and the Soviet constitution has been translated into all languages and is known to every worker" (1993, 293; 1958–1965, 39:329). For Lenin, the true success of the Soviet Union lies in the ability to make the notion of the political body of the council or *soviet* not only legible but understandable to the people of the East. In this framing, the translation of the word *soviet* as a metonymy for the multilingual nation provided the ammunition necessary for Soviet soldiers to defeat imperialism. Lenin thus defines translation as the primary strategy for Soviet conquest.

Distinguishing the Soviet conquest from capitalist imperialism, Lenin explains that Soviet ideology and its translation account for the "miracle" (*chudo*) of the Soviet victory (1993, 254; 1958–1965, 39:329). Attributing this military success to the translatability of *soviet*, Lenin blends the secular practice of translation with the spiritual phenomenon of the miracle, investing Bolshevik ideology with both a spiritual and a scientific—that is, both sacred and secular—authority. Lenin's insistence on the *miracle* of the Soviet victory indeed recalls the connection between nineteenth-century Russian imperial expansion and Russian Orthodoxy.[40] However, in mythologizing Soviet colonization, he also implicitly describes the secularization of the former empire as a miracle. Lenin thus links both imperial expansion and secularization to the act of translation. The translation of *soviet* functions for Lenin both as a miracle with its authority rooted in the imperial past and as a secular form of civil governance with its authority secured in the Soviet future. Translation not only mythologizes the *Soviet* but also crucially authorizes a seamless *translatio imperii* from Russian Orthodox imperial hegemony to the scientific gaze of the Soviet colonial enlightenment project. The power of Lenin's rhetorical gesture lies in its capacity to reinscribe an authoritative discourse of Russian imperial rule onto the Soviet's secular political ideology.

The authority of Soviet translation was also shaped by the reception of Marxist-Leninist theory in local intellectual circles in the Caucasus and Central Asia. The word *soviet* encountered its Turkic double in *shura*, which appeared in the titles of coordinating committees of Muslim organizations during the early twentieth century and was the name of one of the most influential Turkic journals in the Russian empire.[41] The shared meaning of *shura* and *soviet* as "council" and the competing secular national and religious local political institutions they represented obscured differences in the power structures of the former Russian imperial territories and the emerging Soviet empire. Furthermore, the term *shura* not only denotes a council but specifically refers to the representative democratic sociopolitical organization of Islam. It emphasizes justice, equality, and dignity and is the name of sura 42 in the Qur'an. The Islamic scholar Fazlur Rahman writes, "To carry on their collective business [government], the Qur'an asks them [Muslims] to institute *shura* [a consultative council or assembly], where the will of the people can be expressed by representation" (2009, 43). The translation of the word thus could simultaneously signify the Soviet government, the postrevolutionary local Muslim committees, and Islamic ideals of justice.

While the congress proceedings indeed commenced with speeches in English, French, German, Russian, Bulgarian, Turkish, Azerbaijani

Turkic, Persian, Chechen, Uzbek, and Kumyk, by the fourth session these had been reduced to three official languages—Russian, Azerbaijani Turkic, and Persian—in order to minimize the disruption of the proceedings. Zinoviev instead requested that delegates within each language group should elect an individual to deliver translations "in the corridors or out in the street" (Riddell 1993, 130). Furthermore, where translation was given, it was often charged as incorrect or incomplete. The lack of Turkic or Persian transcripts makes it impossible to verify mistranslations; however, several delegates alleged that their works had been mistranslated or abridged.[42] Thus, under the auspices of multilingualism, Russian was ultimately centralized as a universal tongue, while minority language groups were literally marginalized on the outskirts of the proceedings and building.

The congress, like Gorodetsky's verse, captured little of the material reality of Baku in 1920. An industrial capital and a major source of oil for the young Soviet state, Baku had only months earlier succumbed to the Red Army's force. Turning away from the present, the conference proceedings instead revived a poetic vision of the Caucasus as the heart of a transcendental revolutionary spirit, which it traced to nineteenth-century Russian orientalist representations of the North Caucasus and Georgia, as well as romantic and biblical messianism. The speeches drew on romantic rhetoric as well as allusions to the "oppositional imperialism" of the Decembrist poets who had been exiled to the Caucasus for their opposition to Tsar Nicholas I. Such romantic orientalist intertexts, which were deeply indebted to the Russian imperial gaze, provided unusual precedents for a Bolshevik anti-imperial campaign aimed at gaining support in Caucasus, Central Asia, Persia, India, and China. However, the speeches resignified these relics of the imperial period as defining features of the temporality of Soviet anti-imperial ideology, which at once sought to redeem an originary Russian revolutionary spirit and distanced itself from Russia's nineteenth-century imperial legacy. While the congress accomplished little in terms of effecting Soviet policy in the Caucasus, it inspired and realized a political platform for the poetics of the avant-garde poets and artists in Baku, as well as the formation of Muslim communist and later Soviet Azerbaijani national narratives.

A sublime image of surging oceans recurs throughout the speeches. Both Pavlovich and Zinoviev invoked the topographical metaphors of estuaries and confluences. For Pavlovich, the rivers signified the cultural achievements of various national groups combining in a "common international ocean of poetry and learning of toiling humanity" (Riddell 1993, 143). Indeed, like the function of translations into Russian, the image of the ocean captures a similarly centralizing vision of Soviet diversity. The Soviet model of incorporation generates its ideological power. This "international ocean," Pavlovich writes, rivals the "old monuments of Russian and Ukrainian literature, such as the works of Pushkin, Lermontov, Tolstoy, Gogol, and Shevchenko," as well as "classical Greece" and the "civilization of the medieval and capitalist epochs" (143). Pavlovich imagines socialism as an empire of minorities that rivals the Greeks, the Russians, and the kingdoms and capitalist nations of Europe. The ocean serves as a metaphor for cultural integration that diffuses the spatio-temporality of the Soviet Union, encompassing the entire European past and present. Expanding on this radical spatio-temporality, Pavlovich devises a mythical form of rail transport, which he dreams will connect great cities and civilizations across space and time, linking Berlin, Byzantium, and Baghdad, as well as Cape Town, Cairo, and Calcutta, and finally Petersburg and Persia (137). These spatio-temporal clusters organize a Eurasian network according to an alliterative logic, realizing a global Soviet revolution through poetic as well as infrastructural innovations (137).

Zinoviev generates a similar image of Soviet expansion through biblical allusions. Like Lenin's recourse to miracle, Zinoviev evokes the importance of religion as a defining feature of discourses of Russian imperialism. He describes the workers' proletariat in Russia and the movement of the oppressed nationalities as two streams that "if cleansed of national prejudices" could be "merged into one single tumultuous, powerful stream that, like the sea, will sweep all obstacles from its path, clearing the land of all the evil from which we have suffered so long" (73). The image indeed recalls the Slavophile philosopher Nikolai Danilevsky's portrait of the cross-fertilization of ancient cultures as streams. This great flood of socialism aims to dissolve landownership and, like in the great biblical flood of Noah's ark, destroy evil to prepare for a new world of harmony and good. For Zinoviev socialism quite literally replaces the Church in shielding workers from the evil floods of capitalism.

Zinoviev not only drew on biblical imagery but also directly championed an Islamic holy war in attempt to rally the largely Muslim crowd.

The term "Holy War" (*Sviashchennaia voina*) appears throughout his speeches, but the Russian term was reportedly substituted for *jihad* or *ghazavat* in the speech's delivery, attributing an orientalist vision of Islamic holy war to the Soviet cause.[43] The use of the term is corroborated by the testimony of a young Azeri soldier who describes the crowd being inspired by the "declaration of holy war against the enemy of revolution; thousands of people, convinced there was no contradiction between being a Bolshevik and a Muslim, joined the Bolshevik ranks" (Riddell 1993, 30).[44] The announcement for the congress also invokes the image of a religious pilgrimage: "Formerly you traveled across deserts to reach the holy places" (40). However, such attempts to rouse support from the Muslim population were not reduced to rhetorical flourish. Local newspapers also reported the slaughter of a hundred sheep and goats in honor of the congress (20). The political efforts to appropriate Muslim cultural symbols for the Soviet cause mirrored the allusions to nineteenth-century romantic orientalist tropes of Decembrist poetry, conferring the rhetorical force of the canon of Russian orientalism on the political-ideological platform of the congress.

Romantic intertexts also appear in the conference speeches in the form of allusions to and citations from the works of Pushkin and Lermontov. Citations from Pushkin and Lermontov exemplify a trend in Russian Orientalism to personify the Caucasian landscape as a romantic force of resistance. At the congress, these images found new currency in the speeches of local delegates from the Caucasus and Central Asia, as triumphal declarations of the completion of the East's emergence as a revolutionary force. Serving as chairman of the congress, Narimanov delivered the opening speech in which he alluded to a short but famous epithet from Azeri poetry. Referring to "the gray-haired East" (*sedovlasyi Vostok*), he simultaneously evoked Axundov's vision of a "white-haired Caucasus" from the Russian version of his 1837 poem "On the Death of Pushkin" and Lermontov's famous 1841 poem, "The Argument."

The reference to the Russian phrase obscures the distance between Axundov's expression of Caucasian sovereignty and Lermontov's popular orientalist image. The evocation of these two works also recalls an intercultural, interlingual, and intertextual encounter from the previous century. Axundov translated his poem into Russian with the help of the poet Bestuzhev-Marlinsky and may well have shared it with Lermontov while instructing him in Azeri. Lermontov, in turn, recalled the epithet when he depicted Elbrus in "The Argument." Appearing finally in Narimanov's speech, the trope of the wise Caucasus connects the poetic worlds of the leading figures of Azeri and Russian literature of the nineteenth century to the political agenda of the congress. Referring not only to the famous trope but to the history of its linguistic and cultural translation, Narimanov realizes the Eastern International through the politics of translation. He also forges an important linkage between the orientalist image of the Caucasus and the future of the Soviet Union.

Lermontov's poem also appeared in a speech by the chairman of the Bukhara delegation, Ahmed Matushev. Matushev cites directly from "The Argument" as evidence of his vision of a Soviet future in Central Asia, "I don't fear the East, / Answered Kazbek, / There the race of men has slept deeply, / Already for nine centuries" (Не боюся я Востока, / Отвечал Казбек, / Род людской там спит глубоко, / Уж девятый век) (Lermontov 1958–1962, 1:526). Lermontov's famous portrait of the Kazbek and Elbrus Mountains arguing over the destiny of the East offers a curious referent for a vision of postcolonial Central Asia. Citing the work, Matushev argues, "Today we can say with pride that the East is awakening from its centuries-long sleep and coming out onto the common human road of social construction in fraternal unity and contact with the proletariat of the West, embodied in Red Russia" (Riddell 1993, 164). Recalling Lermontov's canonical orientalist image of the sleeping East, Matushev contrasts it with the beginning of a new era. In this way, he reimagines Lermontov's poem as the historical antecedent of a revolutionary ethics. Lermontov's orientalism becomes the foundation for a new Red canon of Soviet anti-imperialist literature. Indeed, the return of nineteenth-century romanticism was an important feature of the Soviet canon well into the 1930s.[45] On the one hand, the reimagination of that canon distinguished the formal innovations of modernism. On the other, the return to romanticism highlighted a continuity between the influence of Decembrist thought on the Caucasus poems of Pushkin and Lermontov and the ethical dimensions of Soviet revolutionary literature.

Matushev's image of the awakening East also echoes many of the Islamic modernist reformers' responses to their orientalist interlocutors of the nineteenth century, from the Persian/Afghani religious scholar and reformer Sayyid Jamāl al-Dīn al-Afghānī to the twentieth-century Azeri thinker Ehmed bey Ağaoğlu (Ağaev). However, for Matushev, the "proletariat of the West" and "Red Russia" serve as agents in this modernization. In "The Argument," Lermontov pinpoints the slumber of the East in the ninth or tenth centuries, a period during which conversion to Islam began in the Caucasus in the aftermath of the Arab conquest of the seventh century.[46] Lermontov represents the East through a vision of Islamic conversion as cultural stasis. However, in his allusion to Lermontov, Matushev instead highlights the awakening of the eastern proletariat. He draws on Troianovsky's theory of the Eastern International and anticipates the charge of Soviet orientalist institutions, which Pavlovich would outline a year later. Matushev's and Narimanov's literary allusions to the romantic orientalist canon generated by Pushkin and Lermontov further exemplify the central role the poetic imaginary of the Caucasus played in generating the material foundations of a Soviet ideology of expansion rooted in Russian orientalism, despite its paradoxical disavowal of imperialism.[47]

Transcaucasian Politics and Universal Poetics

The Congress of the Peoples of the East not only provided an opportunity for politicians to invest in the power of the word but also inspired poetic experiments among the Russian émigré writers in Baku, particularly the avant-garde poetics of *zaum*, or transrational poetry. Alexei Kruchenykh and Velimir Khlebnikov moved from Tiflis to Baku during the summer of 1919. After the invasion of the Red Army in the spring of 1920, they took up work in the new Soviet government. According to Kruchenykh's memoirs, after Sovietization he and Khlebnikov joined the staff at BakKavRosta, writing lines for propaganda posters.[48] Khlebnikov's poetry of the time also invokes Soviet propaganda, as Andrea Hacker argues in her study of Khlebnikov's Baku notebooks; many of the fragments echo sound patterns from the conference proceedings.[49] Khlebnikov's and Kruchenykh's major theoretical development, the "transrational language" of zaum found its full expression in the Caucasus, first in Tbilisi and then in Baku.

One year following the conference, Kruchenykh published a pamphlet titled "The Declaration of the Transrational Language" (Deklaratsiia zaumnogo iazyka) (1967, 179–81). While the avant-garde's interest in multilingualism and wordplay, which were defining features of zaum poetry, developed largely in Tbilisi, the congress confirmed the power of translation to effect politics. In the manifesto, Kruchenykh calls for a worldly poetic language: "The transrational creations can yield an all-worldly poetic language, born organically and not artificially like Esperanto" (Заумные творения могут дать всемирный поэтический язык, рожденный органически, а не искусственно, как эспиранто) (181). Even if inspired by the international face of the congress, the "all-worldly" character of zaum is deceiving, because for Kruchenykh and Khlebnikov, it relied on the hegemonic position of Slavic languages, or rather sound units, as bearers of meaning—a tension that can be traced to Slavophile or Eurasian exceptionalism. The influence of the performance of multilingualism and the creation of an all-worldly meaning at the congress is reflected in Kruchenykh and Khlebnikov's efforts to generate an "organic" worldly language through the ideological union of the proletariats of East and West under Soviet influence.

While zaum entailed a rejection of rational sense, it by no means openly praised similar manifestations in romanticism. An obsessive rejection of the romantic poetry of Pushkin instead became one of the avant-garde's most notable features. Indeed, Katerina Clark discusses this continuity as "Romantic Anticapitalism," describing the St. Petersburg avant-garde's response to anticapitalist revolutionary politics.[50] The paradoxical temporal orientation of the avant-garde: that is, its simultaneous nostalgia for a prerevolutionary past and anticipation of a revolutionary future manifested in an attack on or, in the words of the avant-garde poet and artist David Burliuk, a "dis-construction" (*dis-konstruktsiia*) of the imperial canon and an investment in romantic poetics.[51] Perhaps the most famous example of this campaign was the futurist manifesto of 1912, "Slap in the Face of Public Taste" (Poshchechina obshchestvennomu vkusu), produced by the futurists Kruchenykh, Mayakovsky, Khlebnikov, and Burliuk. The manifesto famously ordered that the Russian canon of writers—including Pushkin, Dostoevsky, and Tolstoy—must be thrown off the "steamship of contemporaneity" (*s parokhoda sovremennosti*) (Maiakovskii 1939–1949, 1:402–3). This simultaneous celebration and rejection of the imperial canon was coupled with the uncertain embrace of technology and industrialization.

Such themes were particularly important to the Baku writings as the subject of much of the romantic orientalist writings of the nineteenth century, as well as the focus of a Soviet colonial modernity project. Scholars trace the disjuncture between romanticism and modernism in part to the centrality of form in avant-garde art and poetry. However, as Roman Jakobson explains in "Modern Russian Poetry: Velimir Khlebnikov," although romanticism has been historicized as a form of experimentation with the spiritual realm, "the contemporaries of the Romantics thought of the moment exclusively in terms of its formal innovations" (1973, as cited in Gurianova 2012, 95). Jakobson's statement perhaps points to the oversimplification of the notion of a distinctive avant-garde form. Moving beyond romantic poetics, the avant-garde poets instead revived the image of the romantic poet-as-creator and the universalizing force of poetry and art to validate these Soviet modernity discourses.

Khlebnikov's "all-worldly," transrational Transcaucasus was inspired by the figure of Pushkin in the Caucasus. Echoing the evocations of Lermontov's revolutionary Caucasus at the Congress of the Peoples of the East in his notebooks composed in Baku, which reflect his attendance at the congress proceedings, Khlebnikov reveals his preoccupation with Pushkin's Caucasus imaginary. The image of the romantic poet himself provided a model for the ways in which Khlebnikov envisioned space and time on the Soviet Union's frontier. Within Khlebnikov's unpublished notebooks composed in Baku, a *carmen figuratum* takes the form of one of Pushkin's famous self-portraits.[52] Indeed, the poem's subject is appropriate to its portrait of the anti-autocratic Decembrist sympathizer, a revolution centered in the Caucasus and a critique of British imperialism.

Drawing on Pavlovich's fantastic communist railway network and the global topography of the congress's vision of the Eastern International, Khlebnikov generates a network of spatio-temporalities organized around the alliteration of the consonant "B." The expulsive sound "B" echoes in "Baku," "Bombay," "fight" (*boi*), as if creating a figurative "boom" of cannon fire (Hacker 2006, 448). These images of revolution across the Red East are paired with religious "B" images, including references to the Bábist Islamic sect through its leader Mirza Báb and the historic Baku mosque Bibiheybät, named after the daughter of the seventh imam Mūsá al-Kādhim (Kazım), who fled to Baku to escape the persecution of the Abbasid caliph. Both of these symbols signaled a spiritual rupture or revelation from the ruling caliphs and local Islamic institutions, drawing on both religious politics and sound meanings to ground the revolutionary hymn.[53]

Less than ten years after Pushkin was thrown from the "steamship of contemporaneity," the revolution in the East was cast back onto Pushkin as one of the central progenitors of the romantic Caucasus imaginary. However, rejecting an academic analysis of Pushkin and his work, Khlebnikov reconceptualizes a portrait of the man as a world revolutionary. Pushkin's vision of poetry as prophecy and of himself as a "prophet" is central to the *carmen figuratum*. In this way, Khlebnikov relies on Pushkin's self-portrait in order to authorize his own place in the ranks of prophets of Russian and world literature more broadly.[54] Placing the revolution inside Pushkin's self-portrait—and figuratively, his imagination—Khlebnikov maps Pushkin's vision of the Caucasus as a space of freedom onto the Soviet anti-imperial revolution. The image of the prophet that occurs in Khlebnikov's poem not only directly evokes a Russian orientalist fascination with biblical and Qur'anic images but also relates Khlebnikov's utopian vision of the power of technology to unite world languages, connecting space and time through an expansion of the forms in language as the groundwork for transformations in the material world.[55]

While Khlebnikov drew on technology to generate the spiritual energy for his all-worldly language, the symbolist poet and philosopher Viacheslav Ivanov developed a vision of universal poetics. In October 1920, a month after the congress, Ivanov arrived in Baku. Ivanov had been a pivotal figure in the development of modernism in St. Petersburg at the turn of the century, organizing the influential literary salon the Tower, and the poetic workshop the Academy of Verse. Shortly after arriving in Baku, and aided by his former protégé Gorodetsky, he received an appointment from the local division of Narkompros as professor of classical philology and poetics at Baku State University.[56] Unlike Gorodetsky and Kruchenykh, Ivanov occupied a relatively marginal role in the literary and art scene in Baku; however, his appointment at the university provided a forum for émigré writers to organize lecture series. His vision of the relationship between religion and community as connected through sound and verse had a significant impact on the sound experiments and universalist poetic topographies of the avant-garde.

Between November 1920 and June 1924, Ivanov expanded on his theory of universal poetics in his lectures at Baku State University.[57] His history of the development of world poetic forms and aesthetic analysis of their construction engineered his design for the creation of a theory of universal poetic forms. In her analysis of the unpublished course material, Anna Tamarchenko describes the lecture notes as a literary-historical analysis of poetics. Tamarchenko outlines Ivanov's concerns as follows: "the genetics and evolution of poetic forms," the philosophical tradition of aesthetics, and a discussion of the canon as an obligatory code of poetic forms and genres (1986, 85). In particular, she highlights Ivanov's attention to strophes as "the basis of metrical composition" and "simultaneously a finished syntactic and thematic whole" rooted in "speech, consolidated and bound together by the external sound patterns of language" (87, 92–93). It is indeed no coincidence that this theory of poetics bears striking similarities to Mikhail Bakhtin's discussion of the *utterance* and the *chronotope*, as Bakhtin was a great admirer of Ivanov's work. For Ivanov, the strophe, like the *utterance*, is a complete unit of meaning and, like the *chronotope*, provides an image of humanity throughout the ages of world literature (Bakhtin 1997–2012, 3:341–43). Unlike Khlebnikov's and Kruchenykh's theory of the word, poetry for Ivanov does not entail a rejection of rationality but rather its balance with creative intuition, which he casts in terms of Dionysian and Apollonian principles.[58] However, like Khlebnikov and Kruchenykh, Ivanov believed that poetry possessed the power to transform life, albeit not through the inner logic of Slavic sounds but rather through the synthesis of world poetic canons, or styles rooted in speech. Common to both avant-garde visions developed in Baku are an interest in the synergetic and synthetic possibilities of the word and its participation in worldly poetic traditions.

Ivanov calls for a return to collectivity and community through a mystical and mythical experience of art. Perhaps his most important innovation is his synthesis of the Orthodox concept of *sobornost'* with classical philosophy and romantic thought. Like Kruchenykh's and Khlebnikov's reliance on Slavic sounds as the basis of a universal poetics, Ivanov's appropriation of the term *sobornost'* from its Orthodox Christian context privileged a notion of Slavic exceptionalism associated with Slavophilism (Ivanov 2001, xiv).[59] In Ivanov's 1904 treatise "Nietszche and Dionysus," which critiques Nietszche's *The Birth of Tragedy*, he develops a connection between religion (Russian Orthodoxy) and classical myth. Challenging Nietszche's vision of Dionysus as an alternative to Christianity, Ivanov argues that Christ did not betray but rather continued Dionysian pathos. He writes, "The eternal sacrifice and eternal resurrection of the suffering god—this is the religious idea of Dionysian orgiasm" (Ivanov 2001, 180).

In his 1915 essay, "Scriabin's View of Art," he expands on this theme by outlining the relationship between poetry and music. For Ivanov, Scriabin exemplifies a turning point in the consciousness of humanity (Ivanov 2001, 211). He compares Scriabin to the mythic figure of ancient Greece Orpheus, whose "musical" art for Ivanov exemplified the "the indivisible couple Poetry and Music, together with their mentor, Dance" (215). Indeed, the futurist's interest in the musicality of language and the total art of theater grows out of this connection in Ivanov's work. In Ivanov's model faith acts as a "liberating force" that realizes the "collective" (*sobornyi*) and universal ecstasy as a path to universal transfiguration (219). This liberating capacity of art, however, depends on the reciprocal relationship between the artist and art. He writes, "true art is not only free but liberating" because in its very mystery "it is simultaneous creation—with respect to its creator, the artist—and self-creating, *natura naturata* and *natura naturans*" (215). Drawing on Spinoza's *Ethics*, Ivanov replaces God with the figure of the artist-as-creator and nature with art embodying the self-creating power. For Ivanov, art thus structured or reconstructed life, while for futurists such as Khlebnikov, art was linked to a creative power that did not reside outside the self (God) but rather within the cognitive capacity of the artist. These visions of the creative power of art drew on both classical and contemporary philosophy, as well as Russian Orthodox theology.

Ivanov's interest in creative intuition and Khlebnikov's transrational apprehension of meaning can also both be traced to the work of Henri Bergson. Somewhat paradoxically, what is most compelling about Bergson's philosophy is not his influence on the Russian avant-garde but rather his work's resonance with Russian Orthodoxy (Fink 1999, 27–41). Both philosophical traditions reject rational "knowing" and share a common vision of unity through the synthesis of multiple states of consciousness. In both systems, the "I" of the cognizant subject is joined with the "non-I," or object through intuitive knowledge, in turn causing the "I" to exist in harmony with the world (30–31). The subject thus subordinates to the object in order to understand it through the spiritual faith or creative force of intuition. These universalist poetic topographies illustrate the fusion of Orthodox theology and continental philosophy underpinning the spiritual character in the symbolists' and futurists' work.

Returning to Khlebnikov's Baku poems, the states of transrational intuitive consciousness reveal themselves in his poem's parallel structure. In his Pushkin portrait, Khlebnikov creates an internal logic of meaning based on sound patterns. The following segment from his Baku notebooks also echoes the "b" sound in the poem, connecting Baku to the sounds of revolution and religious sites and figures. However, the stanza also juxtaposes the realm of poetry and that of war.

> and they gave him a fight
> Where that word of mine howled
> Horror [howls]
> The howl of cannons—a nightingale.

> и дали ему бой
> Где выло слово мой
> Жуя [воет]
> Вой пушек соловей.
> (cited in Hacker 2006, 452)

Khlebnikov's poem presents two symbolic worlds of poetic love and war within Pushkin's image. Playing on sound and visual symmetry, he juxtaposes "fight," "horror" and "cannons" to the "word" and "nightingale." The "howls," placed in the center, both visually and symbolically connect the worlds of war and love. The second and fourth lines are also joined by the sonance of "word" and "nightingale" (*slovo, solovei*) as elements of love poetry. In the archival notes surrounding the portrait poem, the following verses also evoke the figure of the nightingale: "After all, Pushkin, the tender-throated nightingale, brought out his flute from the throat of the cannon" and "sang the armed nightingale" (as cited in Hacker 2006, 465–66). Khlebnikov thus links the nightingale to the poetic voice of Pushkin as well as to weaponry: "cannons" and "artillery" (*pushki, orudie*).

Pushkin's recurrence as a nightingale emphasizes his symbolic persona as a literary prophet and further articulates his relationship to the orientalist literary canon. The nightingale's song, as a common symbol of pre-Islamic and classical Islamic poetry, represents the poet's songs to the beloved. However, perhaps more relevant to Khlebnikov's portrait of Pushkin is the image of the nightingale that appears in one of his orientalist works from 1824, "The Fountain of Bakhchisarai." The story recounts the life of Qirim Giray, ruler of the Crimean khanate (1758–1764, 1768–1769), and his unrequited love for a Polish captive in his harem (Pushkin 1979, 4:235). While the poem, which is one of Pushkin's most famous works, is set in Crimea rather than the Caucasus, it is replete with references to Islamic poetic symbols, including the songs of nightingales. Indeed, the very first lines offer a quotation from the thirteenth-century Persian poet Sa'dī. Furthermore, Pushkin's source material for this citation has been attributed to Thomas Moore's *Lalla Rookh,* implying a tertiary level of orientalist intertextuality and a commitment to orientalist fashion.[60] Perhaps most fascinating, the recurrent parallels of poetry and war in both Moore and Sa'dī's texts, like Khlebnikov's work, oppose the transience of earthly might to the eternal force of poetry. Invoking Sa'dī and Moore through Pushkin's orientalist fashion, Khlebnikov's portrait of revolution in the East reiterates the political force of poetry. Both spiritual and creative intuition are evoked in the figures of the nightingale and the romantic poet, which for Khlebnikov endure after the cannon fire has settled. Khlebnikov's vision of intuition is not only reliant on the symbols of a single great religious text. Like Ivanov's canons, it refers to the synthesis of worldly symbolic forms from European and Russian orientalism, to Islamic (and pre-Islamic) poetry. While this fusion may not have been as organic as Kruchenykh had hoped, Baku and the Transcaucasus more broadly inspired Khlebnikov's attempts at a corrective to a Russian orientalist vision of the Caucasus, albeit one that inadvertently also called on Soviet internationalist propaganda in its imagination of a utopian transrational worldly poetic language.

The universal topographies that emerged in both Khlebnikov's and Kruchenykh's zaum and Ivanov's Dionysian *sobornost',* as well as the carnivalesque spirit of Gorodetsky's sketches and verse, exemplify the Russian émigrés' utopian visions of art and life on the Soviet eastern frontier. The reciprocal relationship between art and life in Baku was shaped by an emphasis on the creative power of poetry—*poesis*—as well as the role of avant-garde aesthetics in shaping political discourse. The Russian émigré writers thus conceived of art diversely, from Ivanov's neoclassical conception of a spiritual world collectivity to Gorodetsky's vision of the artist as a carnivalesque builder of the new Soviet capital. These avant-garde conceptualizations of the role of the poet and writer in the new society, which had remained on the margins of politics before the revolution, were transformed by the utopian imaginary of the Eastern International. An orientalist image of Baku as a timeless, mysterious, and universal poetic landscape, as if on the threshold between Europe and Asia, indeed suited futurist and symbolist aesthetics. However, placed in the context of the formation of Soviet Azerbaijan and Soviet expansion, representations of Baku in the work of the émigré writers blended state power with a more spiritual or anarchic concept of revolutionary force that had been cultivated in the imperial metropole decades earlier. In this way, the Baku avant-garde harnessed its prerevolutionary creative poetics to generate a new image of the Eastern International centered in Baku.

Art in the Streets: Mayakovsky and Vechorka's Baku

Breaking from Gorodetsky's and Khlebnikov's timeless and all-worldly orientalist imaginary of the revolutionary Caucasus, the poets Vladimir Mayakovsky and Tatiana Vechorka centered their visions of the city around life on the streets. Their innovations on modernist themes emerge from descriptions of the city captured in fragmented images of Baku as a bustling industrial capital. In this way, their poetry also challenges an image of a provincial Baku, representing it instead as a vital Soviet metropole. In 1921 Mayakovsky composed "Order no. 2 to the Army of Arts" (Prikaz no. 2 po armii iskusstv). His first "Order" directed at the arts was delivered in 1918, after the October revolution. This second "Order," which followed three years later, was composed in revolutionary and newly Soviet Baku. Unlike the futurists' transrational vision of an all-worldly language of poetry, Mayakovsky highlights the space of the streets and Baku's industrial landscape as the symbolic building blocks for a new society. He writes:

At each river's source,
Lying with a hole in its side,

The steamship howled through the docks:
"Give (us) oil from Baku!"
While we drag it out and argue,
In search of secret meaning,
The things resound a cry:
"Give us new forms!"

У каждой реки на истоке,
лёжа с дырой в боку,
пароходы провыли доки:
«Дайте нефть из Баку!»
Пока канителим, спорим,
смысл сокровенный ища:
«Дайте нам новые формы!»—
несётся вопль по вещам.
    (Maiakovskii 1939–1949, 2:86–88)

Although the poem is not fashioned around Mayakovsky's memorable stepladder form, its structure highlights the voices of the workers and poets, which emerge from within its body in short interjected orders. Mayakovsky's vision of the city reflects the style of the short slogans and window art he created during his work at both the Moscow and Baku divisions of Rosta. The first actor in the stanza is a steamship, a common image in the avant-garde's poetic lexicon symbolizing the technologies of the twentieth century. Here, the steamship is located alongside a generative romantic symbol—the river's source. However, Mayakovsky's river here does not evoke the romantic, spiritual powers of creation, as do the mythic rivers and streams highlighted at the congress, but rather signifies the colonial infrastructure, delivering steam power and oil. The stanza constructs a parallel between the images of the thoughtful poet and industrial power. The inspirational and life-giving source of the river yields the steamship, which in turn calls out for oil. The speeding steamship similarly alludes both to Baku's location as a Caspian seaport and to the futurist order to throw the nineteenth-century Russian canon off the "steamship of contemporaneity." The order for the colonial product parallels the order for "new forms." Colonial Baku provides oil and poetry as the raw materials for the construction of a new Soviet society. For Mayakovsky, Soviet modernity is thus directed by art. The "new forms" that the world of things cries out for possess the power, literal and figurative, to "pull the republic out of the mud" (2:86–88). As Gorodetsky does in his Hymn, Mayakovsky presents art as a dimension of colonial economics and state building, oriented toward the modernization of the Soviet Union's eastern frontier.

Vechorka's verse also conveys the civic role of art. However, unlike Mayakovsky's emphasis on colonial economics, her poetry reflects the power of art to transform the physical and spiritual space of the city. She describes the power of propaganda in her 1919 poem "The Temptation of Posters" (Soblazn afish):

> On the street of the wasted capital,
> Littered with repainted newspapers,
> A horde of silent poets move
> The pieces of spared pages.

> на улице истощенной столицы
> заваленной перекрашенными газетами
> двинет орда притихших поэтов
> куски сбереженных страниц.
>
> (2007, 95)[61]

Vechorka's "wasted capital" is animated by the movement of paper—newspapers, poetry, and posters. Vechorka's work for BakKavRosta around this time suggests that the posters probably refer to propaganda, linking political events to the "spared pages" of poets such as herself who were experimenting with political art in the service of BakKavRosta. As avant-garde emissaries, she notes that the poems also "will lay theaters instead of roofs," their cultural nourishment serving as a symbolic form of shelter. The final couplet, however, abandons these social concerns, comparing the posters to the romantic and sensual forces of temptation. Vechorka describes the cognitive act of reading a poster through a biological and romantic image—"incombustible nerves"—which contrasts with the image of a fragile vitrine. The power of the posters, Vechorka suggests, lies in their artistic capacity to tempt the physiological and spiritual desire of the viewer.

Tatiana Tol'staia (Efimova) was born in Baku in 1892 and took the penname Vechorka during her school years in St. Petersburg studying sculpture. The name evokes the moon goddesses and sisters Zor'ka,

Vechorka, and Nochka (Dawn, Evening, and Night) from Russian folk-tales (Vechorka 2007, 5). After making connections in the futurist circles in St. Petersburg, she gained prominence in the émigré literary scene in Tiflis, contributing to various avant-garde journals—including *41°*, *Friendship* (*Druzhestvo*), and *Al'fa-Lira*—translating local poets, and writing on local cultural affairs. In 1919 she moved to Baku, where she continued to participate in the avant-garde scene, studying with Ivanov at Baku State University, participating in the Poets' Circle, and publishing poetry alongside Kruchenykh and Khlebnikov in the collections *Zamaul'* (1919) and *The World and the Rest* (*Mir i ostal'noe* [1920]).[62] While in Tiflis and Baku, her work was particularly influenced by zaum poetics. To this end, she notes the importance of sound in her work, "sounds in any order appear as creative materials" (Vechorka 2007, 16). Her poetry indeed exhibits a strong concern for the texture of sound and image, however this experimental form is tempered by an interest in the daily life of the city and often a sculptor's sense of materiality. In addition to her own three poetic collections *Magnolias* (*Magnolii*), *Helpless Tenderness* (*Bespomoshchnaia nezhnost'*), and The *Temptation of Posters*, Vechorka translated works of the Georgian symbolists Grigol Robakidze, Titsian Tabidze, and Paolo Iashvili and the Armenian futurist Hakob Kara-Darvish, among others. Her poetry thus captures a vision of the Caucasus with a certain familiarity and tenderness that softens her futurist poetic flourishes.

As both a woman and a native of Baku, she represents a unique voice within a male-dominated émigré community. Her portraits of the city are marked by both the estranging effect of Russian avant-garde aesthetics and a familiar gaze. The poem "Baku" highlights the transformative force of industrialization and the rise of Bolshevik power. She writes:

Clouds, rough like calico
Lower, their edges sprinkled with rain.
City of oily iron [railway] obelisks,
They say that I was born here.

The port stirs in the dusty smoke . . .
Today's day is clearer than yesterday's.
The birds hover over the Maiden Tower,
And the spring north [wind] brings clay.

Persian blue stores.
The sea—a flat cement veranda . . .
A heavy barge loads,
And buzzes around the hydroplane dock.

A sleepy cool wave
Licks the moss-grown post of the bathhouse.
Women's laughter splashes across the distant cabin,
And breaks off screeching like a string.

The greenery dries and burns.
The dust of the shelly-sandy boulevard.
In the frames of the mourning agit poster:
Twenty-six. Shot commissars.

The smell of oil, fruit, tobacco . . .
The sweat of heat, work, and trade . . .
The asphaltic winged roofs expand
Not a province—a colony—Baku

Облака, шершавые как бязь
опускаются, края дождем опрыскав.
Город нефтянях железных обелисков—
говорят, что здесь я родилась.

В пыльном дыме шевелится порт . . .
День сегодняший яснее, чем вчерашний.
Вьются птицы над Девичьей башней,
и несет саман весенний норд.

Голубые лавки персиан.
Море плоская цементная веранда . . .
Грузится тяжелая шаланда,
и жужжит у дока гидроплан.

Сонная прохладная волна
Лижет обомшелый столб купальни.
Плещет женский смех в кабине дальней,
Обрываясь взвизгом как струна.

Зелень высыхает и горит.
Пыль ракушечно-песочного бульвара.
В рамках траурных плакат-агит:
Двадцать шест. Расстрелянные комиссары.

Запах нефти, фруктов, табаку . . .
Пот жары, работы и торговли . . .
Развернет асфальтовые крылья-кровли
Не провинция—колония—Баку.

(2007, 139)

In contrast to the fantastic symbolic lexicon of "The Temptation of Posters," the simple enclosing quatrains of "Baku" trace the familiar images of the city, highlighting its key industrial features: oil and railroads, as well as its most iconic cultural monument—the Maiden Tower.[63] In her portrait of the mechanization of the city, she exposes the introduction of new industrial materials, lending them a magical quality in her representations of "asphaltic winged roofs," the "oily iron obelisks," "the sea—a flat cement veranda," and "the hydroplane dock." However, unlike Gorodetsky and Khlebnikov's visions of a primordial revolutionary Caucasus, Vechorka captures the movement of the city. She notes the changes in the weather from one day to the next, "Today's day is clearer than yesterday's," and the force of life surrounding the mythic monuments, "The birds hover over the Maiden Tower." She also highlights the lives of common people: "the sweat of heat, work, and trade" and the "Persian blue stores." The tone of the verse captures the loneliness and alienation of the forces of industrialization, while its starkness presents the city in snapshots, preferring a language of daily life to transrational, transnational poetic formations. The style of the poem suits its inclusion in Vechorka's 1927 collection *A Third of a Soul (Tret'dushi)*. However, it was actually penned March 10, 1919, when Vechorka was experimenting with zaum. Among the avant-garde forms that Vechorka's work embraces are the use of archaic compound adjectives characteristic of eighteenth-century verse, untraditional rhythms, and the phonetic enhancement of speech through the repetition of the phonemes *zh, z, ch, shch*, which contrast with the alliteration of *l*.[64]

The second to last stanza of the work reveals the context of its composition amid the rise of Bolshevik power. The final couplet reads, "In the frames of the mourning agit poster: / Twenty-six. Shot commissars." The twenty-six commissars were Bolshevik and Left Socialist Revolutionary members of the Baku Soviet Commune, which was a temporary Soviet Baku government that controlled the city from November 1917 through July 1918. After the overthrow of the commune, the commissars tried to escape by boat, only to be arrested and executed by anti-Bolshevik forces in Turkmenistan. Indeed, as Michael G. Smith writes, "The hagiography for the murdered 'Twenty-six' . . . became one of the most memorable and enduring in all of Soviet political culture (second only to the Lenin cult)" (2001, 379). The executions also coincided with the founding of the Azerbaijan Democratic Republic. In March 1919 several leading party members—including Anastas Mikoyan, who had accompanied the twenty-six and narrowly escaped execution himself—brought news about the deaths, claiming that the British had orchestrated the affair. The myth of the heroic twenty-six thus supported the Bolshevik ideological campaign against British imperialism. Bolshevik agitators organized workers' demonstrations and a memorial for the twenty-six on March 20, the advertisements for which Vechorka describes.[65]

Drawing on these events, Vechorka captures an unstable moment in Bolshevik revolutionary history under the Azerbaijan Democratic Republic and the opening of the local propaganda department at Bak-KavRosta. In Vechorka's work the myth of the commissars as a charge against British imperialism stands alongside the humble details of the sweat of workers, women's laughter in the bathhouses, and the dusty boulevard, which present a vision of daily life in the city. Indeed, she notes the frames of the poster, emphasizing its material qualities as an object in the street. Baku emerges in her words not as a province but rather as a poetic and physical center for change and development. Vechorka's recentering of Baku as a colony presents an ambivalent vision of the city that challenges a stylized conception of a new Eastern International as it places art on the streets and "a horde of silent poets" as the order of a new future.

Iskusstvo: The Total Art of Narkompros

In accordance with his leadership role in BakKavRosta, Gorodetsky served as editor and leading contributor to Baku Narkompros's official journal *Art*, which printed three issues in 1921. Although the original designs for the journal planned for dual-language texts in Russian and Azeri, the project was realized exclusively in Russian, with only two articles on cultural features of Baku by Azeri intellectuals: "Muslim Theater" (Teatr u musulman) by the playwright Abdurrahim bey Haqverdiev and "The Tasks of the Musical Enlightenment of Azerbaijan" (Muzykal'no-prosvetitel'nye zadachi Azerbaidzhana) by the composer Üzeyir Hacıbeyov. The journal outlined Baku Narkompros's aims to unite ethnographic study with the creative faculties of art and the political force of propaganda.[66] The total art of Narkompros thus emphasized the interconnection of the arts—theater, graphic arts, music, and poetry—through the state-building project. It also highlighted an aesthetic will to power, which I argue orchestrated a connection between the ideologies of the Soviet imperial center and the Azerbaijani national Bolsheviks.

Art's content featured a diverse assortment of poetry, ethnography, and reports on the infrastructure and projects of BakKavRosta, including poetry by leading Russian symbolist, acmeist, and futurist poets (including Kruchenykh's "Declaration of the Transrational Language"), an analysis of Baku's historic architecture, the theater repertoire, and descriptions of the divisions of the arts department. The first issue hailed "a struggle between factions—European and Asian—as a collision of two comets—the fabulously dreamed east of manuscripts, frescoes, carpets, and coinage and European cubism, futurism, [and] supremacism" (Chichkanov 1921, 13–15). Echoing these concepts, the cover of the first issue of the journal features a stylized art nouveau black ink print on white paper. The title is framed by two *ashiq* figures, or Caucasus/Central Asian bards, dressed only in linen cloths tied with tasseled belts, turbans, and jackboots.

Like classical muses the bards are depicted with pen, paper, and a stringed instrument resembling the *tar* (an instrument popular in Persia, the Caucasus, and Central Asia). Their contoured bodies trace the arches of the surrounding trees and forest plants. A classic orientalist image is here distinguished by the odd juxtaposition of the jackboots, emphasizing the militarized force of the cultural front of the Eastern International.

Gorodetsky framed the objectives of the journal as a project to recover a "lost eastern past" and institute a new artistic regime for the future. In the journal's first issue he described the aims of the Soviet mission in

Figure 1. Cover art for the first issue of the Baku Narkompros journal *Art*, 1920

Baku as equal parts avant-garde art, ethnography, and Soviet politics. He writes:

> In this advanced revolutionary stronghold of the East, all of the grand chal-
> lenges of new art that are set and resolved in Soviet Russia, acquire partic-
> ular significance here in Baku, Azerbaijan. The East and with it Azerbaijan
> still knows the old art forms that have been forgotten in the West. Here the
> Ashugs still sing, here live musical improvisation has not transcended daily
> life into ornament. In simple forms, art deeply roots itself in the masses. Ar-
> tistic instinct is drunk with mother's milk. Carpets, miniatures, maiolica—
> all that the West admires in its museums in the East is preserved in life. All
> this creates a fertile ground for the development of art in Baku and in Azer-
> baijan . . . The work is not only to implant the techniques of European artis-
> tic works here but also to call for a new life for the great art of the East. And
> if Soviet Russia requires of its artists an enormous charge [*napriazhenie*] of
> creative forces, then in Azerbaijan this charge should double. (1921, 5–6)

Gorodetsky accords value to Baku not only as the Soviet Orient, a reposi-
tory for "ancient knowledge," but as a political capital, a place where challenges are resolved. It is a place that preserves the old and "creates a fertile
ground for the development" of a new form of art through propaganda
deeply rooted in the evolution of the proletarian masses. Gorodetsky's fusion of propaganda and art lies in the structure of his comparison, as well
as in his discourse of social engineering.

Following Gorodetsky's imagery, Soviet avant-garde art and the proletarian masses could be nurtured by the *charge* (*napriazhenie*) of creative
forces rooted in "simple forms" of Azerbaijani culture. The discourse of
social evolution provides a linkage between the natural artistic instinct,
"drunk with mother's milk," and the electrification of Soviet Azerbaijan. The term *napriazhenie*, which belongs to the same semantic field as
lightning (*molniia*) and current or charge (*razriad*), was popular in avant-
garde poetry as well as political speeches at the beginning of the twentieth
century.[67] Similarly, at the Congress of the Peoples of the East the head
of the Communist International, Karl Radek, described the Soviet frontier in the opening rally through this rhetoric, "From here will flow an
electric current of political awareness."[68] In the domain of avant-garde
poetry, the electrical image resonated with several diverse discourses,
which particularly among the futurists were signified simultaneously.
Electric images recalled the eighteenth-century scientist and philosopher
Mikhail Lomonosov's vision of social enlightenment, biblical references to
the apocalypse, the mystical realm of necromancy, and Lenin's project to
bring power to the Soviet Union (Banerjee 2012, 110). In the context of
agitprop, the romantic creationist impulse was connected to the realm of
praxis or action. The trope of electricity thus realized the transformation
of the spiritual and poetic force of creation into political propaganda.

Much of this romantic rhetoric, harnessed to proletarian ends, animated the journal. To this end, the little-known Russian futurist poet
Nikolai Makridin's essay "On Proletarian Art" argued for the function
of poetry as an affective synthesis between experience and the material
world. Makridin writes:

> The artistic form is no other than the equilibrium point between external el-
> ements and internal feeling, between the world and the "I." The suffering,
> ruined soul considers its relationship to the world. The world fills it with

feeling; it feels its experiences in the form of the elements of the wind, the desert, and the river. The elements here not only lend rhythm and words but also the image, as a poetic likeness. In the poetic image, in this pale descendant of the original word, the artistic form completes itself in the synthesis of the world and the "I." (1921, 33)

Although Makridin does not mention the Soviet eastern frontier, his presentation of this theory of poetic synthesis in accordance with the journal's aims echoes much of the work of the historical poetics school, highlighting a continuity in the development of a modernist lyric subjectivity in aesthetic and literary experiments in early Soviet Baku as a central component to the Eastern International propaganda project.

The journal approached this ideal of cultural synthesis through discussions and representations of musical and graphic media. Hacıbeyov's "Problems of the Musical Enlightenment of Azerbaijan" promotes a fusion of Western technological modernity with the "spiritual-aesthetic" (*razvitie dukhovno-esteticheskoe*) power of the culture of the Soviet East (1921, 25–58). In another short entry on the Free Satir-Agit Theater (Svobodnyi satiragit-teatr), Hacıbeyov notes the high illiteracy rates among the Muslims of the Caucasus and argues that music, art, and theater play a seminal role in the success of the Bolshevik enlightenment project. Theoretical analysis of music, he writes, promotes the use of "scientific data" to identify "the exact foundations of oriental music" while concerning the "execution of authentic oriental motifs" Azerbaijanis must access their "spiritual understanding" of the art. Theater similarly connects directly to the worker peasant, "becoming the organizer of the psyche of the proletarian masses" (1921, 37).

The conception of work as a spiritual as well as an ideological ideal was reflected in some of the graphic designs printed through BakKav-Rosta.[69] Indeed, in the banner for the organization—"proletariats of all countries unite!"—"proletariats" was translated into Azeri as "working poor" (*bütün cehan faqra kasabası toplaşık*), reflecting an Islamic conception of work. The term *kasab*, as Sultan Galiev glosses, is one of the important teachings of Islam, "the duty to engage in trade and to work." He outlines this Islamic duty to work in addition to "the absence of private property in lands, waters, and forests" as cultural commandments that would facilitate Bolshevik anti-religious propaganda in the Muslim

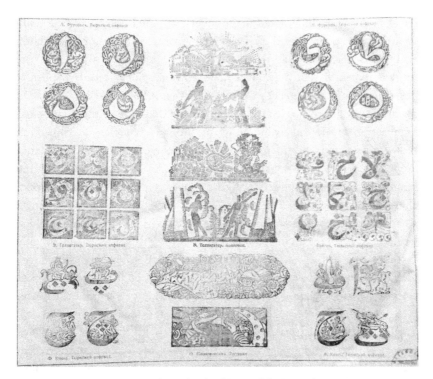

Figure 2. Designs from the third issue of the journal *Art*, 1921

territories ([1921] 1979, 146). Drawing on Sultan Galiev's designs for Muslim communist propaganda, the posters promote the figure of the Muslim communist revolutionary as an avant-garde hero, uniting all countries through a universally understandable community of words, images, and ethical principles.

The last issue of *Art* contains a collection of graphics, including portraits of Lenin and Marx, as well as historic architectural plans of Baku's old city. Some of the most intriguing examples of these prints include a selection of miniature vignettes depicting oil workers, life in the Soviet East, and block designs based on the letters of the old script alphabet.

The letters of the alphabet, adorned by ornate human and animal figures performing various activities—hunting, dancing, cooking, and playing music—are printed alongside Russian script drawn in a fashion to resemble Ottoman-Arabo-Persian calligraphy. The prints most clearly recall the style of illuminated manuscripts, although they place the body of the worker peasant at the center of the sacred text. Although the body is not articulated through the script itself, the designs also evoke the fourteenth-century Hurufi calligraphic tradition, which accords a spiritual power to the script as a veil for God (*Iskusstvo*, no. 2/3 [1921], table VI).[70] As avant-garde agitprop based on a heterodoxic doubling of the illuminated manuscript and Hurufi calligraphy, the designs articulate a connection between the letter and the image, as well as the ethnographic object and modernist art. In this way the spiritual power of letters embodied in the figure of the worker is understood through its investment in the "national character" of the Soviet East.

Soviet anti-imperialist ideology promoted a vision of modernity, which like Klee's *Angelus Novus* remained fixated on a Russian orientalist past. In the minds of the Russian émigré poets and Bolshevik politicians the idea of the new Soviet eastern frontier was thus built on a paradoxical celebration and rejection of the past. This tension persisted in the Soviet celebration of forms of heterodoxy joining the seemingly paradoxical spiritual with the rational, as well as the East with the West, and multilingual with monolingual. The experiments of the Baku émigrés, which included Gorodetsky's interest in the carnival poetics of the prerevolutionary years, the congress's fascination with Decembrist poetry, Khlebnikov's and Kruchenykh's zaum, Ivanov's universal poetics, and Mayakovsky's call for new forms outlined a Soviet eastern imaginary that fused an idea of romantic revolutionary freedom with a utopian vision of an international or universal Soviet language and subjectivity.

Ivanov's and Khlebnikov's theoretical formations, which are echoed in Vechorka's verse, draw an important connection between avant-garde art and Russian Orthodox spirituality that extended beyond a symbolic revival of the Russian imperial past. Ivanov's explicit insertion of Christ in the Nietzschean Dionysian spirit and the more implicit resonances of the bond among spiritual consciousness, intuitive knowledge, and freedom in Khlebnikov's and Ivanov's work envisioned the creative power of art to render legible a vision of Baku as the window onto the formation of a heterodox anti-imperial Soviet colonial politics. In this way, the Soviet orientalist imaginary utilized the physical and symbolic space of Baku—on the threshold between Europe and Asia—to authorize the first years of its anti-imperial colonial expansion. Offering a more nuanced image of Baku from the streets, Vechorka's poetry provides the most grounded portrait of the émigrés working for BakKavRosta. Compared to Gorodetsky's masculinist image of the Harlequin busily drilling and merrily welcoming Sovietization, her vision of the power of art to transform both the physical and the spiritual space of the city anticipates early Soviet propaganda.

The dream of the avant-garde was to create, in the words of Rancière, the "sensible forms and material structures" of an Eastern International and with it a new society, however much it conflicted with the real political conditions of centralization and the subordination of art to the party in the imperial metropole during the late 1920s and 1930s. Despite the poets' active role working for BakKavRosta in Baku, much of the Russian avant-garde poetry produced there between 1919 and 1920 revels in the playful images of prerevolutionary aesthetics. However, the idea of Baku as capital of the new Soviet East nonetheless influenced the creation of universal poetic topographies, including the theoretical formations of Kruchenykh's and Khlebnikov's zaum and Ivanov's symbolist poetics. Vechorka's vision of Baku from the streets instead balances avant-garde forms with snapshots of life "in the colony." While these poetic experiments articulated the tensions within the political structures of Soviet expansion, they also echo much of the official propaganda of BakKavRosta, produced collaboratively by Russian and Azeri artists. These early propaganda experiments generated between 1919 and 1921 not only relied on a connection to an orientalist imaginary of the Caucasus but on the creation of a Muslim communist subjectivity. In this way, the contributions of the Baku émigrés provided linkages between avant-garde anarchist poetics and state-sponsored art while creating a powerful ideological bond between the Caucasus and the Soviet Union as the center of the Soviet East. Soviet Baku thus became a leader in infrastructural development and literary modernity. This political bond rested on the material economic resources of the oil industry, as well as the aesthetic resources of the nineteenth-century Caucasus imaginary. Such a recentering of the Soviet Union in Baku, in turn, cloaked Soviet imperial expansion and the *translatio imperii* in the merry play of the Russian avant-garde and its revolutionary imaginary of the opening of a "window onto the East."

4

BROKEN VERSE

The Materiality of the Symbol
in New Turkic Poetics

Describing the revolutionary writers' circles of the 1920s, the Azeri poet Süleyman Rüstem recalled the Russian poet Vladimir Mayakovsky, whose "great stride and wrestler's build [*pehlevan*]" attracted attention in the Baku streets. Rüstem's description of Mayakovsky's presence fuses the Persianate mytho-poetic hero (*pehlevan*) with the memory of the physicality of the poet's gait. Recalling Mayakovsky's literary salons in Baku, Rüstem describes the agitation of crowds of young intellectuals, engineers, teachers, writers, and students, with creative energies charged to direct the working masses. He quotes Mayakovsky at one such event, "In particular, you Baku poets must work in conjunction with the workers in the plants, factories, and oil fields. Without this it is impossible to create new literature. They are your readers! Without a reader there is no poet" (2005, 2:239). In his portrait of Mayakovsky in Baku, Rüstem imagines his new Turkic Muslim readers through his vision of the arrival of the Russian poet as a familiar mythic hero in the Caucasus. This interpolation of the Russian poet at the helm of a new Turkic tradition indeed recalls

Axundov's image of Pushkin at the center of his rose garden. However, instead of embodying the divine figure of the prophet, Mayakovsky here stands with the weight of a wrestler, ushering in a new poetic tradition by grounding the mythic past in the Baku streets. Rüstem's description of Mayakovsky's legacy in the Caucasus emphasizes the role of literature to excite and organize the Muslim worker-reader as central to the creation of postrevolutionary Azeri poetry under the first years of Soviet control. While Mayakovsky is rarely mentioned by the Azeri poets, his evocation here provides a key to the impact of materialist aesthetics on the formation of the Turkic Soviet poetry of the 1920s.

As I discussed in chapter 3, for the Russian avant-garde Baku occupied an important place in the imagination of a utopian future in the Soviet East and as the site of oil resources crucial to the Soviet state-building project. While many Azeri poets writing under the Azerbaijan Democratic Republic (1918–1920) as well as the new Soviet government (established in 1920) played a major role in the construction of a national-Soviet imaginary, their vision of literary modernity challenged the more static vision of the East generated by the Russian avant-garde. Rather, during the 1920s Azeri poets sustained a prerevolutionary vision of the Caucasus, tied to a history of overlapping cultural and geopolitical interests— Russian, Ottoman, and Persian—as well as heterodox and heteroglossic literary works characteristic of journals produced under Russian imperial rule such as *Molla Nesreddin* and *Enlightenment*.

The dissemination of Bolshevik populist ideologies found echoes in the foregrounding of the figure of the reader as central to the development of new Soviet Azerbaijani verse. The Füyuzat school—with its particular interest in Persian and Ottoman neoclassicism, French Parnassianism, and German romanticism—was often targeted by the Bolsheviks and charged with "distancing the people from today's world" (Quliyev 2008, 213). Much like the Russian avant-garde, Soviet Turkic writers expressed their commitment to "the birth of people's [*xalq*] literature from life," marking their break from the romanticist past in name, although not always conceptually (214). While the Füyuzat school had stressed an interest in the role of intuition in the formation of a community of readers, the literary production of the postrevolutionary years instead emphasized the material and social world as a basis through which philosophical and aesthetic concepts could be worked out.

The Azeri writers' group known as the Red Pens (Qızıl qelemler), which was founded by the Soviet Council for Propaganda in 1925, was ultimately disbanded for perceived nationalist deviations; however, many of its writers continued to play a role in the Azerbaijani Association of Proletarian Writers in the 1930s.[1] This chapter analyzes postrevolutionary Azeri poetry produced by the Red Pens and its members' relationship to the prerevolutionary Füyuzat school, as well as to the formal and philosophical movements of the Russian avant-garde. The Soviet annexation of the Caucasus and subsequent creation of the Azerbaijan Soviet Socialist Republic shaped a twofold vision of Soviet modernity oriented toward the international purview of socialism, understood as the destruction of propertied classes, and étatist nationalism, reliant on the creation of state property.[2] As part of the creation of this new state cultural capital, which also participated in the Soviet Eastern International imaginary, the Soviet government supported the new Turkic poetry movement. This early Soviet Turkic poetry articulated an interest in Marxist-Leninist aesthetics by foregrounding an act of sociopolitical organization as central to the literary project while retaining ties to the romantic symbolism of the Arabo-Persian-Ottoman lyric traditions.

On the one hand, the gradual abandonment of syllabic and *aruz* metrics reflected diminishing cultural ties to the Ottoman tradition and the formation of a Soviet Muslim Turkic tradition. On the other hand, the belated printing in the old (Arabo-Persian) script until 1929, despite the official launch of the alphabet reforms in 1922, generated a sense of continuity with Arabo-Persian and Ottoman poetry while also pragmatically evading centralized Soviet censorship. This ambivalent position in relation to the Arabo-Persian-Ottoman past and the Soviet future articulated a brief period of avant-garde Turkic Muslim communist poetry in the 1920s, during the formation of the Azerbaijan Soviet Socialist Republic. Fixed on this romantic conception of poetic intuition and, at the same time, with a materialist interest in the social world, the Red Pens attempted to articulate a new Turkic poetry, which staged the poetic encounter with a materialist aesthetics.

While writing as a form of technological innovation was central to the construction of a narrative of rationalism, progress, and modernity, a less visible negotiation between the imagination of the material world and a symbolic literary space provided the foundation for poetic developments of the 1920s on the Soviet colonial periphery. To illustrate this transformation, I discuss a series of works written by the Red Pens, beginning with Huseyn Cavid's 1918 play *Iblis*, which represents this period of political and cultural upheaval through an Islamic version of the Faustian myth set against the backdrop of the Middle Eastern theater of World War I. The major figures of the new verse experiments also included Nazim Hikmet, whose collection *Song of the Sun Drinkers* was published in Baku in 1928, and the leading figure of the Red Pens, Süleyman Rüstem. Influenced by Mayakovsky's literary theory and the Turkic folk ballad, Hikmet and Rüstem developed a new Turkic poetics that shaped a vision of Muslim communism during the early formation of the Soviet Union, until Stalinization. These tumultuous years following the 1917 revolution shaped the vision of Turkic Muslim identity within the Soviet Union, articulating a battle over symbols as instruments for the construction of a new society. Although the official Soviet takeover of Baku occurred in 1920, the struggle between conflicting impulses within the largely Russophone Soviet bureaucracy and the Turkophone intelligentsia generated a fragmented transition to Soviet national identity characterized by the reception of materialist aesthetics in Turkic poetry.

The oft-quoted materialist statement, "art is not a mirror to hold up to society but a hammer with which to shape it," has been attributed to both Bertold Brecht and Vladimir Mayakovsky. However, its most concrete citation can be found in Leon Trotsky's 1924 treatise *Literature and Revolution* (*Literatura i revoliutsiia*). In his discussion of Russian Futurism Trotsky writes,

Art, they say, is not a mirror but a hammer: it does not reflect, it transforms. But at present even the mastery of a hammer is taught with the help of a mirror—that is, a sensitive film that captures all the moments of movement . . . If one cannot shave oneself without a mirror, how can one reconstruct oneself or one's life, without seeing oneself in the "mirror" of literature?

Искусство—говорят нам—не зеркало, а молот: оно не отражает, а преображает. Но ныне и молотом владеть учатся и учат при помощи «зеркала», т.е., светочувствительной пластинки, которая запечатлевает все моменты движения . . . Для того чтобы побриться, нельзя обойтись без зеркала. А как же перестроить себя, свой быт, не глядясь в «зеркало» литературы? (1991, 111)

Trotsky summarizes one of the most significant debates within the post-revolutionary avant-garde—whether to envision the new role of art as a tool for destroying the old world order or a field for generating a new society. The vision of art as a hammer evokes the destructive impulse within the avant-garde—its revolutionary momentum—while the mirror and camera express socialist realism's constructive impulse—the power of art to generate social practice through its reflection of the self and social relations more broadly. Indeed, Trotsky reframes Lenin's reflection theory, which outlined cognition as the basis for the reflection of reality. While this materialist theory served as the basis for agitprop and socialist realism, Trotsky's emphasis on the exploration of consciousness also marks a point of transition from the avant-garde to socialist realist projects. Indeed, this vision of art is crucial to understanding the ways in which the Turkic Muslim communist subject was mediated in the process of cultural Sovietization. Competing visions of the role of politics in structuring the formation of a new poetics were further compounded by the task of structuring the new Soviet multinational empire and a cohesive vision of Soviet culture in the Turkic Muslim Caucasus. For the Red Pens, poetry provided a medium to negotiate the Russian-dominant Soviet vision of modern literature with an older romantic Turkic poetic tradition in order to reflect a politically engaged Turkic Muslim communist reader.

In *The Political Unconscious*, Fredric Jameson notably takes up this process of mediation between the inward-focused hermeneutics of the symbol and its external animation through materialist structures. Jameson argues that Marxism, as the universal collective struggle between oppressor and oppressed, often disguised in symbolic form, underlies all the "essential *mystery* of the cultural past" (1981, 20). In this way, he outlines a strategy for "detecting the traces of that uninterrupted narrative, in restoring to the surface of the text the repressed and buried reality of this fundamental history, that the doctrine of a political unconscious finds its function and its necessity" (20). Jameson's political unconscious hinges on a Lacanian model of reading that foregrounds the relationship between the imaginary and symbolic in which the latter designates a mode of criticism that transcends the ideological representation of reality. For Jameson, Lacan provides a means through which psychoanalysis mediates the relationship between the social and the individual without reducing it to a symptomatic reading of individual psychology. Jameson's critical reading practice imagines psychoanalysis not as the symbolic mastery of the subject over object but rather as the *intersubjective* position of the analyst, who both expresses a commitment to desire and a listening distance from it, distinguishing the object of desire from the experience of the desiring subject. Jameson's recuperation of the political content of cultural texts, itself indebted to the tradition of literary and artistic modernism, offers a Lacanian update to Trotsky's reflective principle, albeit one directed toward the restoration of the struggle between oppressor and oppressed to the surface of the textual encounter, rather than the application of poetry to ideological ends.[3]

Jameson's model can be useful for understanding the vision of political art that developed after the October revolution, at a moment when the relationship between literature and politics was still in the process of being reformulated and institutionalized across the multinational empire. The institutionalization of the arts under the new Soviet bureaucracy, and furthermore its colonial apparatus, called for the state sponsorship of art and for the central position of materialist aesthetics to this political project. Art during this period was placed at the forefront of efforts to formulate a new Soviet consciousness. Soviet subjectivity was generated in the discursive exchanges through which Marxist-Leninist ideology operated. As scholars have argued engaging with Foucault, Soviet subjectivity was engineered through the creation of a Stalinist discourse. Most notably, Stephen Kotkin describes the creation of an entire symbolic system that regulated state power. This "speaking Bolshevik" encompassed language, behavior, dress, and a social imagination of a Soviet future that transcended institutional structures (1995, 198–237).[4]

During the first years of Soviet control, the Soviet political unconscious, still in the early years of its formation, operated as a fundamentally intersubjective terrain. In particular, the literature of the Soviet periphery was generated through the constant negotiation of symbols and forms from Russian and Turkic poetry through literary encounters between Moscow and Baku.[5] As I argue in chapter 3, the belated organization of the Soviet bureaucracy in Baku led to the development of alternative avant-garde experiments among the Russian émigrés. In the reception of materialist aesthetics from the writings of Mayakovsky to Alexander Bogdanov, Azeri poetry reflected the conflict between the symbolic imaginations of the supranational Pan-Turkic community and the

Soviet Union. This process occurred through the performance of textual encounters, and the social networks they generated, as the basis for a new Soviet multinational empire. As a formulation of both the Communist International and a Soviet East, a new set of symbols, rhythms, and rhymes imagined a Turkic Muslim communist consciousness. This process took shape through a dialogue about the relationship between the aura of the symbol and materialist aesthetics, which exposed antagonisms between forms of Soviet and Turkic Muslim subjectivity buried in the depths of this new Turkic poetry.

The Organization of the Past: The Myth of Faust and the Theater of World War I

The work of the poet and playwright Huseyn Cavid highlights a line of continuity from intuitive to materialist conceptions of poetry in his Sufi reinvention of the Faust story. Cavid occupied a transitional place in this literary history. Although a follower of the Füyuzat school and its aesthetic vision, in 1922 he joined the literary section of the Baku Soviet Council of Propaganda and its subsequent revolutionary writers' association, the Red Pens.[6] Cavid, like Axundov and Sehhet, was educated in both traditional Islamic and Russian imperial institutions across the Caucasus, including in Persian Tabriz and Ottoman Istanbul, where he studied literature with the Bektashi Sufi philosopher and poet Riza Tevfik. Cavid's engagement with Sufi philosophy echoes Sehhet's interest in intuition as an aesthetic structuring principle.[7] His most famous plays include *Şeyx Senan* (1915), the story of a twelfth-century Sufi who rebels against his faith by falling in love with a Christian woman; *The Devil* (*İblis* [1918]), an Islamic version of the Faust story; and *The Prophet* (*Peyğember* [1922]), the story of the Prophet Muhammad's revelation and propagation of Islam. These plays place figures of the Islamic past in a timeless mythic present, achieved in part by Cavid's preference for an elevated Ottomanized Turkic verse.[8] Central to Cavid's work is the conception of love as the pursuit of divine esoteric knowledge as integral to the formation of political agency. Like Sehhet and Hadi, Cavid's works negotiate a tension between the dual spiritual and political dimensions of art. However, Cavid's work emphasizes the importance of performance, not only in his choice of the genre of theater but in his staging of love as the pursuit of both poetic truth and the organization of politics.

Cavid's works can also be contextualized within the broader formation of Marxist spiritualism that developed during the revolutionary period, in particular the work of the Polish polymath Alexander Bogdanov. A prominent Social Democrat, Bogdanov led the Forward (Vpered) movement, which championed the central role of the arts to organize the intellectual development of workers in the coming revolution.[9] Favoring populist organization and the centrality of the creative impulse of the arts to Lenin's emphasis on parliamentarianism, Bogdanov's writings became a source of inspiration for the work of the avant-garde artists of Proletkul't (Proletarian Culture).[10] Although Azeri writers do not mention Vpered by name, a branch of the group held meetings in Tiflis between 1909 and 1913 as Sehhet penned his *The Suns of the West* in Baku.[11]

Bogdanov identified the power of art to organize emotions and in so doing constitute a political collective. In his 1918 essay "The Proletariat and Art" Bogdanov outlines his theory of art as the "weapon or tool of the social organization of people" (*orudie sotsial'noe organizatsii liudei*) (1924, 118). His description of art frames political organization in terms of a materialist vision of art as both an instrument or weapon of transformation and a social network of agitation. For Bogdanov, the "artistic idea" can be understood through its historical function as a science, which established it as a weapon or instrument of organization. As distinguished from modern science, the power of art lies in its capacity to "organize experience in living images, not abstract terms. Thanks to this wider scope, not only can it organize people's conceptions [*predstavleniia*], their knowledge [*znaniia*] and thoughts [*mysli*], but also their feelings [*chuvstva*] and moods [*nastroeniia*]" (118). This vision of the organizational value of art emphasized the role of cognition in the dissemination and scope of Marxist-Leninist ideology in the cultural sphere.

The notion of art as a technology for mobilizing the emotions of its viewer and thus shaping comradely relations allowed Bogdanov to draw new value from the religious, mytho-poetic symbols of the "bourgeois past." Bogdanov's philosophy, although it provoked contention among Bolshevik circles, inspired a broad range of thinkers and contributed to the development of distinctive visions of proletarian culture. His theory of the organization of things outlined the ways in which art as a creative enterprise structures experience, generates reciprocal understanding and emotional connections, and links forms of knowledge globally to form the comradely relations (*tovaricheskie sviazi*) of a collective proletarian culture ([1920] 1976, 179).[12] Bogdanov, together with his contemporaries Anatoly Lunacharsky and Maxim Gorky, generated a vision of god-building (*bogostroitel'stvo*), which identified the power of religion to organize the moral and social commitment of individuals and announced the founding of a godless proletarian religion that deified the collective.[13] Perhaps most notably, he discusses the myths of the book of Genesis as a starting point for the construction of a future universe. The myths of Genesis establish both the scientific explanation of the origins of the universe and the poetic history of the Jewish people. In this way, for Bogdanov the "Jews were injected into the organization of the world, as it was then understood, the organization of the community and a vital connection with the ancestors" ([1920] 1976, 179). Bogdanov recalls the nineteenth-century trope of the poet as prophet, perhaps most specifically Gogol's vision of the great Russian writers as descendants of the Hebrew prophets. However, here the power of the prophet serves as a basis of the artistic-scientific organization of the new proletarian consciousness.

In this context, Bogdanov argues that Goethe's *Faust* too serves as a foundational myth for the Russian intelligentsia. For Bogdanov, on the one hand Faust was a bourgeois work of the past, but on the other it also revealed the path to "such an organization of the human soul to attain complete harmony among all its powers and abilities" (такой организации человеческой души, чтобы была достигнута полная гармония между всеми ее силами и способностями) (120). Bogdanov's vision of the organizing potential of art is in part generated through the relationship between the material object and its aura, most likely a reference to Schiller. Drawing on the example of the Venus de Milo, he argues that the aura cultivated by the religious community that surrounded it is in turn projected onto the contemporary viewer. The social history of the art object endows it with a transcendental mystical aura, a talismanic quality—which, he argues, can be secularized and harnessed for the formation of future Soviet community. Bogdanov's discussion of Goethe's *Faust* focuses on the less popular second part of the drama. In his retelling, Faust—a soul thirsty for harmony but plagued by the destructive skepticism of Mephistopheles—only finally finds unity with the universe in his work for the benefit of society.

For Bogdanov, Faust serves as an example for the unity of the spiritual, messianic, and prophetic myths of the past with the organization of the proletarian future.

Cavid's interpretation of *Faust* in *The Devil* similarly draws on the power of heterodox spiritual impulses, from romantic dialectics to Sufi symbols, in order to confer power on his political critique of war.[14] Cavid situates his poetic pursuit of truth and love in the global violence and destruction of World War I. His lyric hero, Arif, embarks on a quest to save his beloved Rena from war-torn Baghdad. He can win her love only by discovering the true murderer of her father, which Iblis—taking on the form of various characters—seeks to conceal so that he can steal Arif's soul. Cavid envisions the Middle Eastern theater of the war through the hero's Faustian pact with Satan, rendered in an Islamic-Zoroastrian form as the fiery power Iblis. As a seeker of truth, Arif parallels the figure of Faust; however, Iblis presents a more complex interrogation of the struggle between good and evil, not only as a source of secular sociopolitical mobilization but as a model for social life. Cavid clarifies Bogdanov's vision of the organization of the human soul, in which love and spiritual communion, the symbol's "vital connection with the ancestors," articulates a modern political subjectivity. However, for Cavid this does not depend on the secularization of the mystical aura of the art object so much as on the sublation of the quest for (divine) truth and love in the political realities of war.

Cavid's drama centers around the first part of the Faustian tale—the corruption of the knowledge seeker's soul—and in this way does not offer a vision of a utopian future. Instead, the hopeless violence and destruction of World War I haunt the avant-garde parable of Arif's ultimate corruption. For Cavid, however, Iblis is not a singular force but an omnipresent energy, at once a being and a nonbeing both absent and ever-present. Neither simply an idea, belief, emotion, god, or devil, he is rather the great organizational force that animates the social politics of the terrestrial world. In this way, the play collapses the distance between the aura of the myth and the world that it animates.

The relationship between Iblis and Arif is dialectical, marked by the binary foil, while it also embodies the reciprocal unity of the powers of creation and destruction. This unity of life/death, creation/destruction, and violence/love is in turn realized through the struggle between the philosophical/spiritual world of ideas and the play's setting in war-torn Baghdad. Indeed, this dynamic further extends to the tension between the national and global scale of the war in which the British, Turkish, Arab, and Tatar soldiers collide in Baghdad. The limited stage set and its fluid connection to the audience through a small hut crossed by pairs of symmetrically placed doors and windows echoes Meyerhold's early experiments. *The Devil* shares a concern for the relationship between the world of the stylized, symbolic battle of ideas and the proximity between actor and audience. Arif's symbolic struggle with Iblis thus occurs simultaneously against the bloody realities of war—discussions of offensives, injured soldiers, and armed robberies—with which it shares a stage. The intersection of these worlds is captured in the author's stage directions that open the first scene. Arif lies on a bed in this hut. Behind him,

> There are flashes of lightning and the sound of thunder, trumpets echoing, cannons, rifles, and bomb explosions. At the edge of the stage, there are two screens that display horrible scenes of war engulfed in flames. An officer with a telescope in his hand commands the battle . . . On one of the screens Iblis appears and in the other—an Angel. Silence settles in after the howling.

> ətrafda göy gurultusu, şimşək çaqışı, tranpet sədaları, top, tüfək, bomba patlayışları . . . Qarşıda, səhnənin nihayətində iki böyük göz (pəncərə) atəşlər, alevlər içində dəhşətli bir müharibə təsvir edər. Bir qaç zabit əldə durbin müharibə komandasilə məşğul . . . Gözlərin birində İblis, digərində Mələk görünür. Gurultudan sonra sükut . . . (2005, 3:7)

Arif and the modest hut are positioned between the archetypal powers of good and evil, as well as among the scenes of the battlefield. The historical, terrestrial battle is literally projected onto the Faustian drama.

Despite the clear distinction between the opposing forces of the Angel and Iblis outlined by the stage directions in the battle for Arif's soul, Sufi elements in the story undermine this dualism. The figure of Arif, the "knower"—from the Arabic root 'A-R-F, meaning knowledge—represents the one who has attained divine knowledge through the experience of the Unity of Being (in God) or the *tawḥīd*. Arif, a seeker of wholeness and truth, suffers in the world of appearances and deception orchestrated by Iblis. Indeed, in the opening of the play Iblis's robe brushes Arif's head, signifying the concealment of truth, which Arif tasks himself with exposing over the course of the remainder of the play. In this case the truth, which Arif seeks, is both literally the murder of Rena's father and symbolically the *tawḥīd*, embodied in his search for Iblis and his beloved Rena. Iblis thus functions simultaneously as the cloak or robe concealing truth and truth itself. Like Mephistopheles, he takes on various human forms, from bandits to servants and wise men, but he is also compared to benevolent symbols: an angel, and most notably, the mystical prophet al-Khidr, who initiates people directly into spiritual life from the unseen realms.[15]

Whereas in orthodox Christian and Islamic theology evil is often associated with nonbeing, Cavid again prefers an approach at once neo-Platonic and Sufi, which valorizes the recognition of the Oneness of the Being of God and its creative power not in opposition to but rather through nonbeing. Addressing the heavens, Arif declares, "The thousand aspects of this mysterious reality reveal themselves to me, / And in each of them—darkness . . . / The hymns of nightingales, the hues of flowers / And the brilliant star, / None can inspire my bursting heart. / Oh, he who is nonbeing, his nonbeing more beautiful than Being itself!" (Bin dürlü həqiqət,/ Bin dürlü müəmmalı həqiqət bana xəndan,/ Həpsində də zülmət . . . / Bülbüllərin əlhanı, çiçəklərdəki əlvan/ Ya şö'leyi-əcram,/ Olmaz şu bənim çıldıracaq könlümə əl'an/ Bir mənbəi-ilham./ Ey varlığı yoq, yoqluğu vardan daha dilbər!) (2005, 3:9). Arif's revelation occurs in darkness, through the burning light of the star, as well as other classical symbols associated with the creative faculties of the poet such as the flower garden and nightingale. The symbolic world of poetry—the nightingale and garden—do not serve as the only inspiration for Arif; rather, nothingness itself formulates a source of beauty and creation. For Cavid, the emphasis on the creative force of nonbeing renders Iblis not only a force of chaos but, again paradoxically, the very ordering principle of that chaos. The Angel declares, "O Lord, have a little mercy!/ Humanity is almost in ruin. / The face of the earth is overcome with savagery / Its politics ordered by Iblis" (Ya Rəb, azacıq lütfü inayət!/ Qəhr olmada artıq bəşəriyyət./ Başdan-başa həp yer yüzü vəhşət,/ İblis ilə həmrəngi-siyasət) (2005, 3:2). The politics of the word, the terrestrial realm, manifest in the destructive force of Iblis. Similarly, Iblis's shape-shifting capacities articulate an ethical and theological struggle, exposed at the surface of social relations between characters.

The simultaneous unity and heterodox multiplicity of the universe is emphasized in the end of the play as the townspeople, recognizing Iblis's complicity in the destruction, launch a futile attack, but his simultaneous absence and omnipresence eludes them. This ultimate relativity is realized through a description of the dance of the dead. Before Iblis's dissolution into the atmosphere, he chants:

> All philosophy, every religious sect, every tradition
> Dance without regard to reality or illusion.
> All dance—grief, consolation, love, and death,
> All dance—good, evil, knowledge, and ignorance . . .
> Even that invisible master of the temple dances,
> Even that being-of-nothingness dances.

> Hər fəlsəfə, hər dinü təriqət, bütün adət
> Rəqs etmədə həp olsa xəyal, olsa həqiqət.
> Həp rəqs ediyor hüznü sürur, eşqü fəlakət,
> Həp rəqs ediyor xeyrilə şər, elmü cəhalət . . .
> Rəqs etmədə hətta o görünməz ulu mə'bud,
> Rəqs etmədə hətta o vücudi-ədəmalud.

(2005, 3:102)

Iblis's final monologue imagines this play of binaries to the rhythm of the death dance. The world of symbols and beings, religion, and philosophy are all incorporated into the dance. Cavid's Iblis ultimately corrupts not only Arif's soul but also the entire constellation of binaries that permeate the religious-philosophical system, a veritable death dance of the system of symbols resonates against the endless, meaningless world war.

The heterodoxy of Cavid's *Devil* is most clearly articulated through the play's repeated references to fire in its various forms—stars, weapons, alcohol, and the sun. Cavid situates fire at the center of Iblis's dramatic and symbolic role as the forces of both deception and truth. Indeed, fire is a symbol dear to the spiritual imaginary of the Caucasus. Burning mountains, earth, and streams, which cover the South Caucasus, served as holy places for Zororastrians. To this end, Iblis explains to Arif, "Without fire, trust me, light will not sustain, / Fire, the sun is fire, all humanity is fire, / Every movement, all of primary creation, is fire . . . / Think about Zoroaster, his philosophy, thought, genius / He made people worship fire" (Atəşsiz, inan, nur olamaz sabitü qaim,/ Atəş, günəş atəş, bəşəriyyət bütün atəş,/ Hər bir hərəkət, məbdəi-xilqət bütün atəş . . . / Zərdüştü düşün, fəlsəfəsi, fikri, dəhası/ Həp atəşə tapdırmaq idi zümreyi-nası) (2005, 3:13). Furthermore, the great mythic captive—Prometheus—was chained to the Caucasus Mountains for his symbolic creation of civilization through fire. Fire is here both the gift of civilization and a source of Prometheus's imprisonment. However, fire also catalyzes relations between the characters. Iblis tricks Arif into drinking alcohol by switching *raki* or anisette for water, which Arif exclaims is not water but fire (38). Again tempting Arif to transgress, Iblis offers him gold and fire (in the form of a gun). Iblis with "fiery laughter" mocks, "Creation lives by fire but, alas! / By fire they loose their lives" (Xilqət atəşlə yaşarkən, hey-hat!/ Bunlar atəşlə qılar tərki-həyat) (9). Fire thus generates a symbolic as well as structural unity within the play, driving the action as well as identifying the character of Iblis and his impermanence. The fiery mythic and theological narratives that animate *The Devil* localize *Faust* in the South Caucasus even as they confer a heterodox cultural topography on Arif's search for knowledge.

Although *The Devil* was written before the Soviet takeover, it was frequently performed during the early 1920s.[16] Despite being targeted by the Bolsheviks for his interest in German romanticism and Sufi thought, Cavid successfully staged his plays during the 1920s. This fact can perhaps be attributed to Cavid's involvement in the literary division of the Council of Propaganda, as well as the relatively ineffective censorship apparatus during the early years of Soviet control.[17] This discrepancy between Cavid's controversial source material and his play's popularity can also be attributed to the leftist Bolshevik endorsement (through Bogdanov's and Lunacharsky's writings) of the powerful organizational capacities of *Faust* as a critique of radical individualism. Cavid's drama further foregrounds Arif's quest for truth as a collective social enterprise, which transcends his own physical earthly desires for his beloved Rena. Cavid's portrait of Iblis does not oppose an evil Satan to a truthful God but rather identifies a fundamental structure organizing an endless battle of binaries that stage the senselessness of war. In this way, the work critiques the destructive vision of the individualizing forces of war through the exposure of the radical heterodoxy of Iblis as an organizational force.

Cavid inverts the Bogdanovian vision of the poem as weapon (*orudie*) by projecting the violence of World War I onto his Sufi Faustian drama. The struggle between truth and deception are thus both obscured and clarified in the global violence of war, which constantly interrupts the action of the play. Cavid suggests that the pursuit of truth can be witnessed in the violence of such political realities. Iblis orchestrates the politics of war, and yet the battle for truth is ultimately lost to his powers of deception. Despite this pessimistic vision of the future, the drama culminates—like Memmedquluzade's *The Dead*—in the townspeople's realization of the trap and the unmasking of deception in the public sphere. The political power of poetry is located not only in the play's militant vision of the destruction of the old world order but in its messianic projection of the future and in the revelatory potential of this theater of war to realize Arif's quest for truth.

Victory over the Sun: The Folk Ballad and the People's Poetry

The shift in art from social critique to social mobilization took hold in the 1920s through the work of the Azeri poet Süleyman Rüstem and the Turkish poet Nazim Hikmet. The triumph over the individual was another latent avant-garde theme that characterized the emphasis on the development of new Turkic verse forms. As a leading figure in the Red Pens, Rüstem described Baku as a space where Turkic writers gathered to discuss poetic innovation and studied Soviet literature. "During those years the frequent visits of poets from Moscow to Baku," he recounts, "aided the development of revolutionary poetry" (2005, 2:239). The genre of the Turkic folk ballad, *türkü*, and the central image of the sun expressed the Red Pens' efforts to envision the intersection between a pan-Turkic past and a Muslim communist future. The türkü provided a connection to a pan-Turkic cultural imagination, while reinforcing Bolshevik interests in folk culture as a tool of nationalization. Drawing on Hacıbeyov's analysis of Azeri folk music, which I discuss in chapter 3, the allusion to the türkü evokes a "spiritual-aesthetic" element within the poem.

Rüstem's generation, born following the 1905 revolution, reflected a growing distance from the more traditional religious education received by Sehhet and Cavid and a closer connection to Russian culture. Rüstem was educated at an imperial Russian Russo-Tatar school, then in Moscow. His first collection of works, written during the early and mid-1920s and published in 1927, was titled *From Sadness to Happiness* (*Elemden neşeye*). The dual-language title page carries both the imprint of Soviet government funding and the Red Pens' publishing house. In Russian, under the simplified title *To Happiness* (*K radosti*), the collection is credited to the Association of Proletarian Writers, while the Azeri printed in Arabo-Persian script instead lists the Azerbaijani Literature "Red Pens" Collective as its publisher. In one of its popular poems, "Tomorrow" (Yarın), Rüstem employs a variant of the türkü to envision the direction of new Turkic verse.

> From the horizon of the East, weeping blood,
> An ever-shining sun will rise tomorrow.
> All who find life in its light
> Will strangle the enemy tomorrow.
>
> Burning in the hands of youth,
> Attuned to the sound of death,
> Looking everywhere for help,
> The mother of the East will be free tomorrow.
>
> The nations of power are looking
> Upon their murderous work happily,
> And suddenly that frightening face of the West
> Will turn to dust tomorrow.
>
> The tearful, passionate hearts
> Will weep; the moaning peoples will smile.
> The hands calloused from the garden of work
> Will tear out the thorny roses tomorrow.
>
> Şərqin qan ağlayan ufuklarından
> Sönməyən bir günəş doğacaq yarın.
> Onun, işığıyla can bulan kəslər
> Kəndi düşmanını boğacak yarın.

Cəhlin pəncəsində yanan ekleyen,
Ölüm nəğməsini hər an dinləyən,
ətrafdan özüne imdat gözləyən
şərqin annesı hür olacak yarın.

Gücün millətləri boğup öldürən
Ettiği işinə bakıp sevinən
Qarbın o qorxulu çəhrəsi birdən
Yaprağa dönərək sulacak yarın.

Daima ağlayan tutgun könüllər
Güləcək; güləcək inləyən illər.
Emək bağçasından qabarlı eller:
Tikanlı gülləri yolacak yarın.

(1927, 122)

The opening stanza reflects the generative and destructive powers of the sun, to give life and fuel the inner moral and ethical battles within the self. From the depths of the bloody revolution, the colors of the sunrise reflect the light of "tomorrow." The development of the poem follows the tone of the collection, moving from the terrors of war to tomorrow's happy projections. The poem juxtaposes the rise of the sun in the East in the first stanza against the frightening face of a decaying West, which "turns to water and leaves," implying tomorrow's promise of autumn.

In the final stanza, Rüstem imagines a garden of work, evoking the classical symbol of the rose garden alongside the Soviet iconic image of the worker's calloused hands. This rose garden of work reminds his readers of both the materialist vision of the physical bodies of the working masses and the classical Ottoman-Persian vision of the natural world as a symbolic spiritual-cultural community. The worker, he suggests, tends to this garden of the classical past, freeing it from thorns, and in so doing realizes a victory in the battle against oppressive power. As the poem circulated through subsequent reprintings, Rüstem's contemporaries also echoed this imagery of the sunrise in the east and the calloused hands of the eastern worker tilling the rose garden of the past for a "happy" tomorrow.[18] Following the türkü form, the poem reinforces the word "tomorrow" through the word's repetition and emphatic placement at the end of the final line of each stanza. "Tomorrow" serves in this way ambiguously as both adverb and subject, driving the action of the poem just as the sun drives the movement of the seasons. The material reality of tomorrow is constituted through a concern for the physicality of the body and for the mytho-poetic.

Hikmet also experimented with the folk ballad genre in his famous poem "Song of the Sun Drinkers" (Güneşi içenlerin türküsü), published in a collection by the same name in Baku in 1928 (1928, 6–11). Hikmet's free verse variant of the türkü, stripped of its rhyme and classic syllabic rhythm, instead highlights the thematic of the genre with its chorus of soldiers announcing a raid on the sun. Drawn to the revolutionary spirit, Hikmet traveled to Moscow in 1921 to attend the Communist University of the Toilers of the East. There he read Marxist theory, delivered poetry on stage alongside Mayakovsky, and worked with Meyerhold to plan small drama productions at the university.[19] These connections to the Russian avant-garde left a strong impact on his early style. However, as Rüstem recalled, Hikmet also forged an early connection with the poetic circles in Baku. As Rüstem notes, Hikmet began to discuss the challenges of developing a new poetry in the 1920s, first through a written correspondence and then in 1927 during a visit in which he met with Rüstem, the poet and translator Mikayıl Refili, and others. This historic meeting was captured in a photograph, which Rüstem fondly remembers.[20]

Though Rüstem only mentions this later meeting, it is likely that the poets first met during Hikmet's visit in 1923 (2005, 2:228–32).[21] Hikmet's fervent revolutionary Marxist politics and free verse style made him a favorite among the Red Pens. In turn, Baku served as inspiration for Hikmet's vision of a Muslim communist utopia. He described his journey to Baku from Moscow by train, celebrating the city as a vision of modernization and characterized by the spiritual, social, and industrial power of oil. "I want to kiss the black-eyed workers with their greasy overalls. / I want to prostrate myself on the holy earth of Baku / Taking a handful of oil and drinking it like black wine" (cited in Göksu and Timms 1999, 73). This vision of Baku provides both localized and material images of the city in the figure of the workers, while capturing the spiritual quality of the symbol of Baku's oil as black wine. Pursuing this fusion of spiritual and industrial energy, "The Song of the Sun Drinkers" formulates an appeal to a communal, ecstatic spirit through references to the Russian avant-garde and the symbols of Zoroastrian fire worship. Its

Figure 3. Vladimir Mayakovsky is pictured here with Süleyman Rüstem, Huseyn
Cavid, and other members of the Red Pens during his visit to Baku in 1927. There
is no official record of all persons present at the meeting however, those pictured
likely include: (*front row, left to right*) the Azeri poets Mikayıl Yurin, Huseyn Cavid,
Süleyman Rüstem, Vladimir Mayakovsky, and the documentary filmmaker Roman
Karmen; (*back row*) the writers Məmməd Arif, Abdulla Faruq, the journalist Mikayıl
Dolganov aka "Kamskii," and Şəmsəddin Abbasov. According to Rüstem, the
photograph was taken in the Bregadze atelier in Parapat (Fountain Square) in 1927
(2005, 242). This copy was sourced from the Azerbaijan State Archive of Literature
and Art (Azerbaycan Dövlet Edebiyyat ve İncesenet Arxivi), f. 125, v. 1, s. 10.

form similarly challenges the boundaries between the high art of classical
poetry and the türkü.

The poem introduces a song of a mythical group—the sun drinkers—
who announce a raid on the sun. The poem recalls Nietszche's vision of the
Apollonian force in *The Birth of Tragedy*, which also served as a central
theme for the Russian avant-garde. The theme was most famously taken
up in the 1913 Futurist opera *Victory over the Sun* (*Pobeda nad solntsem*),
a joint production by Mikhail Matiushin, Alexei Kruchenykh, Velimir
Khlebnikov, and Kazimir Malevich.[22] Indeed, the refrain of Hikmet's song
announces, "The victory over the sun is near." For Nietszche, Apollo—
the Greek sun god—represented the world of appearances, the artificial,
and the rational. Perhaps most crucially for the Russian avant-garde, the
Apollonian signified the principle of individuation. The Russian avant-
garde thus rallied for a victory over the primacy of the individual and

the stale, scientific rationality of the past. *Victory over the Sun* chronicles a disjointed series of events about a time traveler who arrives in the thirty-fifth century, where people are waging war against the sun. The sun stands for artificial appearances, sterile rationality, singularity, and finite or closed scientific models. For the futurists, these old forms need to be replaced with alternative epistemologies—literally new sources of energy (Clark 1995, 38–44). Invoking *Birth of Tragedy*, or perhaps more directly Ivanov's "Nietzsche and Dionysus," the play highlights the victory of the Dionysian collective impulse over the Apollonian force of rationality. Like Ivanov, the futurists were inspired by the transformative political potential of the collective experience of ecstasy and its victory over the isolation of radical individualism. Crucially, for the futurists this transformative power lay within the cognitive faculties of the artist or poet. *Victory over the Sun* thus aimed to change the way the viewer sees and experiences the world, collapsing the boundaries between art, the subject, and spectator by mobilizing a politically engaged art.

Hikmet's raid follows this avant-garde thematic presented in the futurist *Victory over the Sun*, invoking the triumph over the principle of individuation (the Nietzschean Apollonian) through a transgression of the boundaries between poetry and song. His imagery also alludes to Dionysus, the god of the grape harvest, "With blood drops of grapes, the red vineyards fume" (Üzümleri kan damlalı kırmızı bağlar tütüyor) (1928, 10). The violence of Hikmet's raid is captured in the visceral image of smoldering vineyards speckled with grapes like droplets of blood. Affect is emphasized in the repetition of the image of the heart. Hikmet directs his readers, "You too, wrest / Your heart from its chest cage . . . Cast your heart beside our hearts!" (Sen de çıkar/ göğsünün kafesinden yüreğini . . . yüreğini yüreklerimizin yanına at!) (1928, 9). The ecstatic moment is embodied in the synaesthetic fusion of sound and light. He writes, "We drink the sun in its voice! / We overflow./ It overflows!" (Güneşi içiyoruz sesinde! / Coşuyoruz. / Coşuyor!) (10). The excitement of the sun drinkers who, incorporating the power of the sun, flow forth like a current, in turn triggers the ecstatic response of the environment around them. This correspondence of human and environment is evident in the warm color pallette of the poem. The earthy tones of the copper feet and beards of the heroes are echoed in the blood-colored grapes, red torches, and copper earth and sky. The image of the sun, which appears prominently in the work of the Red Pens, signifies both Soviet modernity and an emergent Muslim communist subject. This rising sun and its accompanying poetic innovations nonetheless retain a continuity with the past. The sun offers a doubled symbol—evoking at once the images of nature characteristic of neoclassicism and the Füyuzat school, as well as the reception of the West embodied in Sehhet's collection of translations of Western classics, *The Suns of the West*, which I discuss in chapter 2.

Unlike the futurist utopian vision of the mechanized collective, Hikmet's sun drinkers are connected to the spiritual energies of the earth and its elements. Hikmet emphasizes the Dionysian frenzy through the intoxicating transubstantiation of the sun from "earthen cups." He writes:

> We were born from the earth, fire, water, and iron
> Our wives nurse our children with the sun!
> Our copper beards smell of the earth!
> It's hot as blood
>   As hot as
>   That *moment*,
> Burning in the dreams of young lads!

> Biz topraktan, ateşten, sudan, demirden doğduk
> Güneşi emz(d)iriyor çocuklarımıza karımız!
> toprak kokuyor bakır sakallarımız!
> kan kadar sıcak
> delikanlıların rüyalarında yanan
>   o, an,
>   kadar sıcak!

(9)

The heroes are connected to the earth elements, and Hikmet represents the life cycle through the fertile images of the sun's energy as breast milk, blood, and semen. Ejaculation here appears as a temporal and a sensory experience—the sun's heat and that *moment* of climax. Similarly, the red beards of the heroes mirror the fiery earth. Hikmet's insistence on a connection to the sun, despite his attack on the Apollonian, reveals the poem's ties to the central myth of Zoroastrian fire worship. For Hikmet, the sun is both an idea of the past that must be conquered in the name of avant-garde poetry and an expression of unity with the powerful fire of the earth. The song itself is woven into a flame, the path to the sun winds like a fiery flame:

> This is a song that
> Twists
> A braided flame.
> It's bloody like a crimson torch,
> Burns on the dark brows,
> Of the heroes—copper feet bare!
> I also plaited
>   that braid
> I also crossed that bridge with them
>   into the sun

> Bu bir türkü
> Alev bir saç örgüsü
> Kıvranıyor.
> kanlı; kızıl bir meş'ale gibi yanıyor
> esmer alınlarında
> bakır ayakları çıplak kahramanların!
> ben de sardım
>   o örgüyü
> ben de onlarla güneşe giden
>   köprüden geçtim.

(6)

The song transforms into a flame or torch, which in turn alights on the heroes' brows. The lyric subject's journey is also incorporated through the act of braiding, echoing the twisting forms of the flames. Finally, the sun drinkers are compared to hungry wolves and the sound of their singing to howls harmonizing the earth and sky in copper hues. Hikmet's call to the sun drinkers at once wages a battle against the bounded forces of individualization and mechanization, which has stripped the earth of its spiritual power and eclipsed the animalistic and carnal spirit of the poetic song.

The rhythmic repetition of the chorus serves as the main structuring principle of the work, replacing the classic conventions of the *ghazal* and *qaṣīda*. Hikmet conveys his song through fragmentary images suspended in the broken lines of the stepladder form, made famous in part by Mayakovsky's poetry. The cascading lines of the stepladder form, which in Russian verse traditionally articulates a rhythmic space for breath, here in its Turkic context also emulates the sublime descent from the heights of the classical tradition.

> Tearing
> The mouths of the golden-maned lions
>   We stretched
> We leapt
> We rode the lighting winds!
> From the cliffs
>   Breaking from the rocks, the eagles
> Beat their wings gilded in light!
> The flame-wristed riders whipped,
> The horses rear up!!
> There's a raid
>   A raid on the sun!
> We'll conquer the sun
> The victory over the sun is near
>
> altın yeleli arslanların ağzını
> yırtarak
>   gerindik
> Sıçradık şimşekli rüzgârlara bindik!
> Kayalardan
>   kayalarla kopan kartallar
> çırpıyor, ışıkta yaldızlanan kanatlarını!
> Alev bilekli süvariler kamçılıyor,
> şaha kalkan atlarını!!
> Akın var.
>   güneşe akın!
> Güneşi zabt edeceğiz
> güneşin zabtı yakın.

(6–7)

Hikmet builds on the stepladder form with the fantastic imagery of the symbolists and futurists to articulate a new Turkic poetics. The eagle swooping down from the cliffs evokes the Pushkinian sublime; however, instead of following a movement from the sky to earth, the descending lines trace an ascending path from the lion's leap to a mythical army of winged riders raiding the sun. Hikmet abandons classical form and rhyme for free verse. Particular to the Turkic grammatical structure, Hikmet's stepladder highlights action, the end of each line punctuated by a verb. This structure emphasizes the rhythmic qualities of the regular declension pattern and Turkic vowel harmony, generating a distinctive variant of the stepladder that foregrounds action over images. The raid is here repeated through the chorus of the song as well as the vertical movement of the form and syntax of the verse.

The descent from the heights of the aesthetics of the sublime traces the dissolution of the individual lyric subject into a collective raid against the Apollonian. Hikmet's "Song of the Sun Drinkers," like Cavid's *Devil*, however, softens the poetic militancy of verse as a weapon by instead emphasizing the revelatory power of the symbol. This latent interest in symbolism within the Turkic avant-garde marks an inclination toward a Bogdanovian spiritual materialism that envisions comradely social relations through the creative archive of the symbols of the past, that is, both Islamic themes and Turkic folk ballads. In this way, "Song of the Sun Drinkers" articulates the formation of a mythic political consciousness, marked by a celebration of fire worship, which turns on the verticality of the romantic sublime for its revolutionary energy. In Cavid's *Devil* and Hikmet's türkü the thematic of the search for truth, located in a reorganization of the past, in turn generates a new form of lyric subjectivity. This new form, however, is not only characterized by its Russian and German avant-garde allusions but in its capacity to generate a dialogue between modernist visions, which look simultaneously at a mythic past and toward an uncertain future.

Words on a Mission: Mayakovsky and Turkic Free Verse

While much of the Red Pens' work highlights experimentations with forms of spiritual materialism that surfaced in 1920s Baku, aesthetic and personal linkages with Mayakovsky's work also emphasized a direct connection between poetry and the streets of the city. Nina Gurianova (2012) argues that Mayakovsky's work marks a theoretical break in the avant-garde, moving from a prerevolutionary "aesthetics of anarchy" toward a postrevolutionary utopian utilitarianism. Gurianova explains that the October revolution marked a break from an anti-teleological and provocative "aesthetics of anarchy," which sought to understand or visualize the viewer's cognitive experience, to a utopian vision of art that employed tactics of agitation and the often-didactic lesson to transform the viewer's consciousness. She identifies this break in particular with Mayakovsky's collaboration with the former Vpered thinker and later commissar of enlightenment Lunacharsky. Through these institutional linkages Mayakovsky participated on the board of the Narkompros organ *Art of the Commune* (*Iskusstvo kommuny*), where he published his treatise in verse "Order to the Army of Arts."[23] Indeed, this shift characterizes a move away from the chaotic impulse of destruction toward a vision of state building.

On the one hand, this shifting approach to materialist aesthetics marked by Mayakovsky's poetry of the streets follows a political move from revolution to state building. According to much of the scholarship on Soviet culture, the 1920s were characterized by a shift from the pluralistic cultural "soft line" of NEP toward centrally governed cultural institutions during the nationalization of the republics and Stalinization during the late 1920s and early 1930s.[24] In this sense, Mayakovsky's poetics have been described through his connection to his agitational propaganda for Rosta (Kernan 2014, 224–46).

In the context of the Caucasus, artistic production was undergoing contemporaneous institutional shifts in the political and cultural sphere following the Soviet rise to power in 1920. The creation of new institutions such as BakKavRosta were reflected in this particular line of development within the Red Pens' work. Mayakovsky's influence on Azeri poetry articulated the new role of the Soviet institution through poetic innovation. This shift transformed the vision of community from one animated by the pan-Turkic and pan-Islamic symbolism of the rose garden and Bogdanovian spiritual materialism to one commanded by more structuralist forms of materialism linked to an emergent Azerbaijani Soviet national idea. The gradual shift from hermeneutics to materialism was unified by a concern for the continuous narrative of the collective revolutionary struggle. This emphasis on the materiality of the artistic process re-envisioned the mythic past through Marxist-Leninist history and visualized a community of comradely relations in the immediacy of the present.

Mayakovsky explicitly outlined the goals of new poetry in his essay, "How to Make Verse?" (Kak delat' stikhi? [1926]). Unlike the isolated academicism of the past, the goal of new poetry lies in its symbiotic relationship with the social world. Here speech plays a central role: "How do we extract spoken language from poetry and how do we extract poetry from this speech?" (1939–1949, 12:84). Mayakovsky casts aside the versification manual and instead champions a vision of the creative process through materialist modes of production. The writing of verse, he explains, requires a "social command" (*sotsial'nyi zakaz*): that is, a vision of the word as a material solution to world problems, a sense of feeling or desire for one's class, material—words, instruments, or weapons of production—pen and word processing capacities, techniques of elaboration (12:84). Despite its roots in social discourse, this new poetry is also militant. Good rhymes, he argues, function like an attack—unrepeatable and surprising. The social mission is achieved, furthermore, through a poetic charge. Placing the new verse in the context of the Civil War, he writes, "the social mission is to give words to the songs traveling with the Red Army to the Petersburg front" (12:84). Mayakovsky's repetition of the instrument or weapon echoes Bogdanov's vision of proletarian art and Khlebnikov's description of Pushkin's poetry as verbal cannons, but it raises the stakes of such claims from an aesthetic revolution to a social mission. In its reception of Mayakovsky's aesthetic commands, the new Turkic poetry reflected the conflict between a mythic supranational symbolic imagination and new national Bolshevik ideology.

Hikmet described the influence of Mayakovsky on his work through a common vision of poetry's capacity to bring politics into the street. According to the art and theater critic Alexander Fevralsky, Hikmet explained, "What my poetry and Mayakovsky's have in common is breaking down, first, the division between poetry and prose; second, [overcoming] differences in styles (lyrical, satirical, etc); and third, bringing the language of politics into poetry. However, we used different forms. Mayakovsky is my teacher, but I do not write like him" (as cited in Göksu and Timms 1999, 47). Hikmet's interest in blurring the boundaries between poetry and prose as well as literature and politics resonate in his claims to an aesthetic modernity and its corresponding vision of social collectivity in his "Song of the Sun Drinkers." Indeed, "Song" evokes Mayakovsky's 1917 revolutionary anthem "Our March" (Nash marsh). Blending song and verse, "Our March" also embodies the physicality of the poem. Like Hikmet's "Song," the poem acquires a new rhythm, through the beat of the battle march rather than the academic conventions of versification. Mayakovsky's march generates music from his body of words. He writes: "Our heart is our battle drum / . . . Our weapon—our songs / Our gold—the chiming of voices. / . . . / Heart, boom battle! / Our breast—the brass of cymbals" (Сердце наш барабан. / . . . Наше оружие—наши песни. / Наше золото—звенящие голоса. / . . . / Сердце, бей бой! / Грудь наша—медь литавр) (1939–1949, 2:7). The beating of the collective lyric subject is punctuated by the sounds of cymbals clashing against their breasts. The body serves as an instrument of both music and war. For Mayakovsky this translation of sound and lyric into material form is thus achieved through the shared likeness between the body and the instruments or weapons of war and music. However, for Hikmet, verse is not linked to physicality through metaphor but rather reflected across the body, for as he notes, the song burns like a torch on the brows of his heroes.[25]

Hikmet insists on the more lasting influence of Soviet theater on his conception of the relationship between the word and body (Göksu and Timms 1999, 51). The poet Yevgeny Yevtushenko recounted Hikmet's commitment to Meyerhold's theater, "I dreamt of Meyerhold and Mayakovsky . . . it was a street revolution that turned into a stage revolution" (1999, xix). The relationship between the theater and the revolution was, among the arts, most intimately and institutionally intertwined with Soviet propaganda efforts during the 1920s. Indeed, Vechorka's vision of pages of poetry laying theaters instead of roofs also highlights this connection. Conceptually, Hikmet's embodied verse shares Meyerhold's vision of the physical body as an instrument or weapon and as a material through which emotions could be organized and channeled. Meyerhold's biomechanics presented a scientific vision of the body as the mechanized instrument of the actor, artist, and director. However, despite his emphasis on the scientific orchestration of bodily movement, a factor that made Meyerhold's work popular with the Bolsheviks, the *effects* of his system, as Meyerhold's assistants described, instead revealed "the formal display of the emotional" (Braun 1995, 176). Indeed, Meyerhold orchestrates Mayakovsky's poetic bodies in reverse: where for Mayakovsky the body emerges through the contour of the word, for Meyerhold the word emanates through the body. This vision of the body as a conduit for language and emotion—or an energetic charge—appears in Hikmet's understanding of the spiritual value of language as well as a concern for the space of the word on the page—an interest shared by both Mayakovsky and Hikmet. This imagined space of the stage in Hikmet's work articulates the symbolic link between the word and the page through the body.

Hikmet's use of free verse and concern for physicality in "Song" is prefigured by Rüstem's 1923 "The Twelfth International Youth Day" (Ön ikinçi beyn-al-halq gencler günü). Rüstem draws a portrait of a youth demonstration through his vision of marching words. Voices call out from within the verse, like Mayakovsky's army of the arts, reforming the structure of the poem through an emphasis on the utterance. Rüstem writes:

Today
All
The youth of the world demonstrate
—Today, the world hopes for light
From the sunrise
From the land of the victors
We hear voices
—We
Want a revolutionary life
Hey youth!
With firm steps.
Come on!
Forward!
Forward!
Forward!

bu gün
bütün
dünya gəncləri nümayış yapıyorlar
—bu gün doğan günəşdən
işıq umuyor dünya
cahangirlər mənbəyindən
—biz
biz
"yakı həyat istəyoruz
sesleri duyuluyor.

—ay gənclər!
Sərt addımlarla.
Haydi!
İləri!
İləri!
İləri!
     (1927, 94)

Like Hikmet's türkü, the broken lines of Rüstem's free verse are united through the musical quality of the poem. Rüstem and Hikmet draw on the sonance of the Turkic vowel harmony in their opening lines "Today / All" (*bu gün / bütün*) and later "a song / a braid" (*bir türkü / saç örgüsü*). The call and response element of the soldier's song, characteristic of the türkü genre, appears in both Rüstem's appeal to the youths, whose "firm steps" are embodied in the repetition of the commands, "Forward! / Forward! / Forward!" Hikmet's chorus similarly articulates the voices of his sun drinkers through his stepladder line breaks, which seem to trace the bodies of the soldiers on the march through a call and response across the page: "There's a raid. / A raid on the sun!" (*Akın var. / güneşe akın!*). While both poems highlight the rhythm of the soldier's march, they also operate with much of the same imagery, emphasizing nature through the sun and the wind. For Hikmet the wind carries his sun drinkers, "We rode the lighting winds!" (Şimşekli rüzgârlara bindik!), and for Rüstem "—the wind / let it carry these voices / to the distance / to the distance" (—Ruzgar / Aparsın bu səsləri / Uzaqlara / Uzaqlara) (1927, 96). The repetition of "to the distance" resounds like a windswept echo. Mayakovsky's "March" and its vision of the body as instrument is replaced in Rüstem's and Hikmet's work by an emphasis on the natural world in orchestrating the rhythmic repetition of the song. While Mayakovsky emphasizes the body through the rhythms of language, Rüstem and Hikmet make use of the theatricality of the utterance. Rüstem articulates the voices of the youth march through em dashes and interjections "—We / Hey youth! / Come on!" and Hikmet by scattering his sun drinkers victory calls across the page.

The türkü genre emphasizes this connection between Turkic mythopoetic symbol and avant-garde form. Rüstem's and Hikmet's emphasis on the chorus, in turn, highlights the site of enunciation of the speaking subject. Hikmet closes his poem with a primal scream bathed in the sun's light.

> Even
> the earth is copper, the sky is copper!
> Howl the song of the sun drinkers!
> Ho-wl!
> Let me howl!

> Hatta
> Toprak bakır, gök bakır!
> Haykır güneşi içenlerin türküsünü!
> Hay-kır!
> Haykıralım!
>
> (1928, 11)

The rhythm of the howls, which evoke the Dionysian victory over individualism, lays its syllables bare. A reminder of the loss of the syllabic metrical form of the türkü, Hikmet's song draws out syllables instead to materialize the voices of his sun drinkers and the emotional charge of their wild call into the empty abyss of the page.

The imbrication of form and content in Hikmet's and Rüstem's poetry expresses a fluid vision of Turkic identity as bound by cultural and linguistic ties. Although I have chosen to transliterate Rüstem's verse into modern Azeri Latin script from its Arabo-Persian original for the sake of continuity, the differences between his and Hikmet's language are minimal. Indeed, the Red Pens, in keeping with the work of the Füyuzat school, often preferred Turkish pronouns and verbal forms such as the first person Turkish *ben* to the Azeri *men*, as well as the present continuous Turkish—*iyor* form to the Azeri—*ir*. However, as I discuss in the postscript, this continuity was interrupted by the full adoption of the Latin script in 1929, which introduced new boundaries that restructured the imagined community of Azeri verse. These early twentieth-century verse experiments therefore represent a final period of supranational engagement in the poetic sphere, before Soviet cultural institutions began to promote a fixed ideology of Soviet Azerbaijani national identity.

The performative style of Hikmet's and Rüstem's works, in dialogue with Mayakovsky's and Meyerhold's work, exposes the increasing

influence of oral speech in poetry. Their emphasis on recitational per-
formativity coincided with the populist peasant poetry of figures such as
Sergei Esenin but also participated in a broader shift in Turkic poetry during the nineteenth and early twentieth centuries. In *Grammatology and
Literary Modernity in Turkey*, Nergis Ertürk (2011) analyzes these transformations in conceptions of literary writing in Ottoman and modern
Turkish literature, particularly during the transition from the nineteenth
through the early twentieth centuries. She outlines a shift from an emphasis on *logocentrism* in classical poetry, the privileging of speech over writing rooted in God's oral transmission of the Qur'an to the Prophet, to
a nineteenth-century *phonocentrism*, which focuses on the problems of
representing the oral diversity of Turkish in the Arabo-Persian script. The
introduction of phonocentrism, with its anxiety about earlier forms of
logocentrism, she argues, resulted in a mediation of internal foreignness
that characterized the entrance of the Ottoman empire into global capitalist modernity.

The attention to the transformative power of recitation in Rüstem's
and Hikmet's works is thus rooted in the challenges of negotiating an
internal foreignness, generated through the experience of the process of
Soviet nationalization. The poetic interest in speech was accompanied by
the expansion of imperial institutions designed to structure nationalization through vernacularization, which included the study and design of
national written systems for oral languages.[26] In turn, Mayakovsky's and
Meyerhold's work, motivated by its own populist politics, rendered performance and the space of the theater central to the conceptualization of
modern artistic form. In dialogue with this avant-garde aesthetic, the new
Turkic verse of the 1920s returned to a set of neoclassical symbols as the
organizing principles of modern Soviet life.[27]

From Cavid to Hikmet and Rüstem, a strong vision of the instrumen-
tality of art emerges. Similarly, a Bogdanovian conception of the value of
spirituality for revolutionary efforts, a romantic anticapitalism, motivates
the application of the mytho-poetic symbol to the task of shaping the organization of political life. Returning to a quest for love and truth through
the frame of the Faust story, Cavid's *Devil* marks a formal and conceptual transition away from intuition as a pathway between the world and
the poem, characteristic of the prerevolutionary tradition. Cavid instead
foregrounds the performance of the social world in his play in verse as

the ground through which the ethical and moral battles of society can be worked out. In so doing, *The Devil* collapses the distance between the aura of art and the community it describes. For Cavid the theme of love, as the pursuit of divine esoteric knowledge, stages a new political subjectivity, mediated between the chaos of the real world—embodied in war—and the pursuit of truth. *The Devil* envisions the search for unity, not as a battle between good and evil but rather in the convergence of the two in the path to truth. Deconstructing a militant binary worldview, Cavid also challenges a vision of an individual progressivist subject by instead outlining the search for truth through the pursuit of love—that is, the seeker Arif's love for Rena—and the unveiling of the singular within the multiplicity of Iblis's terrestrial manifestations. Fire and the folk song formulate an analogous frame for Hikmet's and Rüstem's vision of progress. Hikmet and Rüstem answer Mayakovsky's call for a social vision for poetry through new free verse experiments. Shaped by the beat of the march and the performative descent of fragmented verse forms across the page, these works visualize the dialogic features of the stage within the text.

Similar to the Russian avant-garde's ambivalent relationship to romanticism, the formation of a new Turkic verse established a stronger continuity with the classical syllabic and *aruz* metrical traditions. In this sense, the Red Pens' evocation of the türkü establishes a linkage with a pan-Turkic supranational oral cultural tradition, albeit one that abandoned more heterodox Persianate lexical and poetic elements, which were popularized during the prerevolutionary period in the journals *Enlightenment* and *Molla Nesreddin*. Indeed, these formal ties to the pan-Turkic elements in the Füyuzat school expose a resurgence in pan-Turkic identity. However, Hikmet and Rüstem invoke the folk foremost as a triumph over individualism by appropriating the folk ballad as collective performance rather than by foregrounding the poet's will to power. The process of retrieving the symbol from its mythic past stages the relationship between intersecting visions of the Russian and Turkic lyric subjects. In this way, it confers the spiritual power of the mythic on the present and a vision of the Soviet future, by making the Turkic symbol resonate through its staging in the new poetic form. Through the materiality of their broken lines and letters, the Red Pens render legible the formation of a national Bolshevik political unconscious, bringing to the surface a new Turkic poetic subject through this literary encounter on the threshold of Eurasia.

POSTSCRIPT

Latinization and Refili's
"The Window" onto Soviet Azerbaijan

As one of the first collections of poetry published in the Latin script, Mikayıl Refili's *The Window*, which opened this book, frames a postscript to the supranational Turkic Muslim identity discourses that persisted during the revolutionary years in the Caucasus. Although Refili had been a member of the Red Pens, this 1929 collection formalized the beginnings of an Azerbaijani Soviet poetic tradition. The Latin script reforms of 1922 and 1929 marked a major break in the development of Turkic poetry, exercising a decisive impact on the conceptualization of the relationship between the poet and society. Rendering many readers of the old script suddenly illiterate, Latinization nationalized Turkic dialects, severing common linguistic ties among Turkic readers, and distanced them from cultural connections to the Ottoman and Persian empires.

The first Latin alphabet was introduced by the New Turkic Alphabet Committee (Yeni türk elifba komitesi) in 1922 but restandardized in 1929 after the Turkish script reforms.[1] Then, in 1939, the writing systems of the Soviet republics were all formally converted to the Cyrillic alphabet with the goal of repressing cultural and linguistic ties to Turkey. Refili was one of the first Red Pen writers to publish in the Latin script. *The Window,* his first single-author published collection of verse, hit the press in 1929 with a new Turkic free verse style that echoed Rüstem and Hikmet's poetry. Although *The Window* was published in the year of the second round of script reforms, it relied on the unstandardized Latin alphabet of 1922, which elided some of the letters k, q, g, and ğ, characteristic of the instability of writing systems during the formation of the national republics. The script reform not only changed access to written texts, rendering both works in the old and new scripts illegible to parts of the population, but also created a distance from the classical poetic forms of syllabic and *aruz* meter. As a technology of the Soviet modernity project, it thus shaped a vision of an Azerbaijani Soviet national literature and in so doing severed ties to other Turkic literary traditions across the Soviet Union and Turkey, marking a departure from the internationalist ambitions of the Eurasian conception of the Eastern International.

The Window envisions a break from the pan-Turkic community through Refili's focus on the monumentality of the local city. The broken script echoing Mayakovsky's, Hikmet's, and Rüstem's verse crawls across the page in a stepladder form. Like Hikmet and Rüstem's poems, utterances call out, as if voiceless orders to an uncertain audience. The title poem, which opens the collection, describes the city as viewed through the poet's window. Its vision of the street recalls Mayakovsky's and Vechorka's imagination of Baku as a colonial capital.

> Today the Gilavar wind is a little quiet;
> The fluttering of the leaves isn't heard . . .
> But the city, the big city,
> Has turned,
>   midnight, yet still
>   doesn't sleep,
>   A hallway
>   was opened white
>   from the window,
> My thoughts are like a handle bound to a shining
>   dagger . . .
> In front of me the big city
> A window.

Gilavar bu gün bir az sakit;
  Yaprakların titrəməsi duyulmayır . . .
  Lakin şəhər, böyük şəhər,
    Gəcə yarı,
      olmuş, fəqət
        uyumayır,
  Bir koridor
    açılmış aq
      pəncərədən,
  Fikrim bir sap kibi ilişmişdur parıldayan bir
      xəncərə . . .
  Önümdəki böyük şəhər
  Bir pəncərə.

                  (1929, 7)

The city emerges as if through a window frame in an interrupted panorama of frozen images. The poem begins and ends with two romantic symbols—the Gilavar wind, a local wind that blows across the Caspian Sea, and the curved dagger (*xencere*). However, the bustling city obscures the natural images that were once the focal points for the poets of the Fuyüzat school. Whereas for Rüstem and Hikmet, the wind brings the revolution, for Refili the sounds of the wind and the leaves are diminished by the repeated references to this "big" city. The stepladder structure of the poem literally creates a distance separating the natural world, poetic thought, and the city street. Indeed, the structural element of the window, which carries the white light into the hallway, eventually becomes not only the source of vision but synonymous with the city itself. Refili, as if answering Mayakovsky's order for new forms, creates a window in the Latin alphabet, through which the "big city" of Soviet Baku emerges.

The most dramatic example of Refili's use of the formal break of the free verse and the stepladder occurs in his poem about the revolution, "When the World Was Crumbling" (Dünya paralanırkan). In this work, not only does the force of the revolution break up the city of Baku, but it literally does violence to his verse, striking out single words in the stairstep form. The first section contains a series of floating fragments, as of torn window signs lost in the rebellion:

```
Revolution:
    Rebellion!
        The workers
            Of the whole universe
                Unite!—
                    they said,
    The sea was tumultuous,
        They were united,
            They awoke,
                They shouted:
Citizen,
    Comrade,
        Are you a friend? Or stranger?

İnqılab:
    İsyan!
        Cumlə cahan
            İşçiləri
                Birləşiniz!—
                    dedilər,
    Dalgalandı dəniz,
        Birləşdilər,
            Oyandılar,
                Bağırdılar:
Vətəndaş,
    Yoldaş,
        Dostsan? Yad?
                        (1929, 11)
```

The calls to the workers stand alone like strangers in an unidentified mass, such as the third person singular "they said," with its implied subject. The next stanza begins with the romantic image of the tumultuous sea as a metaphor for the crowd. Indeed, the stepladder here resembles a series of waves of lonely words caught in a confusing and tumultuous mass. The disorder is emphasized in the third stanza, in which the utterances specu-late who is a friend and who an enemy. The term *vetendaş*, meaning com-patriot, derives from the word for homeland (*veten*) and was often used by the Fuyüzat school to refer to a supranational spiritual, linguistic, and cultural home. Here it parallels the term comrade (*yoldaş*), which became the most common Turkic translation for the Russian *tovarishch*. Refili's stanza seems to question the relationship between the homeland and the Soviet state, confusing friend and foe in the fight.

Breaking the conventions of the *aruz* and syllabic meter, Refili instead repeats fragmented sounds to suggest new relationships among the words and images. The repetition of "q" creates a flood of blood and snow.

> Snow: Blood
>> Will flow
>>> Will color
>>>> The white quilt.

> Qar: Qan
>> Aqar
>>> Boyanar
>>>> Aq yorgan.
>>>>> (1929, 12)

The drawn-out stream of words also visualizes blood flowing out from the snow. Elsewhere in the poem Refili returns to rhymed couplets to create an internal rhythm of chaotic movement. Recalling the image of the Simurgh opening its wings, he writes:

> Boom, bam, bang . . .
>> Rebellion:
>> Opened its wings,
>>> Life!

> Bum, bom, pat . . .
>> Açdı qanat,
>>> İsyan:
>>>> Can!
>>>>> (12)

The rhymed pair, "opened its wings" (*Açdı qanat*) seem to fall down the stair-step line in the onomatopoeic "Bum, bom, pat." Refili imagines the opening of the wings of revolution and perhaps recalls the mythic Simurgh, emerging through a new sound and form. His imagination of the mytho-poetic past here descends the stairs into a new space of revolution. Indeed the "revolution" (*isyan*) rhymes with the old Azeri-Persian word for soul or life (*can*), emphasizing the coexistence of these two worlds.

The final two stanzas of the poem draw a conflicted portrait of the revolution in which the two worlds are suddenly thrown into shock. The red flag rises, designating the victory of the Soviets:

> The flag rose:
> Its color is blood . . .
> The Azan was called:
> Hey bourgeois
>   This is our feast!
>   * * *
> The sun rose:
> Those who rose were many.

> Yüksəldi bayraq:
>   Rəngi qan . . .
>   Çəkildi əzan:
>   Ey burzhui,
>   Bizimdür bu toy!
>   * * *
>   Günəş doğdu:
>   Yuksələn çoxdu.
>   (1929, 13)

Although the tone of Refili's work is celebratory, revealing his pro-Soviet orientation, a sense of the somewhat fractured nature of this victory persists in these final dislocated lines. In a shift away from the stair structure, these last verses seem relatively static, devoid of the chaotic images of tumultuous oceans and flowing blood in the poem's body. The blood-colored flag also lends the victory an ominous tone. In Azeri, the two pairs of internal lines rhyme, linking "The color of blood" (*Rengi qan*) and "The Azan was called" (*Çekildi ezan*), as well as the pairs "Hey bourgeois" (*Ey burzhui*), a transliteration of the Russian term for bourgeois, which in the original Latin script echoes "This is our celebration" (*Bizimdür bu toi*). The Latin script facilitates this rhymed couplet, which imagines the celebration of the rise of Soviet power in Baku through the Islamic call to prayer and local feast, *toy/toi*. In the final lines, the image of the rising sun indicates the rising of a new regime. The crumbling of the world, which Refili so carefully renders in the broken lines of the new script, announces a new era of poetry under the Soviet sun. However, as the bloody flag and call to prayer mark the new era, they remind the reader of the traditions of the past that fight to exist alongside these new poetic worlds.

Refili's collection envisions Soviet Baku through the Latinization reforms and their effects on the shifting form of new Soviet Turkic verse. His preference for the contemporary streets over the mytho-poetic past marks the closure of the imaginary "window onto the East," as well as a shift in Soviet diplomacy away from the Eastern International to state building. Only a few years later, the 1934 Congress of Soviet Writers further pushed to institutionalize an official Azerbaijani Soviet national canon. Unlike the congress of 1920, by 1934 Russian was established as the dominant language of cultural production. The congress also attributed literary greatness to a text's accessibility to Russian and Western readerships, as well as the Soviet Union's role in creating new writing systems (Schild 2010, 126–30). The script reforms were thus instrumental in articulating the gradual disappearance of heterological networks linking the cultural spaces of the Russian, Persian, and Ottoman empires. In this way, Refili's poetic form plays on the tension between the erasure of these linguistic and cultural networks and their instrumentalization in the fashioning of Soviet literary modernity. Although mytho-poetic symbols such as the Simurgh linger in the shadows of his verse, his *Window* envisions the first steps toward nationalization and the crystalization of a Soviet Azerbaijani consciousness.

The revolutionary transition from 1905 through 1929 constituted a brief period in Russian and Soviet imperial history. However, this *translatio imperii* nonetheless represents a foundational moment that set the stage for the formation of a multinational Soviet poetics and politics. Intertextual Turkic and Russian literary encounters produced during this transitional period on the threshold of the empire left a lasting impact on the ways in which forms of ethno-linguistic national identity were conceived in the Soviet Union and in the emergent post-Soviet nation-states. The popularity of romanticism in the constitution of Bolshevik anti-imperial discourses inspired the cultivation of a Turkic, Muslim, and often Marxist Azeri lyric subject through the processes of literary translation and transcription. From this vantage point, Sehhet's and Memmedquluzade's translations unmasked the anti-imperialist façade of the romantic poetics of Soviet expansion in the Caucasus. In turn, the introduction of a new avant-garde image of the Eastern International, as a Marxist-Leninist vision of Eurasia, and the materialist verse of the Red Pens appropriated mytho-poetic forms to mobilize a Turkic Muslim communist subjectivity. Finally, the introduction of the Latin script severed lasting ties between Azeri verse and a supranational archive of classical poetic forms, as it provided a new system for the literary inscription of Soviet Azerbaijan. Despite their attempts to throw the romantic canon from the steamship of modernity, the Russian and Turkic avant-gardes could not turn their gaze from the wreckage of the imperial past. Soviet imperialism, at least in its early years, was in this way a fundamentally avant-garde phenomenon. This brief period of avant-garde Azeri poetry, in its confusion of forms between languages and poetic traditions, produced the very sort of organic synthesis and worldly poetic experiments that the Russian futurists had imagined.

Placing these Russian and Azeri poetic visions of the Caucasus on the threshold reveals not only an orientalist vision of Eurasia and its attendant Bolshevik Eastern International but also the ways in which these discourses informed the creation of a modern Turkic literary subjectivity. The impact of the recurrence of Russian imperial poetry during the revolution and formation of the Soviet Union, through translation and allusion, illustrates the ways in which Azeri poetic resistance to Russian cultural imperialism also relied on a rejection of a singular, monumental national narrative. As an early model of anticolonial literature, these intertextual encounters between Azeri and Russian poetics offer an alternative vision of the "nonaligned" position. The multinational Soviet Union was generated on the discursive threshold between the Eurasian imaginaries, as well as between a Marxist-Leninist aesthetic commitment and the subordination of poetry to Soviet propaganda. The disconnection between postcolonial studies and Soviet literary studies was born out of the ambivalence exercised by the nonaligned countries in response to Moscow's colonial policies, particularly after the Soviet invasion of Budapest in 1956. However, as this book illustrates, the position of the Caucasus on the threshold of the Eurasian imaginary and the Soviet periphery generated aesthetic and political experiments with anticolonial Marxism that preceded the more prominent decolonization movements during the mid-twentieth century.

The construction of a form of supranational Muslim communist subjectivity between these Russian and Azeri literary encounters challenged
a static vision of European modernity through its exploration of poetry's
heterodoxical and heterological revolutionary potential. As an alternative
reading of literary modernity poised on Europe's and Russia's margins,
the Eurasian threshold thus attends to the uneven development of empire,
which has confined the vision of cultural production on the periphery
of the Soviet Union to a singular vision of belatedness and marginality.
Instead, my focus on Azeri and Russian revolutionary poetic encounters in
the dialogic space of the threshold exposes a modernist subjectivity, which
anticipates the material structures of revolutionary history. From the vantage point of the Caucasus, a comparative historical poetics thus poses a
challenge to Eurasianist totality, both its orientalist archive and its deterministic theoretical modality, exposing layers of intertwining, supranational influences at the foundation of this revolutionary poetic encounter.

NOTES

1. "Komsomol" was an abbreviation for the All-Union Leninist Young Communist League (Vsesoiuznyi leninskii kommunisticheskii soiuz molodezhi), founded in 1918 and reformulated in 1922 with the unification of the USSR.

2. In *The Translation Zone*, Emily Apter outlines the relationship between translation studies, *translatio studii*, and imperial succession, *translatio imperii*. Her model of translation zones describes the constellations of power that underlie the process of translation in industrial zones in transition. She describes these zones, drawing on the example of literary modernism, to encompass a "broad intellectual topography that is neither the property of a single nation, nor an amorphous condition associated with postnationalism" but instead "a zone of critical engagement . . . an act of love, and (as) an act of disruption . . . a means of repositioning the subject in the world and in history." In this way, for Apter "translational transationalism" hinges on an understanding of both "translations among small nations or minority language communities," as well as "the point of debarkation to a cultural caesura—a translation—where transmission failure is marked." Apter's emphasis on translation zones, which situates literary texts in historical as well as comparative global frameworks is particularly useful to understanding the context of revolutionary Baku (2006, 5–6, 41–82).

3. The Janus-headed vision of Eurasia, as Dragan Kujundžić writes of Russian historiography, signaled "the hinge of the self-colonizing gesture that inhabits Russian identity from within and, from the earliest times, divides or haunts Russian national genealogy" (2000, 896). Alexander Etkind argues that this discourse was the result of centuries of Russia's

politics of internal colonization. See Etkind 2011, 13–27. For a discussion of the mapping of these cultural and political tropes onto the geographic space of Eurasia, see Dobrenko and Naiman 2003.

4. See the interview with Centre Zahra in Paris (Dugin [Duguine] 2013).

5. Dugin writes, "Neo-Eurasianism was thus enriched by new themes: traditionalism, geopolitics, Carl Schmitt, Martin Heidegger, the Conservative Revolution, structuralism, anthropology, and so on" (2014, 11).

6. The Eurasianist landmass is juxtaposed against European Atlanticist merchantilism. For more on this binary and the role of time as a geopoetic corrective, see Uffelmann 2017, 360–84.

7. This connection between postcolonial theory and right-wing nationalism in the postsocialist world was explored in depth at a recent conference, "Imperial Reverb: Exploring the Postcolonies of Communism," held at Princeton University, May 13–15, 2016. This argument was compellingly explored in the following papers: Zsuzsa Gille, "Postcoloniality in 3D: The Eastern European New Right-Wing's Cognitive Map"; Saygun Gökariksel, "The Misadventures of Transnational Justice: Rightwing Lustration in 'Postcolonial' Poland"; Diana T. Kudaibergenova, "Unidentified Diffusion: The Use and Abuse of Postcolonial Discourse in Post-Independent Kazakhstan"; and Dirk Uffelmann, "Varieties of Nationalism in Polish and Russian Appropriations of Postcolonial Theory."

8. Samira Haj offers a generative framing of Islamic reform through a conception of modernity in dialogue with but independent from the singular structure of a progressivist, individual, Western subject (2009, 1–29). For a discussion of Muslim modernist reform movements in Central Asia, see Khalid 1998.

9. For a discussion of Refili's poem, see the postscript in this volume.

10. Here I refer to the fact that engagement with Marxist or Marxist-Leninist theory no longer accords with communist party membership.

11. See Moore 2001, 111–28; Young 2001, 113–58. Also, for a discussion of Russian Orientalism, see the section "Orientalism on the Threshold" in this volume.

12. Timothy Mitchell framed his intervention drawing on figures such as the Egyptian economist Samir Amin and the sociologist Immanuel Wallerstein (2000, 17).

13. According to Ilya Kliger and Boris Maslov, historical poetics began with Alexander Veselovsky's work from the 1860s to the 1900s and continued into the twentieth century with thinkers such as Mikhail Bakhtin, Olga Freidenberg, and Mikhail Gasparov. They define the movement as "a Russian scholarly tradition that approaches literary form as a recursive and mediated response to historical processes," which influenced both the formalists and the Moscow-Tartu school of semiotics. Kliger and Maslov argue for the explicitly political nature of historical poetics: "Whereas the evolution of form-oriented approaches to art and literature finds parallel in the West, the specific conditions of Russian historical development stimulated an understanding of literature as intricately woven into the fabric of sociopolitical life" (2016, 1, 10).

14. In a 2014 article, Harsha Ram takes up the work of the Georgian Blue Horn poets as an example of the ways in which "peripheral modernisms" have been marginalized from the Western canon. As an example of peripheral modernism, Ram argues that the Blue Horns respond to the process of the uneven modernization of Georgian national culture through a "sense of historical belatedness" that challenges the authority of the metropole in authorizing history and progress. Ram concludes that the movement should not be celebrated as a form of local resistance to colonial modernity due to its "profoundly Eurocentric aestheticism." In contrast, this book takes the vantage point of the South Caucasus to instead expose the impact of a particularly heterodoxic and heterologic space tied to Turkic Muslim cultural discourses on our conceptualization of (post)colonial modernity. See Ram 2014, 343–59.

15. These fields continue to be better represented in the German and French academies. However, excellent scholarship on the Caucasus and Central Asia has been taken up particularly in the disciplines of history and anthropology. See Derluguian 2005, Goff 2014, Gould 2016, Grant 2009, Khalid 2015, and Schild 2010.

16. The so-called Eurasianist movement of the 1920s and 1930s, which largely opposed the Bolshevik revolution and identified a return to Orthodoxy as one of its central values, was formulated through the writings of Nikolai Trubetskoi, Petr Savitskii, Petr Suvchinskii, and Petr Arapov. This movement drew on a pervasive political, geographical, and political ideology that promoted Russia's "half-Asian" Eurasian character. For a discussion of the movement, see Glebov 2011, 103–14. The first Eurasianist work is dated to June 3, 1921, when G. V. Florovsky and N. S. Trubetskoy delivered papers at the Religious Philosophy Circle of Sophia. The collection of ensuing published articles was titled *Turn to the East: Presentments and Fulfillments, the Eurasianists' Affirmation*. The Eurasianists eventually split into two groups: the leftist "clamor group" of intellectuals in exile in the Parisian outskirts including S. Ia. Efron and D. P. S. Mirsky who held notable pro-Soviet sympathies and a larger group in Prague including Trubetskoy, Savitsky, and Jakobson. See Sériot 2014, 24–60.

17. The intelligentsia was a group of civic-minded intellectuals [*intelligenty*] of both noble and non-noble birth, which formed in Russia at end of the eighteenth century under the reign of Catherine the Great. Particularly during the nineteenth century, the ideas of the Russian intelligentsia were in many ways shaped by the influence of French, British, and German culture. See Berlin 1979.

18. In this sense, I refer to the influence of the émigré intellectuals who founded the Eurasianist movement, such as Roman Jackobson on the formation of Slavic studies.

19. For a history of the development of US Slavic studies in response to Cold War policies, see Engerman 2009, 6.

20. However, the first rediscovery of Bakhtin's work in the Soviet Union occurred in the 1950s when a group of students at the Gorky Institute of World Literature, where Bakhtin had defended his dissertation a decade earlier, became interested in his *Problems of Dostoevsky's Art* (*Problemy tvorchestva Dostoevskogo* [1929]). At this time Bakhtin generated an updated version of the manuscript and published it as *Problems of Dostoevsky's Poetics* (*Problemy poetiki Dostoevskogo* [1963]). See Emerson 1997, 42. Bakhtin's work came into vogue in the United States in the 1980s through Caryl Emerson and Michael Holquist's translations and was taken up in postcolonial studies in the 1990s in the work of Homi Bhabha and Robert Young.

21. For a discussion of the notion of "speaking Bolshevik," see Kotkin 1995; Voloshinov 1973, 1976. For a discussion of Bakhtin's flirtations with Marxist theory, see Zbinden 2006, 64.

22. See the debate published in the 1981 special issue on modernism in *New German Critique* (Habermas and Ben-Habib 1981, 3–14).

23. See also Bürger 1984, 49–50.

24. Vasilii Osipovich Kliuchevskii (1841–1911), one of the most famous nineteenth-century historians in the Russian empire, was of Mordvinian origins. Cited in Etkind (2011, 97).

25. See Etkind's extensive discussion of Kliuchevsky 2011.

26. For an interesting discussion of postcolonial politics in the context of transnational poetics, see Harrison 2013, 353–69.

27. The idea of constellations of power refers to Foucault's theorization that the individual subject "is not a pre-given entity which is seized on by the exercise of power" but rather "is the product of a relation of power exercised over bodies, multiplicities, movements, desires, forces" (1980, 74).

28. The word "Russian" encompasses both *russkii*, signifying an ethno-religious identity, and *rossiiskii*, signaling a civic identity. Since *Rossiia* referred to Russia's status as an empire,

rossiiskii also included the non-Russian subjects of the empire. While the Russian imperial administration relied on the legal term *inorodtsy* to distinguish the ethno-religious category of non-Slavic and non-Orthodox subjects of the empire, language remained a potent exterior manifestation of otherness. The legal term *inorodtsy* was used to refer to non-Slavic and non-Orthodox peoples of the empire. See Slocum 1998, 173–90.

29. Similar to the parallel terms *russkii* and *rossiiskii*, the term "Azeri" described an ethnic identity and "Azerbaijani" [*Azerbaycanlı*], a civic one. Indeed, while the latter appeared in the press at the turn of the century, it did not gain circulation in official documents until the mid-twentieth century, between the 1920s and the 1930s. To this end, Harun Yilmaz argues that the term was artificially created by the Soviet government to delimit ties with Persia and Turkey (2013, 1–23).

30. While the term "Muslim" did not account for Sunni, Shi'i, and Sufi religious differences or ethnic distinctions, it expressed a unified sense of belonging to a creed. Sunni and Shi'i Islam historically differ on the question of the succession of the Prophet as the caliph of the Islamic community. Whereas Sunnis believe that Muhammed appointed Abu Bakr, Shi'a believe that he instead appointed 'Ali. Many other distinctions can be made between the groups, including the interpretation of the hadith or the sayings of the Prophet, observations of practice, and the return of the Mahdi—the redeemer of Islam in Islamic eschatology—who the Shi'a call the Twelfth Imam. Practitioners known as ṣūfī belong to different ṭuruq (pl.) or groups, such as the Naqshbandi tariqa. While many studies discuss Sufism as a mystical variant of Sunni or Shi'i Islam, Sa'diyya Shaikh describes it more thoughtfully as "the process by which a believer embraces the full spiritual consequences of God's oneness (*tawḥīd*). The goal of the Sufi path is to enable a human being, through the cultivation of virtuous excellence (*iḥsān*), to commune directly and experientially with her Creator. In the historical development of Sufis, one encounters varied and increasingly sophisticated notions of the mystical path, or *ṭarīqa*. Such a path generally entails that the Sufi aspirant, under the guidance of a spiritual master, follows a practical method of purification and refinement of the self, undergoing many states (*aḥwāl*) and stages (*maqāmāt*) that reveal progressive unveilings of the divine reality (*haqīqa*)." See Shaikh 2014, 35.

31. I thank Altay Göyüşov for this note.

32. The term "Türk" was also used throughout the empire to emphasize a supranational linguistic bond as Turkic speakers. As with the term "Muslim," *Türk* did not account for regional linguistic or cultural differences but rather signified cultural cohesion.

33. The territory of Azerbaijan, which held one brief period of statehood under the Azerbaijan Democratic Republic between 1918 and 1920 and after the fall of the Soviet Union in 1991, is populated by many ethno-linguistic groups, including Tats or mountain Jews, Avars, and the Lesghians—who also inhabit much of the North Caucasus, Chechnya, and Dagestan.

34. As Francine Hirsch notes, Uvarov's choice of the term *narodnost'* reflects his effort to distinguish Russia from other European states (2005, 37).

35. *Sobornost'* is a Russian Orthodox concept that refers to union of individual believers in a unanimous whole, and *tawhid* is a metaphysical concept of the Unity of Being most often attributed to the thirteenth-century Islamic philosophers Ibn Sab'īn and Ibn 'Arabī. These terms are discussed in chapters 1 and 2.

36. I use the term "supranational" to distinguish my description of the social and political histories of the Russian empire and the Soviet Union from Western notions of cosmopolitanism and Marxist notions of internationalism. The term "internationalism" served a crucial Marxist-Leninist ideological role, particularly during the formation of the Soviet Union. Stalin mobilized "cosmopolitanism" as an indictment of dubious cultural or economic loyalties abroad. In his fascinating study on cosmopolitanism in Soviet and post-Soviet Baku, Bruce Grant highlights the social and official histories of the terms "internationalism" and

"cosmopolitanism." Grant argues that after cosmpolitanism's recuperation in the Brezhnev era, in Baku it began to signify ascribed notions of hierarchy and social mobility within the state related to Russification. Indeed, the acquired significance of the term resonates with the introduction of the ideologies of internationalization in the former imperial space of the Caucasus. See Grant 2010, 123–47.

37. Consider the following ethnographic description: "the Caucasus, standing along a stone wall between Asia and Europe" [Kavkaz, stoiaschii kamennoiu stenoiu mezhdu Aziei i Evropoi] (Kovalskaia 1869, 54).

38. See Tolz 2015, 32. Tolz argues that the 1917 revolution did not mark a rupture in orientalist discourses, but rather that Eurasianism illustrates continuities between German and Russian orientalist conceptions of imperial and national identity as well as their evolution through transition from the Russian to the Soviet empire.

39. See Sériot 2014, 159–74.

40. While some Eurasianists supported the Soviet state, such as D. S. Mirsky (who notably worked for the Soviet secret service), many of the members were émigrés who envisioned Eurasianism as an alternative to communism motivated by a religious conception of collectivity. Indeed, this slippage between state and imperial policy and anti-imperial politics is consistent with the nineteenth-century exiled intelligentsia's writings. For more on Mirsky, see Sériot 2014, 24–60.

41. Danilevsky's treatise was first published in essay form in *Dawn* [*Zaria*], 1–6, 8–10 (1869).

42. Castagné writes, "In Russia, the German Weltpolitik is on one of the chosen fields, and as a result of its superior culture of energetic intellectuals at the head of the Soviet regime, Germany can see that the 'Germanophone' Bolsheviks work in reality for her (Germany) in the Muslim Russian countries and furthermore they are formed in the mold of their ethnic doctrines. It is a Muslim Tatar from Kazan who presides over the Muslim Charity Association in Berlin, a spirit of German culture which, under the last three incumbents, led the Soviet Foreign Ministry in Tashkent" (1923, vi). A friend of Kazakh activist and statesman Mustafa Chokay, Castagné held ties to the Prometheus movement and appeared in their publications. See Copeaux 1993, 9–46. On Castagné, see Gorshenina 1997, 255–72.

43. In his 1923 essay, "The Tower of Babel and Confusion of Tongues" [Vavilonskaia bashnia i smeshenie iazykov], Trubetskoy writes, "Several languages belonging to a single geographical and cultural-historical region often exhibit similar features and this resemblance is conditioned by prolonged proximity and parallel development, rather than by common derivation" (Trubetskoy 1991, 153–54).

44. Polytony describes languages in which the opposition of shifting tone pitch distinguishes meaning. Jakobson offers the example of Swedish, Serbo-Croatian, Chinese, and Vietnamese (1962, 156). Consonant palatalization (phonetics) refers to the pronunciation of a consonant by either touching or moving the tongue away from the hard palate (roof of the mouth).

45. Jakobson writes, "Borrowing is just a particular type of convergence. The essential problem in comparing contiguous languages is the problem of development convergence" (1962, 149).

46. In his article on forms of historical time animating revolutionary consciousness, Boris Maslov connects engagements with Darwinian evolution to late imperial consciousness through Marr's work (2016, 29–43).

47. Similarly, in an essay on Pushkin, Dostoevsky describes the figure of the Russian hero, embodied in Pushkin's *Evgenii Onegin*, as the ultimate stranger, who like the Caucasian exiled poets, was estranged from both his native Russia and Europe (1972–1992, 14:425–40).

48. Alexei Khomiakov [Aleksei Stepanovich Khomiakov] (1804–1860) was a theologian, poet, and philosopher, whose writings promoted pan-Slavic unity. Unlike the popular

ethnolinguistic distinction of Aryans and Semites made by the famous French linguist Ernest Renan (1823–1892), Khomiakov's categorization of the Aryan race included Arabs and Persians, defining Christianity as the basis for Russia's Europeanness. In Khomiakov's system, Iranian Russia opposes Kushite China and Germany. Khomiakov's theory not only ironically parallels German philosopher Friedrich von Schlegel's *Philosophy of History* (*Philosophie der Geschichte* [1828]), but also recalls Ernest Renan's religious-linguistic categories in his *General History and Comparative System of the Semitic Languages* (*Histoire générale et système comparé des langues sémitiques* [1855]). Khomiakov's model reverses Renan's categories, aligning monotheistic Islam and Russian Orthodoxy against secular and polytheistic Europe and Asia in many ways closely approximating Schlegel's model, although excluding Germany from the Iranian race. It is also interesting to note that the Iranian's "love of freedom" is counteracted by the Kushites' "mindless conquest." While the structure of Khomiakov's history engages with German and French orientalist models of national Indo-European origins, he appropriates this model to distinguish Russia's Slavic Eurasian identity. See Lim 2006, 166–67; 2013, 109–70.

49. Gasprinsky's familiarity with the Eurasian topos on which his utopia seems to play could have come out of his close friendship with the conservative nationalist journalist Mikhail Katkov. See Fisher 1998, 127–52.

50. This vision of Eurasia as a world apart, neither Europe nor Asia, emerges in the work of the Slavophile linguist ethnographer and geographer V. I. Lamansky (1883–1914). See Sériot 2014, 49.

51. Most notably in his *French and African Letters* Gasprinsky valorizes the French civilizing mission on the modernization of North Africa (Gasprali 2008, 169–206).

52. While the first diplomatic and military ventures in the Caucasus began under the reign of Ivan IV in the sixteenth century, major military campaigns and the appointment of the first Russian viceroy of the Caucasus, Prince Grigory Potemkin, occurred under the reign of Catherine II during the late eighteenth century.

53. This group of orientalists includes the writers Alexander Pushkin, Mikhail Lermontov, Alexander Bestuzhev-Marlinsky, as well as the historian Vasily Bartold, the linguist Nikolai Marr, and those writers who worked for the Imperial Geographical Society (Imperatorskoe russkoe geograficheskoe obshchestvo [1850–1917]). The latter was one of the major organs of Russian orientalist studies in the late nineteenth and early twentieth centuries. For a discussion of lesser-known orientalists, see Layton 1994.

54. The Decembrists, as Andrzej Walicki writes, idealized "ancient Russian liberties" refashioned according to European Enlightenment values (Walicki 1979, 67–68). The work of this group of intellectuals, also known as "the children of 1812," was marked by the Napoleonic invasion and an interest in awakening a distinctive native principle or *samobytnost'*, meaning individuality and independence, popularized in discourses of Russian national identity of the period. In invoking the term "Decembrists," however, I refer more broadly to sympathizers with their critiques of autocratic power.

55. Indeed, these images remained in dialogue with the European trope of "the noble savage." For a discussion of these terms as well as Russian Orientalist portraits of the figure of the North Caucasian Muslim in a comparative context, see Layton 1997, 88–89.

56. Dana Sherry argues that in the Russian imperial administration in the Caucasus the Imperial Russian Geographical Society became one of the most influential orientalist institutions. The Imperial Geographical Society relied on a system for classifying the population in terms of the physical landscape they inhabited. Sherry writes, "in short, geography functioned for Caucasus officials much as race functioned for British officials in India" (2007, 5).

57. While religious freedom was already protected under Catherine the Great's religious toleration, the "freedom of conscience" further liberalized religious practices and in particular conversion (Werth 2014, 207–39).

58. Tiflis is the Russian name for the city of Tbilisi and was used by the Russian imperial administration.

59. See Grant 2010, 123–47.

60. See Mamed 2001; Swietochowski 1995, 31–62.

61. The *ta'ziyeh* is a ritual performance mourning the death of Imam Husayn and anticipating his return as the Mahdi or twelfth Imam (Floor 2005, 129–96).

62. Though the title of the journal is often translated as *Abundance*, the word transliterated as *füyuzat* comes from the root *feyz* meaning prosperity, spiritual nourishment, and enlightenment. Given the aims of the journal, I have chosen to translate it as *Enlightenment*.

63. The public scope of these discourses was, however, limited by low literacy rates.

64. As scholars have noted, the idea of Russian culture in the US academy was defined by a Soviet canon of works and shaped by a singular vision of literature as a space for political and social dissent. William Mills Todd III calls this the centripetal model of Russian culture (1998, 26–40). See also Buckler 2009, 251–63.

65. While other writers such as Tolstoy, Nikolai Leskov, and Vladimir Makanin were important contributors to the Russian orientalist imaginary, with the exception of Tolstoy these figures were less frequently referenced by their Azeri interlocutors. Although Tolstoy appears in the Azeri press, his works were not central to the development of a modern Azeri poetics, which this book traces.

66. Earlier in 1915 they organized a special committee in Istanbul, the Comité pour la Défense des Droits des Peuples Turco-Tatar Musulmans de Russie, whose aims were to protect against violations of civil and religious rights for Muslim, Turko-Tatar nations in Russia.

67. Prometheus was supported by the Polish statesman Józef Piłsudski. For a discussion of the Prometheus movement and journal and the French and Polish role in its formation, see Copeaux 1993, 9–46; Iskhakov 2017. On Rasulzade, see Bennigsen 1985. For articles from *Promethée*, see Rasulzade 2010.

68. Some of the most notable discussions of the literature of the Muslims of the Caucasus in Anglophone scholarship include Grant 2009; Gould 2013, 87–107; and Tyrrell 2001.

69. See Etkind 2011. Monika Greenleaf (1994) discusses Pushkin's vision of Russia's orient through the romantic fragment as an ironic questioning of the intentionality of language; Katya Hokanson (2008) nuances the discussion of discourses of center and periphery in literature about the Russian imperial expansion in the Caucasus; Adeeb Khalid argues that given the influence of European thought in Russia beginning in the eighteenth century, Russian orientalism could be better understood as "variations on a pan-European theme than as inherently different" (2006, 29); Nathaniel Knight highlights the role of discourses of Russia's national uniqueness in shaping orientalist discourses (2006, 37); Maria Todorova (2006) notes that the debate over Russian orientalism highlights a major problematic in Russian historiography. Much like other non-Western historiographies, in the case of Russia there is a tendency either to rely on a standard model of empire and account for the necessary deviations from it or to focus on creating local categories of knowledge. Todorova favors "the universalist idiom (tempered, of course, by a strong grounding in historical specificity)" (2006, 48–49). Vera Tolz argues that Said's conceptual framework as well as the work of authors such as Anouar Abdel-Malek, on which his work relies, remains close to the work of the Russian orientalist Sergei Oldenburg's in their conception of a "unified European/Western identity" with its origins in ancient Greece (2006, 132). Susan Layton's (1994) study is one of the first to discuss the relevance of the Saidian framework to the Russian context.

70. As Suny argues, "Russian historiography's contribution to the national imaginary . . . coincided with the development of an ideology of imperialism, in journals like *Vestnik Evropy* and *Russkii vestnik*, the emergence of Russian schools of ethnography and geography, and the flowering of poetry, novels and short stories, music, and the visual arts" (2001, 24–66). Harsha Ram (2003) echoes this point in his analysis of what he terms the poetics of empire. See Etkind 2011.

71. Adrienne Edgar discusses nomadism in the context of Turkmen nation building, and Douglas Northrop takes up the role of women in the nation-building project, building on Gregory Massell's "surrogate proletariat." See Bustanov 2015; Edgar 2004; and Northrop 2004.

72. Yuri Slezkine argues that nationalities policies were built on the tension between the unity of the Bolshevik revolutionary cause and efforts to foster the diversity of national cultures within the Soviet system through the process of translation. Slezkine frames this tension through a historical comparison to the Ilminsky system's use of national language education to spread Christianity in the nineteenth century (2014, 414–52). The Ilminsky system was a strategy of bilingual education based on the efforts of Nikolai Ilminsky (1822–1891)—a Russian linguist, translator, and missionary who attempted to spread Christianity among the Tatar Muslim population of Kazan through the use of bilingual Turkic and Russian language instruction. See Kreindler 1969.

73. This critique of Eurocentrism is in part directed at the totalizing singularity of Said's model, which as Ali Behdad argues, "leaves no room for the possibility of differences among the various modes of orientalist representation and in the field of power relations" (1994, 11). The major exceptions to this case are the aforementioned works of Etkind and Suny, as well as Young 2001. Robert Young argues that the international character of postcolonialism, which he calls *tricontinentalism,* is predicated on its independence from nationalist reliance on bourgeois class domination. This understanding of postcolonialism through "the fundamental reliance between the proletariat exploited within an imperialist nation and the colonized peoples exploited by that nation," is one that developed in Lenin's writings on national self-determination. Young defines postcolonial critique as the "historical moment of the theorized introduction of new tricontinental forms and strategies of critical analysis and practice" that "looks back to the political commitment of the anti-colonial liberation movements." The term "tricontinental" offers an alternative to the label "Third World," which Young appropriates from Anouar Abdel-Malek's speech at the first conference of the Organization for the Solidarity of the Peoples of Africa, Asia, and Latin America at Havana in 1906 (2001, 113–58).

74. Haun Saussy's (2016) work provides a crucial intervention in correcting the hegemonic position of the genre of the novel in world literature discussions.

75. Said writes, "Orientalism can be discussed and analyzed as the corporate institution for dealing with the Orient—dealing with it by making statements about it, authorizing views of it, describing it, by teaching it, settling it, ruling over it: in short, Orientalism as a Western style for dominating, restructuring, and having authority over the Orient" (1978, 3).

76. Said develops the idea of contrapuntality as a response to the critique of his model's Eurocentrism.

77. These discussions emerged in the 2004 *Boundary 2* collection on "Critical Secularisms." These discussions have been developed in the work of Aamir Mufti, R. A. Judy, Emily Apter, Stathis Gourgouris, Nergis Ertürk, and Bruce Robbins. Aamir Mufti outlines secular criticism as "a practice of unbelief" which provides "an invitation to the crossing of boundaries—boundaries of nation, tradition, religion, race, and language—and carries the implication that the world as a whole can be the only authentic horizon of critical practice" (2004, 2, 4).

78. As Mufti argues, contrapuntality "enacts a complex relationship with the notion of tradition—linguistic, national, civilizational—that it both takes seriously and puts into question by opening up any particular tradition to interaction with other such purportedly discrete entities" (2005, 474, 477).

79. As Bakhtin's translators Caryl Emerson and Michael Holquist note, *slovo* literally means "the word," but more specifically signifies "both an individual word and a method of using words that presumes a type of authority" (Bakhtin 1981, 427).

80. This shift in the value of language, which in part occurred in nineteenth-century linguistic philosophy, is often called the linguistic turn. Caryl Emerson frames this debate in terms of Foucault's *The Order of Things*, linking Bakhtin's interest in the interplay between linguistics and psychology, particularly in Lev Vygotsky's work (1983, 245–64).

81. Said writes, "texts are worldly, to some degree they are events, and even when they appear to deny it, they are nevertheless a part of the social world, human, and of course the historical moments in which they are located and interpreted" (1983, 4).

82. For a discussion of Bakhtin's involvement in Russian Orthodox circles, see Clark and Holquist 1984, 82–84. Wilhelm von Humboldt developed a vision of language as constituted both through a product—that is, a closed sign system (*Werk/ergon*)—and as an expression or activity (*Tätigkeit/energeia*). Von Humboldt, whose work had a significant impact on Soviet linguistics more broadly, influenced Bakhtin's conception of discourse as both the product and the activity of production. Discourse understood in this way not only attempts to decipher the *product* or *ergon* of cultural symbols but also embodies the activity or *energeia* of cultural reproduction itself. These terms were taken from Wilhelm von Humboldt's works, which were translated into Russian in 1858 and popularized by Gustav Shpet in his 1927 *The Internal Form of the Word* and many others throughout the 1920s. For more on this connection, see Smith 1998, 17–18.

83. Nina Gurianova also places Bakhtin's dialogism and Shklovsky's estrangement at the center of avant-garde conception of the function of art and literature, as the provocation of the self-awareness and the reader or audience's self-consciousness response (2012, 2–13).

84. Avant-garde artists inspired by the Commedia dell'arte included Andrei Bely, Alexander Blok, Nikolai Evreinov, Sergei Gorodetsky, Elena Guro, Viacheslav Ivanov, Vladimir Mayakovsky, and Igor Stravinsky. See Clayton 1993; Gurianova 2012, 253–75.

85. According to Julia Kristeva's definition, intertextuality not only signifies the "banal sense of the 'study of sources'" but "this transposition of one (or several) sign-system(s) into another" (1986, 111).

86. Karine Zbinden argues that Kristeva's misreading of Bakhtin in part stems from her appropriation of a Lacanian linguistic model in which the self is constituted by and through language, thus Kristeva translates Bakhtin's intersubjectivity as intertextuality (2006, 19–21).

87. This passage is taken from Bakhtin's posthumously published revisions for *Problems* from 1961.

88. In a related discussion Madina Tlostanova introduces Bakhtin's border or threshold chronotope to read transcultural writings penned under colonial power (2007, 409).

1. Parodic and Messianic Genealogies

1. An earlier, abbreviated version of this chapter was published in *Slavic Review* (Feldman 2016a). While Gogol perhaps owes his early fame to his contemporary critic Vissarion Belinsky, his writings gained new popularity, particularly in the North American academe, through the work of the Russian formalists and semioticians during the first part of the twentieth century. These include Tynyanov's, Eikhenbaum's, Chizhevsky's, and Bakhtin's essays from the 1920s and Lotman's work from the 1960s. See Bakhtin 1984; Bakhtin and Sollner 1983, 34–50; Chizhevsky 1979, 137–60; Eikhenbaum 1979, 101–18; Lotman 1990, 199–241; Tynyanov 1979.

2. David Engerman connects Cold War state department funding in the 1960s to the formation of a specific literary canon in US Slavic departments (2009, 6).

3. Celil Memmedquluzade (1866–1932) was a dramatist, poet, prosaist, and literary critic. In 1887 he graduated from the Gori Pedagogical Seminary and taught at local schools in the Georgian countryside. In 1903 he moved to Tbilisi to work as a correspondent for the leading Azeri language newspaper *The Russian East (Şerq-i Rus)*, which was edited by his friend Mehemmed ağa Şahtaxtinski. When the paper closed, he bought the press and founded the Azeri language satirical paper *Molla Nesreddin* in 1906. His most notable works include the short stories: "The Events in the Danabash Village" (Danabaş kendinin ehvalatları), "The Russian Girl" (Rus Qızı), "Freedom in Iran" (İranda hürriyyet), "Qurbaneli bey," and "The Postbox" (*Poçt qutusu*), as well as the plays *The Dead (Ölüler)* and *My Mother's Books (Anamın kitabı)*. *Molla Nesreddin* was published between 1906 and 1917 in Tbilisi, in 1921 in Tabriz, and between 1922 and 1931 in Baku. See Bennigsen 1962, 505–20; Bennigsen and Lemercier-Quelquejay 1964; Mirehmedov 1980.

4. Indeed, the importance of Gogol's work for Memmedquluzade is demonstrated by the presence of a copy of Gogol's masterwork *The Wanderings of Chichikov or Dead Souls* in his personal library. His Russian-language books are collected in the Institute of Manuscripts of the Azerbaijan National Academy of Sciences in Baku [Elyazmalar Institutu] f. 6, v. 552, s. 319.

5. In particular, Mitchell (2002) points to the influence of Gaston Bachelard, Martin Heidegger, Henri Lefebvre, Michel de Certeau, and Michel Foucault on Harvey's *Justice, Nature, and the Geography of Difference*. Mitchell (2000) explicitly uses the term "geopoetics" in his introduction to a volume of *Critical Inquiry*.

6. Indeed, a collection of recent scholarship has made important efforts to expand the canon. Examples of such interventions include Caffee 2013; Grant 2009; Gould 2013; Haber 2003; Murav 2008, 642–61; Ram and Shatirshvili 2004, 1–25; Schild 2010; and Yountchi 2002.

7. As Thomas de Waal's article in *Foreign Policy* attests, Gogol's work is still called on to explain Soviet and post-Soviet geopolitics. De Waal (2012) writes: "How about skipping the political science textbooks when it comes to trying to understand the former Soviet Union and instead opening up the pages of Nikolai Gogol, Anton Chekhov, and Fyodor Dostoyevsky?" The Jordan Center at New York University hosted two blog entries from contemporary Slavicists discussing the 2014 revolution in Ukraine through Gogol's oeuvre. Edyta Bojanowska's entry from April 22, 2014, "All the King's Horses: Ukraine, Russia, and Gogol's Troika," traces the troika as a symbol for Russian messianism from Gogol's work in the nineteenth century to the recent Olympic program. In a post from March 2, 2014, titled "Russia and Ukraine: Stupidity, Cynicism, or Both?" Eliot Borenstein concludes his critique of the historical inaccuracy of US media representations of Ukraine by turning to Gogol to explain the fruitlessness of disputes over identity, citing both Gogol's Russified and Ukrainainized names, "You said it, Nikolai! Or Mikola. I really don't care which one."

8. Notable scholarship on Russian/Soviet imperial connections with pan-Turkic culture includes the work of Michael Reynolds, Holly Shissler, Samuel J. Hirst, Nergis Ertürk, and Azade-Ayse Rorlich.

9. Postcolonial readings of Gogol (most notably those of Myroslav Shkandrij and Edyta Bojanowska) conceptualize representations of Ukraine through the conflicting forces of exoticization and domestication. Russian imperial narratives presented Ukraine through divergent and often anachronistic discourses of Romantic nationalism, westernization, and Orientalism, marking its geopolitical linkages to Russia, Poland, and the Caucasus. Shkandrij's (2001) *Russia and Ukraine: Literature and the Discourse of Empire from Napoleonic to Postcolonial Times* is structured around a comparative Orientalism, linking representations of Ukraine to the Caucasus in Russia's Asiatic or oriental imperial periphery. Indeed, as Shkandrij highlights, Ukraine and its inhabitants were often described as "Asian" (2001, 79). Bojanowska's (2007) *Nikolai Gogol: Between Russian and Ukrainian Nationalism* also

dramatizes the tension between these conflicting identity discourses and geopolitical alignments in Gogol's writings, focusing in particular on the ways in which Gogol's works project the culture of the periphery onto their vision of metropolitan Petersburg. While Gogol has been the most popular focus of postcolonial readings, post-Soviet scholarship has also considered the topic of Pushkin's blackness. See Nepomnyashchy, Svobodny, and Trigos 2006.

10. In his compelling discussion of translations and productions of Shakespeare in postrevolutionary Russia, Aydin Dzhebrailov (1991) highlights the ways in which these adaptations reveal a dynamic interplay between avant-garde and socialist realist aesthetics and Stalinization. Dzhebrailov notes the influence of Caucasian productions of *Othello* on Stalinist kitsch aesthetics. Although he focuses largely on the individual cult of Stalin and his role as a master censor, he nonetheless identifies the production of the play in the Caucasus and its thematic concern for political marginality as motivation for its ascension to prominence in the Soviet canon.

11. Kujundžić engages with Mikhail Bakhtin's discussion of parody in *Problems of Dostoevsky's Poetics* as the force generating the renewal or rebirth of the novelistic genre (1997, 40–41).

12. Etkind argues that postcolonial criticism not only clarifies Gogol, but that similarly Gogol explains Bhabha's theory of "colonial doubling." He appropriates the term from Bhabha's influential essay "Of Mimicry and Man: The Ambivalence of Colonial Discourse" in his 1994 book *Location of Culture* (2011, 14–15).

13. Despite their common interest in Bhabha, methodologically Etkind's analysis, which focuses on Bhabha's and Said's unmarked Russian sources, diverges from Kujundžić's reading of parody, which crucially reflects back on Russian colonization through its belated reverberations in Mikhail Bakhtin's theoretical reception of Nietzsche as well as his own reception by the semiotician Yuri Lotman at a conference in Estonia.

14. These included the series of uprisings across the Russian empire in 1905–1906, the Persian Constitutional Revolution of 1906–1907, and the Young Turk Revolution of 1908.

15. Leslie Sargent (2010) argues that the 1905–1906 so-called Azeri-Armenian war should be contextualized within a broader context of violent uprisings that occurred more systematically throughout the empire. As Sargent demonstrates, the "ethnic violence" that occurred between Azeris and Armenians cannot be attributed either to a struggle for territorial domination or to an ancient history of ethnic hatred as it is usually framed. Rather, the violence, which may have begun as individual acts of terror that expanded into full-scale riots, was exacerbated by reporting of the event in pamphlets and newspapers. This reporting then promoted the further polarization of ethnic divisions and contributed to the institutionalization of Azeri and Armenian national identities. Indeed, she argues that even after 1906 more fluid formations of identity persisted. To this end, she cites how Dashnaks and Azeris continued to collaborate for constitutional reform, participating in both the Young Turk movement and the Iranian Constitutional movement.

16. For more information about the mobilization of oil workers in the Caucasus and the recognition of the Hümmet—the first all-Muslim Social-Democratic Party—at the Sixth Congress of the Russian Social Democratic Workers' Party in 1906, see Bennigsen and Wimbush 1979, 14; Kleveman 2003, 11–30.

17. Indeed, the play was performed six times in Tbilisi in 1906 and thus would have been familiar to the journal's readers (Mamed 2001, 91).

18. For a discussion of the particular reform agenda of the jadids, see Khalid 1998. This interest in reform as such can be read as analogous to the Russian avant-garde's interest in revolution as such. On this topic, see Nina Gurianova's (2012) discussion of the "aesthetics of anarchy."

19. For instance, to a Persian an Azeri might be called a "Turk," whereas for a Georgian, Armenian, or Russian an Azeri speaker would be called "Muslim." This shift was particularly relevant after the Russian annexation of the Caucasus brought more "gaurs" or unbelievers (as Russians were called) to the region. The term "Muslim" would have also been used to refer to both Sunnis and Shi'a.

20. See Swietochowski 1995, 30; Altstadt 1983, 199–209.

21. Gogol's line completes his satire of the provincial imperial bureaucracy when the mayor breaks the fourth wall to address the audience. He inquires of the audience, "What are you laughing at? You are laughing at yourselves!" (Chemu smeetes'? Nad soboiu *smeetes'*) (2003, 4:94). The trope of self-reflection also alludes to the play's epigraph, which reads, "There is no blaming the mirror if your face is crooked" (*na zerkalo necha peniat', koli rozha kriva*) (IV. 4).

22. The Sufi writer and thinker Idries Shah (1990, 1993) discusses the importance of the Molla figure in Sufi teachings.

23. The early figures of the Ukrainian national movement include the poet Taras Shevchenko (1814–1861) and the ethnographer Mykola Kostomarov (Nikolai Ivanovich Kostomarov) (1817–1885). In his seminal Ukrainian nationalist ethnography, "Two Russian Populations" (Dve russkie narodnosti), Kostomarov distinguished the autocracy and collectivism of *Northern* or Great Rus (Russia) from the liberty and individualism of *Southern* or Little Rus (Ukraine) (1861, 33–80; 1996, 122–45).

24. The vision of literature as social critique is indebted to a genealogy of nineteenth-century Russian social and aesthetic theory, including the work of Gogol, Vissarion Belinsky, and Nikolai Chernyshevsky. To this end, Chernyshevsky described this engaged literary tradition as "the Gogol period in Russian literature" (Chernyshevskii 1855, 1–2, 4, 7, 9–12; 1953).

25. Eikhenbaum describes this in particular as "imitative *skaz*" (1979, 119–21).

26. Kujundžić (1997) illustrates the seminal role of Nietzsche in Russian Formalist thought.

27. The term "Tatar language" was used by Russian officials and orientalists to refer generally to Turkic Muslims of the Russian empire. However, the term designates distinct ethnolinguistic groups of Turkic Muslim communities inhabiting the Crimea, the Volga region, and Siberia.

28. The Muslim modernist thinker Jamāl Al-Dīn Al-Afghāni used the term to signify Islamic socialist governance. See Moazzam 1984, 34.

29. Aziz Sharif (1937) describes Memmedqul'uzade, citing his pen name Molla Nesreddin, as "the Azerbaijani Gogol." Sharif affirms that a comparison between "The Carriage" and "Qurbaneli Bey" would provide "the best means of determining the degree of the Gogolian influence on the Azerbaijani writer." Sharif also cites Memmedqul'uzade's attention to language, his capability to "masterfully construct his artistic language, which excites the reader's passionate indignation regarding [these] events and their participants" as a distinguishing feature of his work.

30. Gogol's story was originally published in Alexander Pushkin's journal *The Contemporary* (Sovremennik). Memmedqul'uzade's story was originally published in a booklet form by the publisher Qeyret in Tbilisi, Georgia. See Memmedqul'uzade 2004.

31. Priscilla Meyer argues that Gogol drew on elements of Honoré de Balzac's fiction as material for his descriptions of city life, combining elements from Balzac's psychological sketches with supernatural and fantastic traces of German Romanticism and Ukrainian culture when writing the Petersburg tales. Among the formal features of Balzac's prose, his metonymic description of the carriage in *La Comédie humaine* (1815–1830), as Meyer argues, forms the basis for Gogol's "The Overcoat" (1842). See Meyer 2008, 26–33; Fanger 1965, 101–29.

32. The term "meat [mincing] knives" refers to the specific knife used for preparing *kat-let*, a Russian dish made of ground meat, formed in a patty, and pan-fried.

33. For a discussion of the semiotics of food and dining, see Brown 1978; LeBlanc 1999. Indeed, Memmedquluzade, like Gogol, often employs food and drink to externalize repressed unconscious thoughts and desires. See Koropeckyj and Romanchuk 2003, 539; LeBlanc 1999.

34. Despite any efforts by the imperial government to co-opt Muslim religious figures into the Russian civil-military system, the military administrators' approach to Islam was marked by apprehension toward nonorthodox sects, specifically those they identified as sufi by their *tariqa*, or order, and public displays of worship such as the *zikr*. The performance of the *zikr* as well as the space of the Caucasus politicized an image of the freedom-fighting Muridist in the Russian imagination. In this way, Russian orientalists elided diverse Sufi groups throughout the Caucasus with those in Chechnya who challenged the authority of the imperial Russian state. See Blauvelt 2010, 244–50; Jersild 2002, 20.

35. This collection contains nonfiction ethnographies as well as excerpts from Russian literature, such as the following line from Pushkin's *Journey to Arzrum*: "The dagger and the sword are parts of their body, an infant begins to master them before he can prattle" (Semenov 1869, 23).

36. I compare the Russian term *kinzhal* to general term *nozh*, which also signifies knife or dagger. The Russian word is most likely a borrowing from the Georgian *khanjali*, which itself was derived from the Persian *khanjar*.

37. See Bojanowska 2007, 189–210.

38. As Dragan Kujundžić argues, the very idea of the false inspector in Gogol's work recalls the series of pretenders to the Russian throne, alleged sons of Tsar Ivan the Terrible, a tradition that "profoundly affected Russian genealogical, patrilinear certainty" (2000, 897).

39. See Edward Said's discussion of the dissemination of literary canons as the transformation of naturally filial to systematically affilial relationships, securing a system through which a Western canon retains an authority to determine literariness (1983, 1–30).

40. For Sharif (1937) the major differences between the authors lie in their comedic presentation. He argues that tragicomedy was central to Gogol's work, while Memmedquluzade showed no mercy for his characters, remaining indifferent to their plight. He argues that while Memmedquluzade is often "cruel to his characters, merciless to them," his authorial success lies in his capacity to generate his "desired mood in the reader, shaking him with the horror of the truth, cause in him resentment against this truth, and direct his will to fight for its destruction."

41. For a discussion of the role of *sobornost'* in *Revizor*, see Malik 1990; Robey 1997, 235; Shapiro 1993, 40–58. For a discussion of the *ta'ziyeh* tradition, see Floor 2005, 129–96.

42. The Azeri citation may be a translation of an apocryphal quotation in a popular and widely disseminated book on Goethe from the turn of the century in which the latter allegedly explains to Herder, "The theater can become a temple, when the right priest is found, just as the church can become a playhouse, if such a one is missing there" (*Auch das Theater kann ein Tempel werden, wenn der rechte Priester sich findet, sowie die Kirche ein Schauspielhaus werden kann, wenn hier ein solcher fehlt*) (Ohorn 1898, 107). I thank Brigitte Rath for this citation.

43. One of the cartoons in a 1910 issue of *Molla Nesreddin* pictured a "modern" Azeri reformer captioned "education with arms" who takes aim at the specter of a conservative molla. The caption reads, "The solar eclipse: Russian missionaries always say that the reactionary mollahs are our brothers in spirit" (Slavs and Tatars 2011, 155).

44. Adeeb Khalid (1998) traces a similar trend in the work of the *usul-i jadid* or new school method of reform in Central Asia.

45. The article was printed in the May 1, 1916, issue of the Azeri journal *The Free (Open) Word (Açiq söz)*.

46. Malik al-Mutakallimin, also Haj Mirza Nasrallah (?–1908) was an early twentieth-century Muslim modernist thinker who studied with Sayyid Jamāl al-Dīn al-Afghānī and was a leader in the Iranian Constitutional Revolution of 1906. Bábism (1844–1852) was founded by Sayyid 'Alí Muhammad Shirazi, who took the title Báb or "gate" from a Shi'i theological term. The Báb's claims to the creation of a new revelation signified a rupture from the Islamic clergy. The religion was persecuted, and the Báb was shot. Those who accepted Bahá'ulláh as the new messiah and split from the Azali Bábís into a new sect known as the Bahai faith. See Amanant 2000.

47. Judith Robey draws her reading of *sobornost'* as "a unanimity, a synthesis of authority" and "the liberty in love with unites believers" from Sergei Bulgakov (1997, 235).

48. Describing the portrait of Pompeii moments before death, Gogol writes, "their communal movement constitutes [the painting's] beauty" (*v svoem obshchem dvizhenii uzhe sostavliaiut krasotu*) (2003, 4:112); See Robey 1997, 237; Bodin 1987, 5–16; Mann 1978, 119.

2. Aesthetics of Empathy

1. Cited in Sandler 2004, 197.

2. Sabukhi was Axundov's penname. All citations of "Na smert' Pushkina" are taken from Axundov 1837, 297–304.

3. This treaty changed the political, physical, and cultural geography of the region, dividing the Azeri people between Persia and Russia along the Araz River. In particular, the Turkic cultural center of Tabriz was separated from the rest of Azerbaijan. Mirze Feteli Axundzade is known as Axundov (Akhundov) in Soviet and Russian scholarship and Axundzade in Iranian and contemporary Azerbaijani scholarship.

4. Drawing on Edward Said's *Orientalism*, Katya Hokanson presents the Russian empire as a series of power relations marked by the binaries of center and periphery. See Hokanson 2008, 3–22; Bassin 1991, 1–17.

5. The etymology of "vernacular," from *verna*, meaning home-born slave, evokes the notion of subaltern speech and serves as a crucial reminder of the class and racial dynamics underlying vernacular literary production. Axundov's plays, written in Azeri, were hailed as the first examples of the modern prose tradition.

6. I discuss Kazy-Girei's short fiction in "Orientalism on the Threshold: Reorienting Heroism in Late Imperial Russia" (Feldman 2012, 161–80).

7. This chapter is in many ways in dialogue with Aamir Mufti's discussion of the emergence of a modern Urdu lyric subject in Faiz Ahmed Faiz's *ghazals*. Drawing on Adorno's conception of the lyric, Mufti argues that Faiz's lyrics make visible the social life of the subject and enable a critical discussion of Indian literary modernity in the context of the partition (2007, 210–43).

8. In *The Translation Zone*, Emily Apter discusses a similar relationship generated between translation studies, or *translatio studii*, and imperial succession, or *translatio imperii*. Her model of translation zones describes the constellations of power that underlie the process of translation amid geopolitical and industrial zones in transition (2006, 5–6, 41–82).

9. Ricoeur calls this process "linguistic hospitality" (2004, 23).

10. The belated publications and translations of these works in the 1970s still preceded Ricoeur's study by a decade.

11. Ricoeur (1984–1988) does not directly engage with the chronotope but does discuss Bakhtinian dialogism in *Problems in Dostoevsky's Poetics* as a radically different type of emplotment. For a discussion of Bakhtin's and poststructuralism, see Kujundžić 1997, 52–56. For an extended comparison of Bakhtin and Ricoeur, see Collington 2001, 221–31.

12. Bakhtin outlines his theory of ethics primarily in his earlier works penned in the 1920s. "Art and Answerability" (Iskusstvo i otvetstvennost'), "Author and Hero in Aesthetic Activity" (Avtor i geroi v esteticheskoi deiatel'nosti), and "Toward a Philosophy of the Act" (K filosofii postupka).

13. Ricoeur similarly critiques structuralism and semiotics for its preference for rules over history (1984–1988, 2:29–60).

14. Axundov's first works in Azeri Turkic include the play *The Story of Monsieur Jordan the Botanist and the Famous Dervish Mastali Shah* (*Hekayeti-müsyö Jordan hekiminebatat Derviş Mesteli şah caduküni-meshur* [1850]) and his novella *The Deceiver of the Stars* (*Aldanmış Kevakib* [1857]).

15. Axundov's 1857 treatise on language reform, *The New Alphabet* (*Elifba-yi cedid*), can be seen as a precursor to the Soviet alphabet reforms of the 1920s.

16. The Gori Teachers Seminary was a school to educate teachers in Georgia sponsored by the Russian imperial government and developed collaboratively with local intellectuals. At the school, young men from the Caucasus (including Azeris, Armenians, and Georgians) were instructed in Russian language and culture, as well as literature and religious studies in their native languages. The Gori seminars educated some of the most important writers and politicians of the twentieth century, including Celil Memmedquluzade, Üzeyir Hacıbeyov, Nariman Narimanov, and Stalin. See Gafarova 2015.

17. For a biography of Axundov, see Algar 1984; 2000, 186–90).

18. According to Algar (1984), Axundov was born to a wealthy Persian former noble-turned-tradesman and the descendant of an African servant to Nader Shah.

19. Adol'f Petrovich Berzhe (1828–1886) was a Russian orientalist who specialized in the South Caucasus. Berzhe's most notable work was *Chechnya and the Chechens* (*Chechniia i chechentsy*), published in Tbilisi in 1859. The German orientalist Friedrich Martin von Bodenstedt (1819–1892) infamously published the works of Vazeh under his own name in *Songs of Mirze Şefi Vazeh* (*Die Lieder des Mirza Schaffy* [1851]).

20. For a discussion of the creation of oriental studies in Russia, see Layton 1994, 75–79; Schimmelpenninck van der Oye 2008, 443–58; 2010.

21. A Russian translation was published the following year (Uvarov 1811, 32–33). Susan Layton notes that Uvarov wrote this essay in collaboration with the German orientalist Heinrich Julius Klaproth (1994, 76).

22. Indeed, for many years the original manuscripts were thought to be lost. A photograph of the manuscript was first published on November 18, 1936, in *Bakinskii rabochii*, no. 267 (1936). The historians Aziz Sharif and Shikhali Kurbanov (1979) discuss its publication history. Translations and photographs of the original manuscripts can also be found in Kurbanov 1959. A transliteration of the Persian version is in Âdamiyat 1970, 273–76.

23. For a detailed discussion of the Russian translations and commentary surrounding the publications, see Caffee 2013, 70–79.

24. See also Kurbanov 1959, 115–16.

25. For an introductory discussion of the *qaṣīda* genre, see Esgerli 2005, 2–23.

26. See Andrews 1985, 131–73.

27. The text was originally written in Persian. See Floor and Javadi 2009.

28. The linguistic/cultural space does not coincide with state sovereignty here.

29. The term "Tatary" (or "Tartary") is a geographic designation used by Russian and European orientalists from the Middle Ages through the twentieth century to designate the steppe from the Caspian Sea and Ural Mountains to the Pacific Ocean. The term was also used by Russian orientalists to refer to the Muslim population of this area as the Turkic descendants of the Mongols. This geographic, ethnic, religious, and linguistic categorization misrepresents what is a diverse group of Muslims (Shi'i, Sunni, and Sufi) who speak distinct dialects

of a Tatar language group (Crimean Tatar, Volga Tatar, etc.) as well as other languages with related grammatical structures and word borrowings including Azeri, Turkmen, etc.

30. For a discussion of the Sokolov translation, see Caffee 2013, 70–79; Kurbanov 1959, 119. For a discussion of the Pushkin monument, see Martin 1988.

31. In the Soviet Union Axundov was promoted as atheist and anti-imperialist, while contemporary scholarship presents him as a westernizer and apologist for Russian colonialism. For the Soviet scholarship on Axundov, see Kurbanov 1959; Guseinov 1949. For contemporary discussions of Axundov and religions, see Cole 1996; Kia 1995; Sanjabi 1995; Zeynalova 2008.

32. Manuscripts of Axundov's treatise are collected at the Institute of Manuscripts of the Azerbaijan National Academy of Sciences in Baku: f. 2, v. 21, s. 1–283. The papers are written in old script Azeri and Russian in black ink on white paper. They contain the author's edits. Included is a letter addressed from Axundov to a St. Petersburg publisher Iakov Alekseevich Isakov dated February 12, 1875.

33. Though a similar correspondence existed between personages of the same name it markedly does not contain the same discussions of religion, which are presented in Axundov's work. See Memmedquluzade (2004, <?> 1:279).

34. The tension between the imagined original (to which his reader has no access) and the translation is central to Axundov's heterodoxy. Brigitte Rath (2014) frames the pseudotranslation as a world literature phenomenon, as a "*mode of reading* that oscillates between seeing the text as an original and as a translation pointing towards an imagined original, produced in a different language and culture for a different audience."

35. Although Mehrdad Kia describes the role of Axundov's religious education in shaping his philosophy, he describes Axundov's critique of religion as if he "turned his back on Islam" (1995, 427).

36. Cited in Guseinov 1949, 275.

37. Axundov mentions North American and European Protestantism in *Three Letters* and his autobiography.

38. David Fieni (2006) argues compellingly for the centrality of a romantic rhetoric of decadence in the work of the French orientalist Ernest Renan and the Islamic scholar Sayyid Jamāl al-Dīn al-Afghānī. For a more detailed discussion of the romantic elements of German orientalism, see Marchand 2009.

39. The origins of the term *jadid* [*cedid*] can be traced to the reforms of the Muslim school and the introduction of the phonetic method [*üsuli-cedid*] for teaching the alphabet. Ismail Gasprali (Gasprinsky) launched the first of these schools in Crimea (Gasprali 2008, 19). For a discussion of Jadidism in the Russian empire, see also Rorlich 1986; Khalid 1998. For a discussion of the role of *ijtihad* in Islamic revivalist thought, see Dallal 1993.

40. The article, "Mirze Feteli Axundov: On Religions" (Mirze Feteli Axundov dinler haqqinda), was first printed in a 1928 issue of the reformist women's journal *The Eastern Woman* (*Şerq Qadını*) (Memmedquluzade 2004, 1:279).

41. See also Axundov 1953, 105–8. For the Azeri version, see Axundov 2005, 1:17–129.

42. See Shaikh 2014; Nasr 2006, 156.

43. A surah is a division of the Qur'an, which could be likened to a chapter. There are 114 in total. "1. Say: He is God, / The One and Only; 2. God, the Eternal, Absolute; 3. He begetteth not, / Nor is He begotten; 4. And there is none / Like unto Him" (*Holy Qur'an* 1983).

44. The Ottoman constitutional reforms marked the conclusion of the *Tanzimât*, a series of modernization campaigns of the legal and administrative infrastructure in the Ottoman empire between 1839 and 1876.

45. Max Müller defines the Turanian language group alongside the Semitic and Indo-European groups as "comprising the dialects of the nomad races scattered over Central and

Northern Asia, the Tungusic, Mongolic, Turkic, Samoyedic, and Finnic, all radii from one common centre of speech" (1862, 43).

46. Cited in Swietochowski 1995, 59.

47. For a discussion of the contributions of *Enlightenment* to the Azeri cultural sphere, see Veliyev 1999. The New Literature movement gathered around the Turkish journal *Scientific Wealth (Servet-i Fünûn)*, founded in 1891 by Ahmed Ihsan (Toköz) (1868–1942). Its influence lasted from 1896 through 1901, only to be overtaken by the Dawn of the New Age group (*Fecr-i Âti*) (1909–1912). Both groups integrated the French Decadent tradition of the Parnassians with Ottoman poetic forms, drawing on Persian and Arabic grammatical, lexical, and poetic structures. See Ertürk 2011, 21, 68.

48. Ram's (2003) reading not only highlights a tension between imperialism and a challenge to the tsars' authority but attends to the generation's sense of futility in its attempts to effect social change after the Napoleonic Wars and the failed Decembrist revolt.

49. Nancy Condee also uses this term in her formulation of a Slavic postcolonial (2006, 829–31).

50. See Andrews 1985, 63.

51. See also Sa'diyya Shaikh's discussion of Sufi states of revelation and the search for divine reality (2014, 1–33).

52. Elsewhere in Pushkin's poetry about the Caucasus he uses the term "chamois" (*serna*), a reference to Zhukovsky's and Derzhavin's poems, which he cites in "Kavkazskii plennik." Again following orientalist fashion, Pushkin uses *serna* to describe Maria as a form of the beloved in "Poltava." In Azeri the term *ceyran* refers specifically to the animal preferred in the poetic tradition.

53. For a discussion of the evolution of the prophetic trope from the eighteenth century ode to the Decembrists and finally Pushkin, see Ram 2003, 63–212.

54. Ram's work highlights this connection between the poetics and politics of empire and the *prophetic* sublime (2003, 63–212).

55. Pamela Davidson argues that "the Decembrist poets turned to the figure of the prophet as a powerful rhetorical image to buttress their authority as the proponents of radical social and political reform" (2002, 490).

56. See Davidson 2002, 495. Pushkin's ignorance of the history of the scripture of Islam is evident, as the Qur'an was said to have been revealed to the prophet Mohammad over a period of twenty-three years, the last of which occurred during his final pilgrimage.

57. See Belinskii 1953–1959, 1:48; Gogol 2003, 8:50–55.

58. See Kia 1995, 427.

59. For a discussion of early Soviet propaganda produced in Baku and the appropriation of the apocalyptic trope of Israfil's horn, see Feldman 2016, 221–49.

60. This essay was first published in the fourteenth issue of *Heyat* on February 23, 1905.

61. Ram discusses the Russian sublime in relation to Hegel's characterization of oriental art (2003, 14–15, 22).

62. The poem appears both in "Toward a Philosophy of the Act" and "The Author and Hero in Aesthetic Activity" (Bakhtin 1997–2012, 1:62–64, 74–75).

3. A Window onto the East

1. See Kazemzadeh 1951; Suny 1972; Swietochowski 2004.

2. See Baberovski 2010, 211.

3. For a discussion of the belatedness of Georgian modernism, see Ram 2014, 343–59.

4. Katerina Clark also frames the avant-garde's politics as a continuation of romantic aesthetics through the poets' sense of social alienation from capitalism, which she calls "Romantic Anticapitalism" (1995, 17).

5. See Gurianova 2012, 253–75.

6. Within Rancière's (2000) hierarchy these functions are constituted through two political subjectivities: the *archi-political* concerning the party and the *meta-political* concerning the distribution of the sensible. For Rancière, the role of the aesthetic regime of the arts in inventing sensible forms for a future community hinges on Schiller's notion of the *aesthetic education of man*, which connected the activity of thought with sensible receptivity as a single reality.

7. Joshua Neese-Todd discusses the immigration of Russian writers from Tiflis to Baku (2006, 54).

8. The university was originally established in Tiflis in 1918 as the multilingual, multiethnic Transcaucasian University under the Transcaucasian Federation. After the collapse of the Transcaucasian Federation, it was relocated to Baku and named Baku State University (Atakişiyev 1991, 75).

9. The propaganda posters were produced by BakKavRosta at the Artistic Union of Baku Workers (Khudozhestvennoe Ob"edinenie bakinskikh rabochikh) between 1921 and 1923. The State Free Satirical Agitprop Theater/Free Critique Propaganda Theater opened in 1920 and was renamed the Baku Worker's Theater (Bakinskii rabochii teatr) in 1923. See Efendiev 1931; Rehimli 2005, 355–58.

10. The Bat was a touring revue group directed by the Russian-Armenian director and performer Nikita Baileff, which traveled throughout Russia, France, and the United States during the early 1900s.

11. Azim Azimzade made his name a decade earlier, publishing drawings in *Molla Nesreddin*.

12. For a discussion of the Russian émigré community in Tiflis, see Nikol'skaia 2000.

13. For more on the history of these networks see Neese-Todd 2006, 34.

14. Information about this hymn can be found in the album of the socialite Vera Sudeikin-Stravinsky, who collected memories, poems, and art during the time she spent in the South Caucasus during the Civil War. A copy of the original poem with accompanying designs can be found in figure 125b of Bowlt 1995.

15. For descriptions of Gorodetsky's radical political shift, see the accounts of the poet Georgii Ivanov and journalist Carl Bechhofer cited in Bowlt 1995. Bechhofer explains this abrupt change in Gorodetsky's political opportunism (73, 85).

16. Leonid Strakhovsky observed that only a year earlier Gorodetsky had worked for a propaganda division for the White army leader General Denikin while in Tiflis. See Neese-Todd 2006, 27.

17. For more on BakKavRosta, see Bobrovnikov 2013, 31–35. Solomon Benediktovich Telingater (1903–1969) was a graphic designer born in Tiflis and active in the Transcaucasian futurist scene. According to some sources, Telingater founded BakKavRosta; from 1921 to 1925 he led the Baku artists union. In 1925 he moved to Moscow to study at the Moscow Higher Art and Technical Studios (VKhutemas) and continued to produce books and graphic designs there.

18. The connection between the spleen and a melancholy temperament is rooted in ancient Greek medicine and the theory of the humors. However, it was most memorably popularized by romantic poets, perhaps most notably the nineteenth-century French poet Charles Baudelaire.

19. Although the Merry Harlequin lasted for only a few months, in December 1920 it was revived as the Satirical Agit Theater by a section of the Bat, and in 1923 became the Baku Workers Theater (Bowlt 1995, 85).

20. Evreinov writes: "Ladies and gentlemen, I forgot to tell you that neither your applause nor your hissing of the piece is likely to be taken seriously by the author, who preaches

that nothing in life is worth taking seriously. And I suggest that if truth is on his side, then you should hardly take his play seriously, all the more as Harlequin has probably risen from his deathbed already, and, perhaps, is already tidying himself in anticipation of a call, because, say what you like, but the actors can't be responsible for the freethinking of the author. (Exit.)" (1916, 33).

21. Douglas Clayton discusses this trend in terms of the influence of Max Nordau's theory of the degeneration of European society, which was translated into Russian at the turn of the century and became an influential text for the early avant-garde (1993, 3–15).

22. A copy of the original poem can be found in Bowlt 1995, fig. 106. My translation offers revisions of Bowlt's.

23. For a more detailed discussion of the development of imperialism and colonialism in Marx and Lenin's writings, see Young 2001, 101–12.

24. The first speech was an "Appeal of the Council of Peoples Commissars to the Muslims of Russia and the East," delivered not long after the revolution on December 3, 1917. The second was an "Address to the Second All-Russian Congress of Communist Organizations of the Peoples of the East," given on November 22, 1919. In 1918 Stalin created the Commissariat for Muslim Affairs (Muskom), which in turn generated the Central Bureau of the Communist Organizations of the Peoples of the East, its international department, and the Turkestani All-Russian Central Executive Committee, which organized propaganda in Central Asia, the Caucasus, and the Middle East (Kirasirova 2014, 45–50).

25. The term "Tricontinent" offers an alternative to the label "Third World," which Robert Young appropriates from Anouar Abdel-Malek's speech at the first conference of the Organization for the Solidarity of the Peoples of Africa, Asia, and Latin America at Havana in 1906 (2001, 125).

26. However, as the historian Masha Kirasirova argues, by 1925 the notion of a global East had waned, giving way to a vision of two easts. She exposes this transition in Stalin's 1925 lecture given to the KUTV, "The Political Tasks of the University of the Peoples of the East," in which he outlined a Soviet and a non-Soviet East. This division signaled a new conceptualization of Soviet polity and the move away from a revolutionary mode of global agitation toward a more centralized focus on state building (2014, 3).

27. The work of Ignác Goldziher (1850–1921) had become popular through the Russian orientalist Baron Viktor von Rosen (1849–1908) who had, in turn, studied with German Arabist Heinrich Fleischer (1801–1888). Kirasirova suggests that Troianovsky may have also drawn on the work of Sir Halford John Mackinder's "Geographical Pivot of History" (2014, 38–39). For more on the instrumentalization of Islam by the Russian imperial administration, particularly to attack sectarian groups, see Crews 2006, 31–92; Keller 2001, 1–68.

28. Kazim bey/Kazembek (1802–1870) was born in southern Azerbaijan/northern Iran. After receiving a religious education during his early years in Derbend (present-day Dagestan), he met Scottish Presbyterian ministers who convinced him to convert to Christianity, taking as his new name Aleksandr. He was one of the first lecturers who taught Russian orientalism in Russian (previously Latin and German were the only available languages). He held appointments at both the Kazan and the St. Petersburg schools and worked to make St. Petersburg the center for Russian orientalism. Like Axundov and Bakıkhanov, Kazim bey held a double identity as an imperial bureaucrat, scholar, and writer. Kazembek's most influential works include *General Grammar of the Türco-Tatar Language* (1848); *Muridism and Shamil* (1859); and *Bab and the Babis, or Political and Religious Uprising in Persia from 1845–1853* (1866). See also Schimmelpenninck van der Oye 2008, 443–58.

29. The work blends the disciplines of history and fiction, announcing its task to "recount stories of Muridism." Throughout these recollections or stories—as the ambiguity of the term *povest'* suggests—the author reports dramatic dialogues between himself and Imam Shamil,

as well as his own experiences in the Caucasus (1985, 22). Indeed, the convention of blending the genres of historical writing and fiction became popular with Nikolai Karamzin's *History of the Russian State* (*Istoriia gosudarstva Rossiiskogo* [1816–1829]), which cited literary works to authenticate the history of the formation of the Russian empire. His synthesis of history and memory further contributed to the construction of an idea of Russian identity as a hybrid fusion of the myths and folk culture of its colonies in the Caucasus.

30. Indeed, one hundred years later under the Soviet Union, Heydar Huseynov was removed from the Academy of Sciences and stripped of his awards for his 1949 book, *From the History of Social and Philosophical Ideas in Azerbaidjan during the Nineteenth Century* (*Iz istorii obshchestvennoi i filosofskoi mysli v Azerbaidzhane XIX veka*) and its alleged idealization of Muridist principles. Huseynov was criticized in particular for the following statement: "As is known, Muridism had a place in Azerbaijan. As a social movement, Muridism was directed against the colonial oppression of tsarism and also against Azerbaijani feudalism." For drawing the same historical continuity between antiauthoritarian sentiment and Sufi ideas, Huseynov, like many Azerbaijani writers and thinkers during the Russian empire and the Soviet Union, was accused of supporting revolutionary sentiment and critiquing authoritarian regimes (Guseinov 1949, 288).

31. In 1918 Mirsaid Sultan Galiev was appointed head of Muskom, a division of Narkomnats, which was created in 1917 to manage the work of local pro-Bolshevik leaders. In 1920, Nariman Narimanov was elected chairman of the Azerbaijani Revolutionary Committee (Azrevkom), then chairman of the Council of People's Commissars (Sovnarkom) of the new Azerbaijan Soviet Socialist Republic. The Bolsheviks created Narkomnats even before the revolution, in June 1917, to promote an anti-imperial ideological stance. Building on this policy, in the 1920s the Soviet government instituted the nativization reforms, known as *korenizatsiia*, literally "taking root." For a discussion of *korenizatsiia* policies in the Caucasus, Central Asia, Siberia, Crimea, and the Volga region, which included the promotion of local administrators to Soviet posts and the institutionalization of local languages in government and educational sectors, see Martin 2001, 129–81.

32. Narimanov writes in particular that "comedy is the mirror of life" (1988, 1:46).

33. See Narimanov for a discussion of this campaign against Tağıyev (1990, 47).

34. Indeed in a 1902 letter Narimanov appealed to Tağıyev to defer school costs he was unable to pay (1988, 1:53–54).

35. In 1920 Narimanov agreed to help secure Baku's oil for Moscow in exchange for leadership of the Sovnarkom. However, this arrangement fell apart after Soviet troops secured power in Baku, and in 1923 Narimanov was sent to Moscow to further curtail his influence. Sara Brinegar calls this Narimanov's "oil deal" (2017, 372–94).

36. Narimanov was very active in revolutionary efforts in Persia through Persian social democratic groups such as the oil worker group Adalet and the Mujahid, constitutionalists from the city of Resht who maintained close ties with Russian revolutionaries and were active in organizing uprisings against the shah during the Constitutional Revolution of 1908.

37. The congress organizers included Grigorii Evseevich Zinoviev, Grigol (Sergo) Ordzhonikidze, Mirsaid Sultan-Galiev, Anastas Mikoyan, and Nariman Narimanov. For details about the conference organization and proceedings, see Riddell 1993, 164.

38. Narimanov writes: "The general impression of the congress was such: we wanted to show the representatives of the East, to speak at length and with beauty of our photographic work, which reached perfection when the speakers were shot in all poses. Lloyd George received the photograph, in which the representatives of the people of the East, holding in their hands naked blades [*kinzhaly*], revolvers, clubs, and knives threatened European capital. He probably smiled and wrote to Comrade Chicherin: 'we agree to enter into negotiations with Soviet Russia on the topic of trade relations.' After this I received a second letter from

Comrade Chicherin in which he wrote that it is necessary to stop all assistance to the Persian revolutionaries, as it will hinder us in our ties to England" (1990, 21–22).

39. Based on Lenin's discussions of the necessity of national language propaganda, Yuri Slezkine similarly argues that the Leninist paradox was built on the tension between the unity of the Soviet revolutionary cause and efforts to foster the diversity of national cultures within the Soviet system through the process of translation. Slezkine frames this tension through a historical comparison to the Ilminsky system's use of national language education to spread Christianity (1994, 414–52).

40. Orthodoxy was defined as a central component of Russian imperial identity in the nineteenth century, as emblemized by the official state slogan of the 1830s, "Orthodoxy, Autocracy, Nationality" defined by Sergei Uvarov, an adviser to Tsar Nicholas I and minister of education (Knight 2000, 54). Francine Hirsch notes that Uvarov's choice of the term *narodnost'* reflects his effort to distinguish Russia from other European states (2005, 37).

41. While these groups emerged after the 1917 revolution, their creation reflected the new liberties in the postimperial society, not direct affiliations with Bolshevik networks (Khalid 1998, 245–69).

42. These include the British delegate Thomas Quelch, who accused his translator of distorting his speech with anti-imperial rhetoric, and the Azerbaijani delegate Dadash Buniatzade, whose speech was severely abridged in Russian. The excluded portions, critical of Ottoman and German imperialism in the Caucasus, were later translated in response to demands from the crowd (Riddell 1993, 27, 111).

43. Michael Kemper notes this slippage, tracing it to the publication of "Manifesto to the Peoples of the East" that year in *Kommunisticheskii international*, no. 15 (1920), 3141–50 (2010, 435–47).

44. The term *ghazavat* was largely preferred to the term *jihad*, at least in the Northern Caucasus during the nineteenth century. The most famous example of *ghazavat* was the Muslim freedom fighter Imam Shamil's holy crusade against Russian imperialism.

45. For a discussion of Pushkin's revival in the Soviet canon of the 1930s, see Clark 2011, 307–44.

46. Varied dates are given for conversion, ranging from the eighth through the tenth centuries. However, conversion was not an event but rather a process that unfolded between the eighth and nineteenth centuries (Lapidus 1988, 48).

47. Harsha Ram also emphasizes the influential role of the nineteenth-century Orientalist imaginary in contemporary media representations of the Caucasus (1999, 1–29).

48. Indeed, given the lack of available housing Khlebnikov lived in the BakKavRosta facilities for a time (Neese-Todd 2006, 48).

49. In her discussion of Khlebnikov's Baku poems, Andrea Hacker relates Khlebnikov's repetition of consonants to Pavlovich's speech (2006, 456).

50. Clark writes that "Romantic Anticapitalism" as "the quest for the authentic," a romantic model of society, in the face of capitalism's "alienation, individualism, and the commodification . . . of culture," in its turn, "was often played out in terms of class" (1995, 16–17).

51. Gurianova traces this term to Burliuk's 1913 poem "Cubism" (2012, 27).

52. For a reproduction of the *carmen figuratum* and a full transcriptions of these fragments from Khlebnikov's notebooks, see Hacker 2006, 447–65.

53. Babism's new revelation signified a rupture from Islamic institutions. Citations from this poem are taken from Hacker 2006, 452–69. Translations are based on Hacker's but have been altered.

54. For a discussion of Khlebnikov and the image of Pushkin as prophet, see Moeller-Sally 1996, 201–25.

55. See Ram 2003, 142–76.

56. See Neese-Todd 2006, 50. Iurii Degen also worked at the university.

57. In her article on Ivanov's lectures, Anna Tamarchenko analyzes the content of his unpublished lecture notes (1986, 82–95).

58. In *The Birth of Tragedy* (1872) Nietzsche argues that the fusion of Dionysian and Apollonian *Kunsttreiben*, or artistic impulses, serve as the foundation for the great Greek tragedies until Euripides' use of Socratic rationalism (Del Caro 1989, 589–605).

59. For a discussion of the relationship between Ivanov's thought and Slavophilism see Ivanov 2001, xiv.

60. On Orientalist fashion in Pushkin, see Greenleaf 1994. Katya Hokanson notes that the reference could have come either from a translation of Sa'di's "The Garden" ("Bustan"), which appeared in 1796, or Moore's text. For a discussion of Pushkin's poem's orientalist themes, see Hokanson 1998, 123–50.

61. The poem forms part of a book by the same name, which was planned for publication in Baku in 1920 but never realized. A cycle of poems by the same title was included in an earlier publication of futurist poetry in Tiflis, *Sofii Georgievne Mel'nikovoi: fantasticheskii kabachek* (1919).

62. Kruchenykh's *Zamaul'* continued in the tradition of the futurist books that he published in Tiflis under the 41° moniker.

63. A considerable amount of lore surrounds the monument, which features on nearly every photograph of the skyline as well as the contemporary currency. It was thought to have been built either between the sixth and eighth centuries as a Zorastrian worship site or during the twelfth century as a watchtower (Ibrahimov 2008, 22–26).

64. These include the aforementioned *Zamaul'* and *The World and the Rest*, as well as Vechorka's essay "On Zaum Poetry" (O zaumnoi poezii). For a discussion of Vechorka's Futurist poetics, see Vechorka 2007, 9–17.

65. For a brief history of these demonstrations and a discussion of Soviet martyrologies in Azerbaijan, see Smith 2001, 363–88.

66. Francine Hirsch defines ethnography (*etnografiia*) as "a broad field of inquiry, which included under its umbrella the disciplines of geography, archaeology, physical anthropology, and linguistics" and shared similarities with European cultural anthropology (2005, 63–98).

67. For a discussion of the trope of electrification in Russian literature, see Banerjee 2012, 90–118.

68. For Radek's speech, see Riddell 1993, 59.

69. For a discussion of some of the posters, see Feldman 2016b.

70. On Hurufism, see Schimmel 1984. For a discussion of Turkish Surrealist interpretations of this theme, see Ertürk 2010, 47–60.

4. Broken Verse

1. There were other groups by the same name formulated across Soviet Central Asia, such as the Qızıl qalam of Uzbekistan, which was officially dismantled by the Soviets, though many of its members also went on to participate in the Association of Proletarian Writers of Uzbekistan. See Bennigsen and Broxup 2011, 43–44.

2. For a summary of this debate, see Louis Dupeux's discussion of 1920s Germany and Mikhail Agursky's analysis of 1920s Russia in Ree 2001, 289–307.

3. The resonances between Jameson's theory and the Russian avant-garde theory described in this chapter highlight the intellectual influence of modernism on the Frankfurt school (Miller 2014, 1–34).

4. Nuancing the approach to the subject, Igal Halfin (2003) describes the interworkings of a "Communist hermeutics of the soul" through which the private thoughts and psyche

of the individual Soviet subject were *read* into the public space of the political community through interpretive practices, interrogation, trials, and the like. See also Halfin and Hellbeck 1996, 456–63.

5. This model builds on Ranjana Khanna's (2003) analysis of the construction of the conscious subject through the institutionalization of psychoanalysis as a colonial discipline. See also Keller 2007; McClintock 1995; Young 1990.

6. At the Congress of the Peoples of the East a Council for Propaganda was created, with branches in Baku and Tashkent. Its leaders were the Russian orientalist Mikhail Pavlovich, the Russian Bolshevik revolutionary Elena Stasova, and the Persian communist Avetis Sultanzade. It published pamphlets in Persian, Arabic, and Turkic. During the first two weeks of its operations it disseminated 1,270 pieces of propaganda: 433 in Persian and 176 in Turkic (Riddell 1993, 30). Previously Cavid had served briefly as a representative of the Araz Republic in Nakhchivan (1918–1919).

7. For a discussion of sufism in Cavid's work, see Mamed 2001, 24.

8. Cavid's complex Ottomanized syntax and lexical register would have been legible to an elite educated Azeri reader. While Sehhet and Memmmedquluzade draw on a Persianate lexicon and syntax, Cavid relies more heavily on Ottoman Turkish.

9. This group of Bolshevik thinkers—which included Bogdanov, Maxim Gorky, and Anatoly Lunacharsky—favored underground populist agitation methods such as workers' clubs, while Lenin's faction preferred more official legal channels. Bogdanov opposed Lenin on both modes of organization and his interest in the central creative role of culture (Mally 1990).

10. Proletkul't was an experimental artistic group that grew out of the 1917 revolution (Mally 1990).

11. Lenin (1914) notes the signatories of the Vpered group.

12. On the role of the aesthetics of easel painting in shaping the conception of comradely social relations, see Lucento 2014.

13. An account of a seminar held by the *bogostroiteli*, see Bazarov et al. 1910.

14. While Cavid's is largely a humanist critique of war, his representation of Arab characters in the play are problematic.

15. For more on al-Khidr, see Shaikh 2014, 14.

16. In 1920 Cavid put on a big production of *The Devil* at the National Drama Theater (Milli Dram Teatrı). For a discussion of productions during the 1920s, see Rehimli 2005, 89.

17. Indeed, one of the most active sections of the Propaganda Council was the Theater Division. This tolerance for Cavid's work was short-lived. In 1937 he was arrested and imprisoned on charges of disseminating anti-Soviet pan-Turkist propaganda.

18. See *Oktyabr alevleri* (1927) and *Qızıl genc kelamler* (1926). For symbolic resonances, see Red Pen writer Almas İldırım's "Yarın" in *Qızıl genc kelamler* 1926, 111.

19. For an account of this period of his biography, see Göksu and Timms 1999, 38–53.

20. The original caption for the archival copy of the photograph reads: "The Famous Poet V. Mayakovsky surrounded by the Azerbaijani Red Pens" (Meşhur şair V. Majakovski Azerbajcan qızıl qelemleri arasında), Azerbaijan State Archive of Literature and Art [Azerbaycan Dövlet Edebiyyat ve İncesenet Arxivi], f. 125, v. 1, s. 10.

21. Hikmet, then living in Moscow, accompanied his partner Nüzhet to visit her brother in Baku.

22. *Victory over the Sun* was the result of a collaboration among Kruchenykh, Khlebnikov, Malevich, and Matiushin (Clark 1995, 38–44).

23. See Gurianova 2012, 253–75.

24. Lenin's New Economic Policy was a mixed approach focused on promoting economic growth after the devastation of the Civil War. In turn, a policy of accommodation toward the intelligentsia ushered in a brief liberal approach to cultural production, which Sheila

Fitzpatrick famously called the "soft" line on culture (1974, 267–87). For more on the articulation of this shift from liberalism and plurality to state control and organization in the field of the arts, see Clark 1991; Read 1990.

25. This vision of the letter inscribed on the body prefigures the symbolist interpretations of the Hurufi calligraphic tradition (Ertürk 2010, 47–60).

26. This trend in Soviet linguistics was championed by N. F. Iakovlev (1892–1974), E. D. Polivanov (1891–1938), A. M. Sukhotin (1888–1942), and L. V. Shcherba (1880–1944). It highlighted the social dimension of the study of sounds and considered "speech as a social fact . . . as a physiological and acoustic process" (Simonato 2008, 341).

27. Ertürk also discusses the influence of the Italian and Russian avant-gardes on Hikmet's poetry, and in particular Mayakovsky's conceptions of *ostranenie*, or defamiliarization, on the formation of an internal foreignness within modern Turkish. To this end, she describes Hikmet's "literary communism" as a "reopening of modern Turkish to Ottoman Turkish, Persian, and Arabic, as well as Russian, Bengali, Chinese, and Italian" (Ertürk 2011, 162–66, 181).

Postscript

1. One of the first publications to introduce a page in the Latin script was *The Eastern Woman*.

REFERENCES

Abasov, Ali. 2008. "At the Original Sources of National Consciousness: The Azerbaijani Enlightenment." *Today and Tomorrow: Azerbaijan in Focus*, no. 1: 54–83.

Abdel-Malek, Anouar. 1981. *Civilizations and Social Theory*. Translated by Mike Gonzalez. Albany: State University of New York Press.

Âdamiyat, Fereydun. 1970. *Andîŝe-hâ-ye Mirzâ Fathali-ye Âkhundzâde*. Tehran: Khârazmi.

Algar, Hamid. 1984. *Encyclopedia Iranica*. "Akhundzada." http://www.iranicaonline.org/articles/akundzada-playwright.

Algar, Hamid. 2000. "Ahundzade." In *Türkiye Diyanet Vakfı Islam Ansiklopedisi*, vol. 2, 186–90. Istanbul: Türkiye Diyanet Vakfı Yayınları.

Altstadt, Audrey. 1983. "The Azerbaijani Bourgeoisie and the Cultural-Enlightenment Movement in Baku: First Steps Toward Nationalism." In *Transcaucasia, Nationalism, and Social Change: Essays in the History of Armenia, Azerbaijan, and Georgia,* edited by Ronald Grigor Suny, 199–209. Ann Arbor: University of Michigan Press.

Altstadt, Audrey. 1986. "Azerbaijani Turks' Response to Russian Conquest." *Studies in Comparative Communism* 19, no. 3: 267–86.

Ammant, Abbas. 2000. "The Resurgence of Apocalyptic in Modern Islam." In *The Encyclopedia of Apocalypticism*. Vol. 3: *Apocalypticism in the Modern Period and the Contemporary Age,* edited by Stephen J. Stein, 237–46. New York: Continuum.

Andrews, Walter G. 1985. *Poetry's Voice, Society's Song: Ottoman Lyric Poetry.* Seattle: University of Washington Press.

Apter, Emily. 2006. *The Translation Zone: A New Comparative Literature.* Princeton: Princeton University Press.

Arjomand, Said Amir. 1993. "Millennial Beliefs: Hierocratic Authority, and Revolution in Shi'ite Iran." In *The Political Dimensions of Religion,* edited by Said Amir Arjomand, 219–40. Albany: State University of New York Press.

Atakişiyev, Aslan. 1991. *M. E. Resulzade adına Bakı Dövlet Universitetinin Tarixi.* Baku: Universiteti Neşriyyatı.

Axundov, M. F. 1837. "Na smert' Pushkina: sochinenie v stikhakh sovremennogo persidskogo poeta Mirzy Fatkh-Ali Akhundova." *Moskovskii nabliudatel',* no. 11: 297–304.

Axundov, M. F. 1938. *Sochineniia: Vstupitel'naia stat'ia, redaktsiia i kommentarii Aziza Sharifa.* Tbilisi: Zaria Vostoka.

Axundov, M. F. 1953. *Tri pis'ma Indiiskogo printsa Kemal-ud-Dovle k Persidskomu printsu Dzhelal-ud-Dovle i izbrannye filosofskie proizvedeniia 1850–64,* edited by M. Kasumova. Baku: Akademiia nauk Azerbaidzhanskoi SSR.

Axundov, M. F. 2005. *Eserleri 3 cildde.* Baku: Şerq-Qerb.

Axundov, M. F. Manuscripts of M. F. Axundov, f. 2, v. 21, s. 1–283. Institute of Manuscripts of the Azerbaijan National Academy of Sciences in Baku (Elyazmalar Insitutu).

Baberovski, Iorg [Jörg Baberowski]. 2010. *Vrag est' vezde: Stalinizm na Kavkaze.* Translated by V. T. Altukhova. Moscow: Rosspen.

Bakhtin, Mikhail. 1981. *The Dialogic Imagination: Four Essays by M. M. Bakhtin,* edited by Michael Holquist. Translated by Caryl Emerson and Michael Holquist. Austin: University of Texas Press.

Bakhtin, Mikhail. 1984. *Problems in Dostoevsky's Poetics.* Translated by Caryl Emerson. Minneapolis: University of Minnesota Press.

Bakhtin, Mikhail. 1986. *Speech Genres and Other Late Essays, edited by Caryl Emerson and Michael Holquist.* Translated by Vern W. McGee. Austin: University of Texas Press

Bakhtin, Mikhail. 1997–2012. *Sobranie sochinenii v semi tomakh,* edited by S. G. Bocharov and L. A. Gogotishvili, Moscow: Russkie slovari.

Bakhtin, Mikhail, and Patricia Sollner. 1983. "Rabelais and Gogol: The Art of Discourse and the Popular Culture of Laughter." *Mississippi Review* 11, no. 3: 34–50.

Banerjee, Anindita. 2012. *We Modern People: Science Fiction and the Making of Russian Modernity.* Middletown: Wesleyan University Press.

Bassin, Mark. 1991. "Russia between Europe and Asia: The Ideological Construction of Geographic Space." *Slavic Review* 50, no. 1: 1–17.

Baudelaire, Charles. 1974. "Correspondances." In *Oeuvres complètes,* 1–11. Paris: Gallimard.

Bazarov, V., Ia. Berman, A. Lunacharskii, P. Iushkevich, A. Bogdanov, I. Gel'fond, and S. Suvorov. 1910. *Ocherki po filosofii Marksizma: Filosofskii sbornik.* Moscow: Zveno.

Behdad, Ali. 1994. *Belated Travelers: Orientalism in the Age of Colonial Dissolution.* Durham: Duke University Press.

Belinskii, Vissarion Grigor'evich. 1953–1959. *Polnoe sobranie sochinenii v trinadtsati tomakh.* Moscow: Nauka.

Benjamin, Walter. 1968. "Theses on the Philosophy of History." In *Illuminations*, edited by Hannah Arendt, translated by Harry Zohn, 253–64. New York: Schocken Books.

Bennigsen, Alexandre. 1962. "'Molla Nasreddin' et la presse satirique musulmane de Russie avant 1917." *Cahiers du monde russe et soviétique* 3, no. 3: 505–20.

Bennigsen, Alexandre. 1984. "Pan-Turkism and Pan-Islamism in History and Today." *Central Asian Survey* 3, no. 3: 39–49.

Bennigsen, Alexandre, and Marie Broxup. 2011. *The Islamic Threat to the Soviet State.* New York: Routledge.

Bennigsen, Alexandre, and Chantal Lemercier-Quelquejay. 1964. *La presse et le mouvement national chez les musulmans de Russie avant 1920.* Paris: Mouton.

Bennigsen, Alexandre, and S. Enders Wimbush. 1979. *Muslim National Communism in the Soviet Union: A Revolutionary Strategy for the Colonial World.* Chicago: University of Chicago Press.

Berlin, Isaiah. 1979. *Russian Thinkers.* New York: Penguin.

Berzhe, Adolf Petrovich. 1868. "Neskol'ko slov o Zakavkazskikh musul'manskikh poetakh." *Kavkaz.* Cited in Samir Gachizade, *Russkaia i evropeiskaia pechat' o M. F. Akhundove.* Baku: Iazchy, 1987.

Berzhe, Adolf Petrovich. 1874. Introduction to "Vostochnaia poema na smert' A. S. Pushkina." *Russkaia starina*, no. 11: 76–78.

Bhabha, Homi. 1994. *The Location of Culture.* New York: Routledge.

Blauvelt, Timothy. 2010. "Military-Civil Administration and Islam in the North Caucasus 1853–83." *Kritika: Explorations in Russian and Eurasian History* 11, no. 2: 221–55.

Blok, Aleksandr. 1997. *Polnoe sobranie sochinenii v dvadtsati tomakh.* Moscow: Nauka.

Bobrovnikov, Vladimir. 2013. "Grazhdanskaia voina i mechty o mirovoi revoliutsii." In *Plakat sovetskogo Vostoka 1918–1940*, 31–35. Moscow: Izdatel'skii dom Mardzhani.

Bodin, Per-Arne. 1987. "The Silent Scene in Nikolaj Gogol's *The Inspector General.*" *Scando-Slavica* 33, no. 1: 5–16.

Bogdanov, Aleksandr. 1924. "Proletariat i iskusstvo." In *O proletarskoi kul'ture, 1904–1924*, 117–24. Moscow: Kniga.

Bogdanov, Alexander [Aleksandr]. (1920) 1976. "The Paths of Proletarian Creation." In *Russian Art of the Avant-Garde: Theory and Criticism, 1902–1934*, edited and translated by John Bowlt, 178–82. New York: Viking.

Bojanowska, Edyta M. 2007. *Nikolai Gogol: Between Russian and Ukrainian Nationalism.* Cambridge, MA: Harvard University Press.

Bojanowska, Edyta M. 2014. "All the King's Horses: Ukraine, Russia, and Gogol's Troika." *Jordan Center at NYU* (blog), April 22. http://jordanrussiacenter.org/news/kings-horses-ukraine-russian-gogols-troika/#.U15Wf-ZdURe/.

Borenstein, Eliot. 2014 "Russia and Ukraine: Stupidity, Cynicism or Both?" *Jordan Center at NYU* (blog), March 2. http://jordanrussiacenter.org/news/russia-ukraine-stupidity-cynicism/#.Uyh9o61dV4U.

Bowlt, John E., ed and trans. 1995. *The Salon Album of Vera Sudeikin-Stravinsky.* Princeton: Princeton University Press.

Braun, Edward. 1995. *Meyerhold: A Revolution in Theatre.* London: Methuen Drama.

Brinegar, Sara. 2017. "The Oil Deal: Nariman Narimanov and the Sovietization of Azerbaijan." *Slavic Review* 76, no. 2: 372–94.

Brown, James. 1978. "On the Semiogenesis of Fictional Meals." *Romanic Review* 69, no. 4: 332–46.

Buckler, Julie. 2009. "What Comes after "Post-Soviet" in Russian Studies?" *PMLA* 124, no. 1: 251–63.

Bürger, Peter. 1984. *Theory of the Avant-garde.* Translated by Michael Shaw. Minneapolis: University of Minnesota Press.

Bustanov, Afrid K. 2015. *Soviet Orientalism and the Creation of Central Asian Nations.* New York: Routledge.

Caffee, Naomi. 2013. "Russophonia: Towards a Transnational Conception of Russian-Language Literature." PhD diss., University of California, Los Angeles.

Castagné, Joseph. 1923. *Russie slave et Russie turque: Les chances d'une politique islamique allemande.* Paris: Revue du monde musulman LVI.

Cavid, Hüseyn. 2005. "Iblis." In *Eserleri, beş cildde,* 7–105. Baku: Lider.

Chakrabarty, Dipesh. 2010. "Legacies of the Bandung: Decolonization and the Politics of Culture." In *Making a World after Empire: The Bandung Moment and its Political Afterlives,* edited by Christopher Lee, 45–68. Athens: Ohio University Press.

Chernyshevskii, Nikolai. 1855. "Ocherki gogolevskogo perioda russkoi literatury." *Sovremennik,* no. 12: 1–12.

Chernyshevskii, Nikolai. 1953. "Essays on the Gogol Period of Russian Literature." In *Selected Philosophical Essays,* 1–12. Moscow: Khudozhestvennaia literatura.

Chichkanov, P. 1921. "Griaduschee iskusstvo." *Iskusstvo,* no. 1: 13–15.

Chizhevsky, Dmitri. 1979. "On Gogol's 'The Overcoat,'" in *Dostoyevsky and Gogol: Texts and Criticism,* 137–60. Ann Arbor: Ardis.

Clark, Katerina. 1991. "The 'Quiet Revolution' in Soviet Intellectual Life." In *Russia in the Era of the NEP: Explorations in Soviet Society and Culture,* edited by Sheila Fitzpatrick, Alexander Rabinowitch, and Richard Stites, 210–30. Bloomington: Indiana University Press.

Clark, Katerina. 1995. *Petersburg: Crucible of Cultural Revolution.* Cambridge, MA: Harvard University Press.

Clark, Katerina. 1998. "Meyerhold's Appropriation of Gogol for 1926 in the Soviet Union." *Theatre* 28, no. 2: 27–33.

Clark, Katerina. 2011. *Moscow the Fourth Rome: Stalinism, Cosmopolitanism, and the Evolution of Soviet Culture, 1931–1941.* Cambridge, MA: Harvard University Press.

Clark, Katerina, and Michael Holquist. 1984. *Mikhail Bakhtin.* Cambridge, MA: Harvard University Press.

Clayton, J. Douglas. 1993. *Pierrot in Petrograd.* Montreal: McGill-Queen's University Press.

Cole, Juan R. I. 1996. "Marking Boundaries, Marking Time: The Iranian Past and the Construction of the Self by Qajar Thinkers." *Iranian Studies* 29, no. 1–2: 35–56.

Collington, Tara. 2001. "Space, Time, and Narrative: Bakhtin and Ricoeur." *Space and Culture,* nos. 7–9: 221–31.

Condee, Nancy. 2006. "The Anti-Imperialist Empire and After: In Dialogue with Gayatri Spivak's 'Are You Postcolonial?'" *PMLA* 120, no. 3: 829–31.

Copeaux, Étienne. 1993. "Le movement 'prométhéen,'" *Cemoti* 16, no. 1: 9–46.

Crews, Robert. 2006. *For Prophet and Tsar: Islam and Empire in Russia and Central Asia.* Cambridge, MA: Harvard University Press.

Dallal, Ahmad. 1993. "The Origins and Objectives of Islamic Revivalist Thought, 1750–1850." *Journal of the American Oriental Society* 113, no. 3: 341–59.

Davidson, Pamela. 2002. "The Moral Dimension of the Prophetic Ideal: Pushkin and His Readers." *Slavic Review* 61, no. 3: 490–518.

De Waal, Thomas. 2012. "How Gogol Explains the Post-Soviet World (and Chekhov and Dostoevsky): The Case for Re(reading) Russia's Greatest Literary Classics." *Foreign Policy*, no. 192: 106–11.

Del Caro, Adrian. 1989. "Dionysian Classicism, or Nietzsche's Appropriation of an Aesthetic Norm." *Journal of the History of Ideas* 50, no. 4: 589–605.

Derluguian, Georgi M. 2005. *Bourdieu's Secret Admirer in the Caucasus: A World System Biography.* Chicago: University of Chicago Press.

Dobrenko, Evgeny, and Eric Naiman, eds. 2003. *The Landscape of Stalinism: The Art and Ideology of Soviet Space.* Seattle: University of Washington Press.

Dostoevskii, F. M. 1972–1992. *Polnoe sobranie sochinenii v tridtsati tomakh.* Leningrad: Nauka.

Dugin, Aleksandr. 2000. *Osnovy geopolitiki: Geopoliticheskoe budushchee Rossii. Mysit' prostranstvom.* Moscow: Arktogeia.

Dugin, Aleksandr. 2010. *Martin Khaidegger: Filosofiia drugogo nachala.* Moscow: Akademicheskii proekt.

Dugin, Aleksandr. 2012. *The Fourth Political Theory.* Translated by M. Sleboda and M. Millerman. London: Arktos.

Dugin, Aleksandr. 2013. "Interview de Alexandre Douguine." YouTube video by Centre Zahra. Filmed May 25, Paris, 23:47. Published May 29. https://www.youtube.com/watch?v=KLRdV9x-5qY.

Dugin, Alexander. 2014. *Eurasian Mission: An Introduction to Neo-Eurasianism.* London: Arktos.

Dzhebrailov, Aydin. 1991. "The King Is Dead. Long Live the King! Post-Revolutionary and Stalinist Shakespeare." Translated by Cathy Porter. *History Workshop* 32, no. 1: 1–18.

Edgar, Adrienne. 2004. *Tribal Nation: The Making of Soviet Turkmenistan.* Princeton: Princeton University Press.

Efendiev, Mamed-Sadyk. 1931. *Chto dolzhen znat' Bakinskii rabochii o svoem Tiurkskom rabochem teatre.* Baku: Azerneşer.

Eikhenbaum, Boris. 1979. "How Gogol's 'The Overcoat' Is Made." In *Dostoevsky and Gogol: Texts and Criticism,* edited by Priscilla Meyer and Stephen Rudy, 119–21. Ann Arbor: Ardis.

Emerson, Caryl. 1983. "The Outer Word and Inner Speech: Bakhtin, Vygotsky, and the Internalization of Language." *Critical Inquiry* 10, no. 2: 245–64.

Emerson, Caryl. 1997. *The First Hundred Years of Mikhail Bakhtin.* Princeton: Princeton University Press.

Engerman, David. 2009. *Know Your Enemy: The Rise and Fall of America's Soviet Experts.* New York: Oxford University Press.

Ertürk, Nergis. 2010. "Surrealism and the Turkish Script Arts." *Modernism/Modernity* 17, no. 1: 47–60.

Ertürk, Nergis. 2011. *Grammatology and Literary Modernity in Turkey*. Oxford: Oxford University Press.

Esgerli, Zaman. 2005. *XIX esr Azerbaycan şeri antologiyesi*. Baku: Şerq-Qarb.

Etkind, Alexander. 2011. *Internal Colonization: Russia's Imperial Experience*. Cambridge: Polity.

Evreinov, Nikolai. 1916. "A Merry Death, a Harlequinade." In *Five Plays with One from Ukrainian*, edited and translated by C. E. Bechhofer, 1–33. New York: Dutton.

Fanger, Donald. 1965. *Dostoevsky and Romantic Realism: A Study of Dostoevsky in Relation to Dickens and Balzac*. Cambridge, MA: Harvard University Press.

Feldman, Leah. 2012. "Orientalism on the Threshold: Reorienting Heroism in Late Imperial Russia." *Boundary 2* 39, no. 2: 161–80.

Feldman, Leah. 2016a. "Reading Gogol in Azeri: Parodic Genealogies and the Revolutionary Geopolitics of 1905." *Slavic Review* 75, no. 2: 256–78.

Feldman, Leah. 2016b. "Red Jihad: Translating Communism in the Muslim Caucasus." *Boundary 2* 43, no. 3: 221–49.

Fieni, David. 2006. "Decadent Orientalisms: Configuring the Decay of Colonial Modernity in French and Arabic." PhD diss., University of California, Los Angeles.

Fink, Hilary. 1999. *Bergson and Russian Modernism, 1900–1930*. Evanston: Northwestern University Press.

Fisher, Alan W. 1998. *The Tatars of Crimea: Return to the Homeland*, edited by Edward A. Allworth. Durham: Duke University Press.

Fitzpatrick, Sheila. 1974. "The 'Soft' Line on Culture and Its Enemies: Soviet Cultural Policy, 1922–1927." *Slavic Review* 33, no. 2: 267–87.

Floor, Willem. 2005. *The History of Theater in Iran*. Washington DC: Mage Publishers.

Floor, Willem, and Hasan Javadi, trans. 2009. *The Heavenly Rose-Garden: A History of Shirvan and Daghestan by Abbas Qoli Aqa Bakikhanov*. Washington: Mage Publishers.

Foucault, Michel. 1980. *Power/Knowledge: Selected Interviews and Other Writings, 1972–1977*. Translated by C. Gordon, L. Marshal, J. Mepham, and K. Sober. New York: Pantheon Books.

Gafarova, Garatel. 2015. "The Transcaucasian Teachers Seminary in Gori." *Visions of Azerbaijan*. http://www.visions.az/history,430/.

Galiev, Mirsaid Sultan. (1921) 1979. "Methods of Anti-religious Propaganda among the Muslims." In *Muslim National Communism in the Soviet Union: A Revolutionary Strategy for the Colonial World*, edited by Alexandre Bennigsen and S. Enders Wimbush, 146–58. Chicago: University of Chicago Press. Reprint of *Zhizn' national'nostei*, vol. 29, no. 127 and vol. 20, no. 128.

Galiev, Mirsaid Sultan. 1979. "The Social Revolution in the East." In *Muslim National Communism in the Soviet Union: A Revolutionary Strategy for the Colonial World*, edited by Alexandre A. Bennigsen and S. Enders Wimbush, 132–38. Chicago: University of Chicago Press.

Gasprali, Ismail Bey. 2008. *French and African Letters, 1887–1891*. Translated by Azade-Ayse Rorlich. Istanbul: Isis.

Gasprinskii, Ismail Bey. 1881. *Russkoe musul'manstvo*. Simferopol': Tipografiia Spiro.

Gille, Zsuzsa, Saygun Gokariksel, Diana T. Kudaiberenova, and Dirk Uffelmann. 2016. "Imperial Reverb: Exploring the Postcolonies of Communism." Conference held at Princeton University, May 13–15. https://imperialreverb.princeton.edu/.

Glebov, Sergei. 2011. "The Mongol-Bolshevik Revolution: Eurasianist Ideology in Search of an Ideal Past." *Journal of Eurasian Studies* 2, no. 2: 103–14.

Goff, Krista. 2014. "What Makes a People? Soviet Nationality Politics and Minority Experience after World War Two." PhD diss., University of Michigan.

Gogol', Nikolai. 2003. *Polnoe sobranie sochinenii i pisem v dvadtsat' trekh tomakh*. Moscow: Nauka.

Göksu, Saime, and Edward Timms. 1999. *Romantic Communist: The Life and Work of Nazim Hikmet*. London: Hurst & Co.

Gorodetsky, Sergei. 1920. *Alaia neft*. Baku: Izdanie aztsentropechati.

Gorodetsky, Sergei. 1921. "Nashi zadachi." *Iskusstvo*, no. 1: 5–6.

Gorshenina, Svetlana. 1997. "Un précurseur de l'archéologie et de l'ethnologie françaises en Asie Centrale: Joseph-Antoine Castagné (1875–1958)." *L'Académie des inscriptions et belles-lettres* 141, no. 1: 255–72.

Gould, Rebecca. 2013. "Topographies of Anticolonialism: The Ecopoetical Sublime in the Caucasus from Tolstoy to Mamakaev." *Comparative Literature Studies* 50, no. 1: 87–107.

Gould, Rebecca. 2016. *Writers as Rebels: The Literature of Insurgency in the Caucasus*. New Haven: Yale University Press.

Grant, Bruce. 2009. *The Captive and the Gift: Cultural Histories of Sovereignty in Russia and the Caucasus*. Ithaca: Cornell University Press.

Grant, Bruce. 2010. "Cosmopolitan Baku." *Ethnos* 75, no. 2: 123–47.

Greenleaf, Monika. 1994. *Pushkin and Romantic Fashion: Fragment, Elegy, Orient, Irony*. Stanford: Stanford University Press.

Groys, Boris. 2011. *The Total Art of Stalinism*. Translated by Charles Rougle. London: Verso.

Gurianova, Nina. 2012. *The Aesthetics of Anarchy: Art and Ideology in the Early Avant-garde*. Berkeley: University of California Press.

Guseinov, Geidar [Huseynov, Heydar]. 1949. *Iz istorii obshchestvennoi i filosofskoi mysli v Azerbaidzhane XIX veka*. Baku: Izdatel'stvo Akademii nauk Azerbaidzhanskoi SSR.

Haber, Erika. 2003. *The Myth of the Non-Russian: Isgander and Aitmatov's Magical Universe*. Oxford: Lexington Books.

Habermas, Jürgen, and Seyla Ben-Habib. 1981. "Modernity versus Postmodernity." *New German Critique*, no. 22: 3–14.

Hacıbeyov, Üzeyir. 1921. "Muzykal'no-prosvetitel'nye zadachi Azerbaidzhana." *Iskusstvo*, no. 1: 25–28.

Hacker, Andrea. 2006. "To Pushkin, Freedom, and Revolution in Asia: Velimir Khlebnikov in Baku." *Russian Review* 65, no. 3: 447–65.

Hadi, Mehemmed. 2005. "Vakhtın sesi ve heyatın sözü." *Seçilmiş eserleri*. Baku: Şerq-Qerb.

Haj, Samira. 2009. *Reconfiguring Islamic Tradition: Reform, Rationality, and Modernity.* Stanford: Stanford University Press.

Halfin, Igal. 2003. *Terror in My Soul: Communist Autobiographies on Trial.* Cambridge, MA: Harvard University Press.

Halfin, Igal, and Jochen Hellbeck. 1996. "Rethinking the Stalinist Subject: Stephen Kotkin's 'Magnetic Mountain' and the State of Soviet Historical Studies." *Jahrbücher für Geschichte Osteuropas* 44, no. 3: 456–63.

Harrison, Olivia C. 2013. "Cross-Colonial Poetics: Souffles-Anfas and the Figure of Palestine." *PMLA* 128, no. 2: 353–69.

Hikmet, Nazim. 1928. *Güneşi içenlerin türküsü.* Baku: Azer neşr.

Hirsch, Francine. 2005. *Empire of Nations: Ethnographic Knowledge and the Making of the Soviet Union.* Ithaca: Cornell University Press.

Hokanson, Katya. 1998. "Pushkin's Captive Crimea: Imperialism in *The Fountain of Bakhchisarai.*" In *Russian Subjects; Empire, Nation, and the Culture of the Golden Age,* edited by Monika Greenleaf and Stephen Moeller-Sally. Evanston: Northwestern University Press.

Hokanson, Katya. 2008. *Writing at Russia's Borders.* Toronto: University of Toronto Press.

The Holy Qur'an. 1983. Translated by Abdullah Yusuf Ali. Brentwood, MD: Amana Publications, 1983.

Hüseynzade, Ali bey. (1906–1907) 2007. *Füyuzat,* no. 5. Reprint, *Füyuzat,* ikinci neşr. Baku: Çaşıoğluç.

Hüseynzade, Ali bey. 2007. "Turan." In *Seçilmiş eserleri,* 32–44. Baku: Şerq-Qerb.

Ibrahimov, Kamil. 2008. "The Mystery of the Maiden Tower." *Visions of Azerbaijan* 3, no. 1: 22–26.

İldırım, Almas. 1926. "Yarın." In *Qızıl genc kelamler.* Baku: Communist gazeti.

Iskhakov, Salavat. 2017. "Rol' Pol'shi v sud'be Azerbaidzhana." Interview. *Radio Azadlyg.* https://www.radioazadlyg.org/a/24595326.html.

Ivanov, Viacheslav. 2001. *Selected Essays: Viacheslav Ivanov,* edited by Michael Wachtel. Translated by Robert Bird. Evanston: Northwestern University Press.

Jakobson, Roman. 1962. "K kharakteristike evraziiskogo iazykovogo soiuza." In *Selected Writings I,* edited by Roman Jakobson, 144–201. The Hague: Mouton.

Jakobson, Roman. 1973. "Modern Russian Poetry: Velimir Khlebnikov." In *Major Soviet Writers: Essays in Criticism,* edited by E. J.Brown, 58–82. Oxford: Oxford University Press.

Jameson, Fredric. 1981. *The Political Unconscious: Narrative as a Socially Symbolic Act.* Ithaca: Cornell University Press.

Jersild, Austin. 2002. *Orientalism and Empire: North Caucasus Mountain People and the Georgian Frontier.* Montreal: McGill-Queen's University Press.

Karamzin, Nikolai Mikhailovich. 1818–1829. *Istoriia gosudarstva Rossiiskogo.* St. Petersburg: Tipografiia H. Grecha.

Kazembek, Mirza. 1985. "Muridizm i Shamil." In *M. Kazem-Bek: Izbrannye proizvedeniia,* edited by A. K. Rzaev, 22–65. Baku: Elm.

Kazemzadeh, Firuz. 1951. *The Struggle for Transcaucasia, 1917–1921.* New York: Philosophical Library of New York.

Keller, Richard C. 2007. *Colonial Madness: Psychiatry in French North Africa.* Chicago: University of Chicago Press.

Keller, Shoshana. 2001. *To Moscow, not Mecca: The Soviet Campaign against Islam in Central Asia, 1917–1941.* Westport: Praeger.

Kemper, Michael. 2010. "Red Orientalism: Mikhail Pavlovich and Marxist Oriental Studies in Early Soviet Russia." *Die Welt des Islams* 50, nos. 3–4: 435–47.

Kernan, Ryan James. 2014. "The *Coup* of Langston Hughes's Picasso Period: Excavating Mayakovsky in Langston Hughes's Verse." *Comparative Literature* 66, no. 2: 224–46.

Khalid, Adeeb. 1998. *The Politics of Muslim Cultural Reform: Jadidism in Central Asia.* Berkeley: University of California Press.

Khalid, Adeeb. 2006. "Russian History and the Debate over Orientalism." In *Orientalism and Empire in Russia*, edited by Michael David-Fox, Peter Holquist, and Alexander Martin, 23–31. Bloomington: Slavica Publishers.

Khalid, Adeeb. 2015. *Making Uzbekistan: Nation, Empire, and Revolution in the Early USSR.* Ithaca: Cornell University Press.

Khanna, Ranjana. 2003. *Dark Continents: Psychoanalysis and Colonialism.* Durham: Duke University Press.

Kia, Mehrad. 1995. "Mizra Fath Ali Akhundzade and the Call for Modernization of the Islamic World." *Middle Eastern Studies* 31, no. 3: 422–48.

Kirasirova, Masha. 2014. "The Eastern International: The 'Domestic East' and the 'Foreign East' in Soviet-Arab Relations, 1917–1968." PhD diss., New York University.

Kleveman, Lutz. 2003. *The New Great Game: Blood and Oil in Central Asia.* New York: Grove.

Kliger, Ilya, and Boris Maslov. 2016. *Persistent Forms: Explorations in Historical Poetics*, edited by Ilya Kliger and Boris Maslov. New York: Fordham University Press.

Knight, Nathaniel. 2000. "Ethnicity, Nationality, and the Masses: *Narodnost'* and Modernity in Imperial Russia." In *Russian Modernity: Politics, Knowledge, Practices*, edited by David L. Hoffman and Yanni Kotsonis, 41–64. New York: Palgrave Macmillan.

Knight, Nathaniel. 2006. "On Russian Orientalism: A Response to Adeeb Khalid." In *Orientalism and Empire in Russia*, edited by Michael David-Fox, Peter Holquist, and Alexander Martin, 32–46. Bloomington: Slavica Publishers.

Koropeckyj, Roman, and Robert Romanchuk. 2003. "Ukraine in Blackface: Performance and Representation in Gogol's 'Dikan'ka Tales.'" *Slavic Review* 62, no. 3: 525–47.

Kostomarov, Mykola. 1996. "Two Russian Nationalities." In *Towards an Intellectual History of Ukraine: An Anthology of Ukrainian Thought from 1710 to 1995*, edited by Ralph Lindheim and George S. N. Luckyj, 122–45. Toronto: University of Toronto Press.

Kostomarov, Nikolai Ivanovich. 1861. "Dve russkie narodnosti." *Osnova*, no. 3: 33–80.

Kotkin, Stephen. 1995. *Magnetic Mountain: Stalinism as Civilization.* Berkeley: University of California Press.

Koval'skaia, E. P. 1869. "Kavkaz: Ocherki etnografii Kavkaza." In *Priroda i liudi na Kavkaze i za Kavkazom*, edited by P. Nadezhdin. St. Petersburg: Otdel'noe izdanie.

Kreindler, Isabelle. 1969. "Educational Policies toward the Eastern Nationalities in Tsarist Russia: A Study of the Il'minskii System." PhD diss., Columbia University.

Kristeva, Julia. 1986. "Revolution in Poetic Language." Translated by Margaret Waller. In *The Kristeva Reader*, edited by Toril Moi, 89–136. Oxford: Blackwell.

Kruchenykh, Aleksei Eliseevich. 1967. "Deklaratsiia zaumnogo iazyka." In *Manifesty i programmy russkikh futuristov*, edited by Vladimir Markov, 179–81. Munich: Fink.

Kujundžić, Dragan. 1997. *The Returns of History: Russian Nietszcheans after Modernity*. Albany: State University of New York Press.

Kujundžić, Dragan. 2000. "'After' Russian Post-Colonial Identity." *MLN* 115, no. 5: 892–908.

Kurbanov, Shikhali. 1959. *A. S. Pushkin i Azerbaidzhan*. Baku: Azerbaidzhanskoe izdatel'vo detskoi i iunosheskoi literatury.

Lapidus, Ira. 1988. *A History of Islamic Societies*. Cambridge: Cambridge University Press.

Laruelle, Marlène. 2012. *Russian Eurasianism: An Ideology of Empire*. Baltimore: Johns Hopkins University Press.

Layton, Susan. 1994. *Russian Literature and Empire: Conquest of the Caucasus from Pushkin to Tolstoy*. Cambridge: Cambridge University Press.

Layton, Susan. 1997. "Nineteenth-Century Mythologies of Caucasian Savagery." In *Russia's Orient: Imperial Borderlands and Peoples, 1700–1917*, edited by Daniel Brower and Edward Lazzerini, 80–99. Bloomington: Indiana University Press.

LeBlanc, Ronald D. 1999. "Food, Orality, and Nostalgia for Childhood: Gastronomic Slavophilism in Mid-nineteenth Century Russian Fiction." *Russian Review* 58, no. 2: 244–67.

Lee, Steven. 2015. *The Ethnic Avant-Garde: Minority Cultures and World Revolution* New York: Columbia University Press.

Lenin, Vladimir Il'ich. 1914. "Letter to the Editor." Marxist Internet Archive. https://www.marxists.org/archive/lenin/works/1914/jan/31b.htm.

Lenin, Vladimir Il'ich. 1958–1965. *Polnoe sobranie sochinenii v piatidesiati piati tomakh*. Moscow: Gosudarstvennoe izdatel'stvo politicheskoi literatury.

Lenin, Vladimir Il'ich. 1993. "Address to the Second All-Russia Congress of Communist Organizations of the Peoples of the East." In *To See the Dawn: Baku, 1920: First Congress of the Peoples of the East*, edited by John Riddell, 253–65. New York: Pathfinder.

Lermontov, Mikhail. 1958–1962. *Sobranie sochinenii v chetyrekh tomakh*. Moscow: Izdatel'stvo Akademii nauk SSSR.

Lim, Soojung. 2006. "East Asia in Russian Thought and Literature, 1830s–1920s." PhD diss., University of California, Los Angeles.

Lim, Susanna Soojung. 2013. *China and Japan in the Russian Imagination, 1685–1922: To the Ends of the Orient*. London: Routledge.

Lotman, Iurii, and Boris Uspensky. 1985. "Binary Models in the Dynamics of Russian Culture." In *The Semiotics of Russian Cultural History*, edited by Alexander Nakhimovsky and Alice Stone-Nakhimovsky, 3–35. Ithaca: Cornell University Press.

Lotman, Yuri M. 1990. "Artistic Space in Gogol's Prose." Translated by S. Toumanoff. *Russian Literature Triquarterly*, no. 24: 199–241.

Lucento, Angelina. 2014. "Painting for the Collective: Art, Politics, and Communication in Russia, 1918–19." PhD diss., Northwestern University.

MacMaster, Robert. 1954. "Danilevsky and Spengler: A New Interpretation." *Journal of Modern History* 26, no. 2: 154–61.

Maiakovskii, Vladimir Vladimirovich. 1939–1949. *Polnoe sobranie sochinenii v dvenadtsati tomakh*. Moscow: Khudozhestvennaia literatura.

Makridin, Nikolai. 1921. "O proletarskom iskusstve." *Iskusstvo*, no. 2–3: 33.

Malik, Madhu. 1990. "*Vertep* and the Sacred/Profane Dichotomy in Gogol's Dikanka Stories." *Slavic and East European Journal* 34, no. 3: 332–47.

Mally, Lynn. 1990. *Culture of the Future: The Proletkult Movement in Revolutionary Russia*. Berkeley: University of California Press.

Mamed, Takhira Gashamkyzy. 2001. *Azerbaidzhanskaia natsional'naia dramaturgiia*. Tbilisi: Iskusstvo.

Mann, Iurii. 1978. *Poetika Gogolia*. Moscow: Khudozhestvennaia literatura.

Marchand, Susan. 2009. *Orientalism in the Age of Empire: Religion, Race, and Scholarship*. New York: Cambridge University Press.

Martin, D. W. 1988. "The Pushkin Celebrations of 1880: The Conflict of Ideals and Ideologies." *Slavonic and East European Review* 66, no. 4: 505–25.

Martin, Terry. 2001. *The Affirmative Action Empire: Nations and Nationalism in the Soviet Union, 1923–1939*. Ithaca: Cornell University Press.

Maslov, Boris. 2016. "Evoliutsionizm kak problema revoliutsionnogo soznaniia." In *Russkaia intellektual'naia revoliutsiia*, edited by S. Zenkine and E. Shumilova, 29–43. Moscow: NLO.

McClintock, Anne. 1995. *Imperial Leather: Race, Gender, and Sexuality in the Colonial Contest*. London: Routledge.

Memmedquluzade, Celil. (1906–1931) 1996–2014. *Molla Nesreddin, 10 cildde*, edited by Eziz Mirehmedov. Baku: Azerbaycan dövlet neşriyyatı.

Memmedquluzade, Celil. 2004. *Eserleri 4 cildde*. Baku: Önder neşriyyat.

Memmedquluzade, Celil. Library of Celil Memmedquluzade. Institute of Manuscripts of the Azerbaijan National Academy of Sciences in Baku (Elyazmalar Insitutu), f. 6, v. 552, s. 319.

"Meşhur şair V. Majakovski Azerbajcan qızıl qelemleri arasında." Azerbaijan State Archive of Literature and Art (Azerbaycan Dövlet Edebiyyat ve İncesenet Arxivi), f. 125, v. 1, s. 10.

Meyer, Priscilla. 2008. *How the Russians Read the French: Lermontov, Dostoevsky, Tolstoy*. Madison: University of Wisconsin Press.

Miller, Tyrus. 2014. *Modernism and the Frankfurt School*. Edinburgh: Edinburgh University Press.

Mirehmedov, Eziz. 1980. *Azerbaycan Molla Nesreddini*. Baku: Yazıçı.

Mitchell, Timothy. 2000. "The Stage of Modernity." In *Questions of Modernity*, edited by Timothy Mitchell, 1–34. Minneapolis: University of Minnesota Press.

Mitchell, W. J. T. 2000. "Geopoetics: Space, Place, and Landscape." *Critical Inquiry* 26, no. 2: 173–74.

Mitchell, W. J. T. 2002. "Preface to the Second Edition of *Landscape and Power*." In *Landscape and Power*, vii–xv. Chicago: University of Chicago Press.

Moazzam, Anwar. 1984. *Jamāl Al-Dīn Al-Afghāni: A Muslim Intellectual*. New Delhi: Naurang Rai Concept Publishing.

Moeller-Sally, Betsy F. 1996. "Masks of the Prophet in the Work of Velimir Khlebnikov." *Russian Review* 55, no. 2: 201–25.

Moeller-Sally, Stephen. 2002. *Gogol's Afterlife: The Evolution of a Classic in Imperial and Soviet Russia*. Evanston: Northwestern University Press.

Moore, David Chioni. 2001. "Is the Post- in Postcolonial the Post- in Post-Soviet? Toward a Global Postcolonial Critique." *PMLA* 116, no. 1: 111–28.

Mufti, Aamir. 2004. "Critical Secularism: A Reintroduction for Perilous Times." *Boundary 2* 31, no. 2: 1–9.

Mufti, Aamir. 2005. "Global Comparativism." *Critical Inquiry* 31, no. 2: 472–89.

Mufti, Aamir. 2007. *Enlightenment in the Colony: The Jewish Question and the Crisis of Postcolonial Culture*. Princeton: Princeton University Press.

Mufti, Aamir. 2010. "Orientalism and the Institution of World Literatures." *Critical Inquiry* 36, no. 3: 458–94.

Müller, Max. 1862. *Lectures on the Science of Language Delivered at the Royal Institution of Great Britain in April, May, and June, 1861*. New York: Charles Scribner.

Murav, Harriet. 2008. "Violating the Canon: Reading Der Nister with Vasilii Grossman." *Russian Review* 63, no. 1: 1–25.

Nasr, Seyyed Hossein. 2006. *Islamic Philosophy from Its Origin to the Present: Philosophy in the Land of Prophecy*. New York: State University of New York Press.

Neese-Todd, Joshua. 2006. "A Southern Silver Age: Baku, Tiflis, and the Institutions of Literary Modernism in War and Revolution." MA thesis, Central European University.

Nepomnyashchy, Catharine, Nicole Svobodny, and Ludmilla Trigos, eds. 2006. *Under the Sky of My Africa: Alexander Pushkin and Blackness*. Evanston: Northwestern University Press.

Narimanov, Nariman. 1988. *Izbrannye proizvedeniia v dvukh tomakh*. Baku: Azerbaidzhanskoe gosudarstvennoe izdatel'stvo.

Narimanov, Nariman. 1990. *K istorii nashei revoliutsii v okrainakh*. Baku.

Nikol'skaia, Tat'iana. 2000. *Fantasticheskii gorod: Russkaia kul'turnaia zhizn' v Tbilisi, 1917–1921*. Moscow: Piataia strana.

Northrop, Douglas. 2004. *Veiled Empire: Gender and Power in Soviet Central Asia*. Ithaca: Cornell University Press.

Ohorn, Anton. 1898. *Schiller und Goethe*. Glogau: C. Flemming.

Oktyabr alevlerı. 1927. Baku: Azgiz.

Pavlovich, Mikhail. 1922. "Zadachi vserossiiskoi nauchnoi assotsiatsii vostokovedeniia." *Novyi vostok*, no. 1: 3–15.

Pushkin, Aleksandr. 1979. *Polnoe sobranie sochinenii v desiati tomakh*. Leningrad: Nauka.

Pushkin, Alexander. 1974. *Journey to Arzrum*. Translated by Birgitta Ingemanson. Ann Arbor: Ardis.

Rahman, Fazlur. 2009. *Major Themes of the Qur'an*, 2nd ed. Chicago: University of Chicago Press.

Qızıl genc kelamler. 1926. Baku: Communist gazeti.

Quliyev, Cemil. 2008. *Azerbaycan Tarixi yeddi cildde*. Vol. 6. Baku: Elm.

Ram, Harsha. 1999. "Prisoners of the Caucasus: Literary Myths and Media Representations of the Chechen Conflict." Berkeley: Berkeley Program in Soviet and Post-Soviet Studies, University of California, Berkeley.

Ram, Harsha. 2003. *The Imperial Sublime: A Russian Poetics of Empire*. Madison: University of Wisconsin Press.

Ram, Harsha. 2014. "Decadent Nationalism, 'Peripheral' Modernism: The Georgian Literary Manifesto between Symbolism and the Avant-garde." *Modernism/Modernity* 21, no. 1: 343–59.

Ram, Harsha, and Zaza Shatirshvili. 2004. "Romantic Topography and the Dilemma of Empire: The Caucasus in the Dialogue of Georgian and Russian Poetry." *Russian Review* 63, no. 1: 1–25.

Rancière, Jacques. 2000. *The Politics of Aesthetics: The Distribution of the Sensible*. Translated by Gabriel Rockhill. New York: Continuum.

Rasulzade, Mamed Emin. 2010. *Sbornik proizvedenii i pisem*, edited by S. Iskhakov. Moscow: Flinta.

Rath, Brigitte. 2014. "Pseudotranslation." *The 2014–2015 ACLA Report on the State of the Discipline of Comparative Literature*. http://stateofthediscipline.acla.org/entry/pseudotranslation.

Read, Christopher. 1990. *Culture and Power in Revolutionary Russia: The Intelligentsia and the Transition from Tsarism to Communism*. London: Macmillan.

Ree, Erik van. 2001. "The Concept of 'National Bolshevism': An Interpretive Essay." *Journal of Political Ideologies* 6, no. 3: 289–307.

Refili, Mikayıl. 1929. *Pencere*. Baku: Azerrneşr.

Rehimli, Ilham. 2005. *Azerbaycan teatr tarixi*. Baku: Çaşioglu.

Ricoeur, Paul. 1984–1988. *Time and Narrative*. 3 vols. Translated by Kathleen McLaughlin and David Pellauer. Chicago: University of Chicago Press.

Ricoeur, Paul. 2004. *On Translation*. Translated by Eileen Brennan. New York: Routledge.

Riddell, John, ed. 1993. *To See the Dawn: Baku, 1920: First Congress of the Peoples of the East*. New York: Pathfinder.

Robey, Judith. 1997. "Modeling the Reading Act: Gogol's Mute Scene and Its Intertexts." *Slavic Review* 56, no. 2: 233–50.

Rorlich, Azade-Ayse. 1986. *The Volga Tatars: A Profile in National Resistance*. Stanford: Hoover Institution Press.

Rüstem, Süleyman. 1927. *Elemden neşeye / K radosti*. Baku: Azerbaycan edebiyyatı 'Qızıl Qelem' cemiyyeti neşriyyatı.

Rüstem, Süleyman. 2005. *Şeçilmiş eserleri üç cildde*. Baku: Sherk-Qerb.

Said, Edward. 1978. *Orientalism*. New York: Vintage.

Said, Edward. 1983. *The World, the Text, and the Critic*. Cambridge, MA: Harvard University Press.

Said, Edward. 1994. *Culture and Imperialism*. New York: Vintage.

Said, Edward. 2002. "Invention, Memory, and Place." In *Landscape and Power* 2, edited by W. J. T. Mitchell. Chicago: University of Chicago Press.

Said, E. V. 2006. *Orientalizm: Zapadnye kontseptsii Vostoka*. St. Petersburg: Russkii mir.

Sandler, Stephanie. 2004. "Pushkin and Identity." In *National Identity in Russian Culture: An Introduction,* edited by Simon Franklin and Emma Widdis, 197–217. New York: Cambridge University Press.

Sanjabi, Maryam. 1995. "Reading the Enlightenment: Akhundzada and His Voltaire." *Iranian Studies.* 28, nos. 1–2: 39–60.

Sargent, Leslie. 2010. "The 'Armeno-Tatar War' in the South Caucasus, 1905–1906: Multiple Causes, Interpreted Meanings." *Ab Imperio,* no. 4: 143–69.

Saussy, Haun. 2016. *The Ethnography of Rhythm: Orality and Its Technologies.* New York: Fordham University Press.

Schild, Kathryn. 2010. "Between Moscow and Baku: National Literatures at the 1934 Congress of Soviet Writers." PhD diss., University of California, Berkeley.

Schimmel, Annemarie. 1984. *Calligraphy and Islamic Culture.* New York: New York University Press.

Schimmelpennick van der Oye, David. 2008. "Mirza Kazem-Bek and the Kazan School of Russian Orientology." *Comparative Studies of South Asia, Africa, and the Middle East* 28, no. 3: 443–58.

Schimmelpennick van der Oye, David. 2010. *Russian Orientalism: Asia in the Russian Mind from Peter the Great to Emigration.* New Haven: Yale University Press.

Sehhet, Abbas. 2005. *Seçilmiş eserleri.* Baku: Lider Neşriyyat.

Sells, Michael Anthony. 1996. *Early Islamic Mysticism: Sufi, Qur'an, Miraj, Poetic and Theological Writings.* Mahwah: Paulist Press.

Semenov, Dmitrii Dmitrievich. 1869. "'Abrek' iz otechestvovedenia." In *Priroda i liudi na Kavkaze i za Kavkazom,* edited by P. P. Nadezhdin. St. Petersburg: Otdel'noe izdanie.

Sériot, Patrick. 2014. *Structure and the Whole: East, West, and Non-Darwinian Biology in the Origins of Structural Linguistics.* Translated by Amy Jacobs-Colas. Berlin: De Gruyter Mouton.

Shah, Idries. 1990. *The Way of the Sufi.* New York: Penguin.

Shah, Idries. 1993. *The Pleasantries of the Incredible Mulla Nasrudin.* New York: Penguin.

Shaikh, Sa'diyya. 2014. *Sufi Narratives of Intimacy: Ibn 'Arabī, Gender, and Sexuality.* North Carolina: University of North Carolina Press.

Shapiro, Gavriel. 1993. *Nikolai Gogol and the Baroque Cultural Heritage.* University Park: Pennsylvania State University Press.

Sharif, Aziz. 1937. "Gogol' i Molla Nasreddin." *Bakinskii rabochi* (March).

Sharif, Aziz and Shikhali Kurbanov, eds. 1979. *Pushkin v strannakh zarubezhnogo vostoka.* Moscow: Nauka.

Sherry, Dana. 2007. "Imperial Alchemy: Resettlement, Ethnicity, and Governance in the Russian Caucasus, 1828–1865." PhD diss., University of California, Davis.

Shkandrij, Myroslav. 2001. *Russia and Ukraine: Literature and the Discourse of Empire from Napoleonic to Postcolonial Times.* Montreal: McGill-Queen's University Press.

Simonato, Elena. 2008. "'Social Phonology' in the USSR in the 1920s." *Studies in East European Thought* 60, no. 4: 339–47.

Slavs and Tatars. 2011. *Molla Nasreddin: The Magazine That Would've, Could've, Should've.* Zürich: Christoph Keller Editions.

Slezkine, Yuri. 1994. "The USSR as a Communal Apartment, or How a Socialist State Promoted Ethnic Particularism." *Slavic Review* 53, no. 2: 414–52.

Slocum, John. 1998. "Who, and When, Were the Inorodtsy? The Evolution of the Category of 'Aliens' in Imperial Russia." *Russian Review* 57, no. 2: 173–90.

Smith, Michael G. 1998. *Language and Power in the Creation of the USSR, 1917–1953*. New York: Mouton de Gruyter.

Smith, Michael G. 2001. "The Russian Revolution as a National Revolution: Tragic Deaths and Rituals of Remembrance in Muslim Azerbaijan (1907–1920)." *Jahrbücher für Geschinchte Osteuropas* 49, no. 3: 363–88.

Sperl, Stefan, and Christopher Shackle, eds. 1996. *Qasida Poetry in Islamic Asia and Africa*. Vol. 2. Leiden: E. J. Brill.

Spivak, Gayatri Chakravorty. 2003. *Death of a Discipline*. New York: Columbia University Press.

Suny, Ronald Grigor. 1972. *The Baku Commune, 1917–1918: Class and Nationality in the Russian Revolution*. New York: Columbia University Press.

Suny, Ronald Grigor. 2001. "The Empire Strikes Out: Imperial Russia, 'National' Identity, and Theories of Empire." In *A State of Nations*, edited by Ronald Grigor Suny and Terry Martin, 24–66. Oxford: Oxford University Press.

Swietochowski, Tadeusz. 2004. *Russian Azerbaijan, 1905–1920: The Shaping of National Identity in a Muslim Community*. Cambridge: Cambridge University Press.

Swietochowski, Tadeusz. 1995. *Russia and Azerbaijan: A Borderland in Transition*. New York: Columbia University Press.

Tageldin, Shaden. 2011. *Disarming Words: Empire and the Seductions of Translation in Egypt*. Berkeley: University of California Press.

Tamarchenko, Anna. 1986. "The Poetics of Vyacheslav Ivanov: Lectures Given at Baku University." In *Vyacheslav Ivanov: Poet, Critic and Philosopher*, edited by Robert Louis Jackson and Lowry Nelson Jr., 83–95. New Haven: Yale Center for International and Area Studies.

Tlostanova, Madina. 2007. "The Imperial-Colonial Chronotope: Instanbul-Baku-Khurramabad." *Cultural Studies* 21, nos. 2–3: 406–27.

Todd III, William Mills. 1998. "Russian Literature: Projects for the Future." *Stanford Humanities Review* 6, no. 1: 26–40.

Todorova, Maria. 2006. "Does Russian Orientalism Have a Russian Soul? A Contribution to the Debate between Nathaniel Knight and Adeeb Khalid." In *Orientalism and Empire in Russia*, edited by Michael David-Fox, Peter Holquist, and Alexander Martin, 47–57. Bloomington: Slavica Publishers.

Tolz, Vera. 2006. "European, National, and (Anti-)Imperial: The Formation of Academic Oriental Studies in Late Tsarist and Early Soviet Russia." In *Orientalism and Empire in Russia*, edited by Michael David-Fox, Peter Holquist, and Alexander Martin, 107–34. Bloomington: Slavica.

Tolz, Vera. 2015. "The Eurasians and Liberal Scholarship of the Late Imperial Period: Continuity and Change across the 1917 Divide." In *Between Europe and Asia*, edited by Mark Bassin, Sergey Glebov, and Marlène Laruelle, 27–47. Pittsburgh: Univerity of Pittsburgh Press.

Tri ognia: Baku v izobrazitel'nom iskusstve 19–20 vekov. Katalog vystavki. 2000. Moscow: Pinakoteka.

Troianovskii, Konstantin. 1918. *Vostok i revolutsiia: Popytka postroeniia novoi politicheskoi programmy dlia tuzemnykh stran vostoka—Indii, Persii i Kitaia*. Moscow: Atid.

Trotskii, L. D. 1991. "Futurizm." In *Literatura i revoliutsiia: Pechataetsia po izdaniiu 1923 goda*, 97–112. Moscow: Izdatel'stvo politicheskoi literatury.

Trubetzkoy, N. S. 1991. *The Legacy of Genghis Khan and Other Essays on Russia's Identity*, edited by Anatoly Liberman. Ann Arbor: Michigan Slavic Publications.

"Tsekh poetov." 1919. *Azerbaidzhan*, no. 266 (December).

Tynyanov, Yuri. 1979. "Dostoyevsky and Gogol: Towards a Theory of Parody." In *Dostoevsky and Gogol: Texts and Criticism*, edited by Priscilla Meyer, 101–18. Ann Arbor: Ardis.

Tyrrell, Maliheh S. 2001. *Aesopian Literary Dimensions of Azerbaijani Literature of the Soviet Period, 1920–1990*. Oxford: Lexington Books.

Uffelmann, Dirk. 2017. "Eurasia in the Retrofuture: Aleksandr Dugin's 'Tellurija' and the Benefits of Literary Analysis for Political Theory." *Welt der Slaven* 62, no. 2: 360–84.

Uvarov, S. S. 1810. *Project d'une académie asiatique*. St. Petersburg: L'imprimerie de l'Academie imperiale des sciences.

Uvarov, S. S. 1811. "Mysl' o zavedenii v Rossii Akademii Aziatskoi." *Vestnik Evropy* 1, no. 55: 32–33.

Vechёrka, Tat'iana. 2007. *Portrety bez retushi, Stikhotvoreniia, stat'i, dnevnikovye, zapisi, vospominaniia*, edited by Aleksandr Parnis. Moscow: Dom-Muzei Mariny Tsvetaevoi.

Veliyev (Körpülü), Şamil. 1999. *Füyuzat edebi mekebi*. Baku: Elm, 1999.

Veselovsky, Alexander. (1904) 2016. "The Age of Sensibility." Translated by Boris Maslov and Lev Blumenfeld. In *Persistent Forms: Explorations in Historical Poetics*, edited by Ilya Kliger and Boris Maslov, 255–73. New York: Fordham University Press.

Voloshinov, Valentin. 1973. *Marxism and the Philosophy of Language*. Translated by Ladislav Matejka and I. R. Titunik. Cambridge, MA: Harvard University Press.

Voloshinov, Valentin. 1976. *Freudianism: A Marxist Critique*. Translated by I. R. Titunik. Edited by Neal Bruss. New York: Academic Press.

Walicki, Andrzej. 1979. *A History of Russian Thought from the Enlightenment to Marxism*. Translated by Hilda Andrews-Rusiecka. Stanford: Stanford University Press.

Wehr, Hans. 1980. *A Dictionary of Modern Written Arabic*, edited by J Milton Cowan. Beirut: Librairie du Liban.

Werth, Paul W. 2014. *The Tsar's Foreign Faiths: Toleration and the Fate of Religious Freedom in Imperial Russia*. Oxford: Oxford University Press.

Yevtushenko, Yevgeny. 1999. "Preface." In *Romantic Communist*, edited by Saime Göksu and Edward Timms and translated by Robin Milner-Gulland, xiii–xxiv. New York: Palgrave Macmillan.

Yilmaz, Harun. 2013. "The Soviet Union and the Construction of Azerbaijani National Identity in the 1930s." *Iranian Studies: Journal of the International Society of Iranian Studies* 46, no. 5: 1–23.

Young, Robert J. C. 1990. *White Mythologies: Writing History and the West.* New York: Routledge.

Young, Robert J. C. 2001. *Postcolonialism: An Historical Introduction.* Oxford: Blackwell.

Yountchi, Lisa. 2002. "An Ode to Great Friendship: Russia, Iran, and the Soviet Tajik Writer." *Clio* 41, no. 2: 173–96.

Zarrinkoob, Abdol-Hosein. 1970. "Persian Sufism in Its Historical Perspective." *Iranian Studies* 3, no. 3–4: 169.

Zbinden, Karine. 2006. *Bakhtin between East and West: Cross-Cultural Transmission* Oxford: Legenda.

Zeynalova, Sevinc. 2008. "M. F. Axundzade ve Avropa medeniyyeti." *Azerbaijan*, no. 1. http://www.azyb.net/cgi-bin/jurn/main.cgi?id=325.

INDEX

Page numbers in *italics* indicate illustrations. Unless otherwise indicated, titles of works will be found under the author.

CPSIA information can be obtained
at www.ICGtesting.com
Printed in the USA
LVHW090015031019
632979LV00006B/123/P